Spatial Dimensions of Development Administration

Spatial Dimensions of Development Administration

James J. Heaphey   Henry C. Hart
Emmette Redford   Jerry Hough
John C. Shearer   Bertram M. Gross

Edited by James J. Heaphey

Published in cooperation with the Comparative Administration
Group of the American Society for Public Administration
Duke University Press, Durham, North Carolina   1971

Printed in the United States of America
by the Kingsport Press, Inc., Kingsport, Tenn.

Preface

This volume contains the papers that were presented and critically discussed at the Seminar on Spatial Aspects of Development Administration held at the Graduate School of Public and International Affairs, University of Pittsburgh, from the middle of June to the end of July 1965. It is a companion volume to *Development Administration: Temporal Aspects* edited by Dwight Waldo, which contains papers that were presented at the Seminar on Temporal Aspects of Development Administration held at the University of California, Berkeley, at about the same time as the Pittsburgh seminar. Both seminars were held under the auspices of the Comparative Administration Group of the American Society for Public Administration and the two host universities. A Ford Foundation grant to the Comparative Administration Group made these seminars possible.

The decision to investigate spatial and temporal aspects of development administration was made by the Comparative Administration Group's Program Committee. As with other decisions by that committee, the hope for this one was that it would generate new approaches that could add up to systematic knowledge of development administration in a comparative perspective. The committee felt that although space and time are considered in most writings on development administration, they have not been sufficiently featured.

To emphasize spatial aspects of development administration is not to make a claim to know *the* spatial aspects and all their implications for development administration. Rather, it is to use the idea of spatial aspects as a perspective. There are, without doubt, many spatial characteristics of development not treated in this volume, and many more that are treated but inadequately covered. The purpose of the volume is not to be definitive. No exhaustive coverage of the theme is claimed here. Nevertheless, the intention was to cover major spatial characteristics of national development. Unfortunately, as is often the case, the seminar group discovered only after considerable discussion that some things required greater attention than was being given them in the papers as planned. To some extent this was remedied in revisions of the papers, but revision could not take care of all the rich thought that emerged in the discussions. It is hoped that students of the participants and readers of other articles and books by the participants will benefit from what could not be included in this volume.

Readers of this volume who are unfamiliar with writings published by, or under the auspices of, the Comparative Administration Group may be surprised by the breadth of phenomena covered under the term "development administration." This breadth is a natural outcome of a kind of commitment (sometimes explicitly stated, and always implicit) to regard administration as part of a context undergoing change. The group began with no predetermined idea about how administration relates to development, and vice versa. Rather, it began with a commitment to study development as a total process involving, inter alia, administration. Needless to say, the group tries to concentrate on administration but not at the expense of comprehending it as part of a development gestalt.

The level of generalization and abstraction might also be surprising to someone unfamiliar with the style of approach followed by the Comparative Administration Group. While the group recognizes that ultimately development administration is practical action taken in practical ways, it is committed to expansion of the knowledge base upon which rational action can be undertaken, rather than with specific prescriptions for action. Thus, although in the final chapter of this volume we suggest some practical aspects of what precedes it, the major contribution of this volume, we hope, is expansion of the knowledge base for action.

The cosponsor of the seminar, the Graduate School of Public and International Affairs, provided numerous service facilities, in addition to space, for the meetings of the participants and for the individual participants. But most of all, it provided an ideal atmosphere. Under the leadership of Dean Donald Stone, the school has reached a place of prestige and respect throughout the world in the field of development administration. Professor Milton Esman, who was at the time chairman of the school's programs in economic and social development, was the person mainly responsible for bringing the seminar to Pittsburgh and was a major contributor of ideas during the planning stages.

A few papers discussed at our Pittsburgh meetings do not appear in this book, not because they were lacking in quality, but because, in my judgment, they did not really fit in with the whole enterprise. I should mention the authors of those papers, because they contributed so much to our efforts. I should mention the many persons at the University of Pittsburgh who facilitated our meetings. But I shall trust that they know who they are and find sufficient gratifications for their efforts in the publication of this book.

We gathered together in the summer of 1965 for six weeks of discussion; our efforts would have reached print much sooner if I had not been forced by many things to delay getting this manuscript to the publisher. Thus, I should be held responsible for any datedness of statistics or other materials. A six-month period following the seminar as a senior specialist at the East-West Center enabled me to write the introductory and concluding chapters for the volume. I am also grateful to the Graduate School of Public Affairs, State University of New York at Albany, for the secretarial services it provided, and to my colleagues there for helping me sharpen my ideas about development administration.

JAMES J. HEAPHEY

Albany, New York
June 24, 1969

Contributors

James J. Heaphey is a professor of public administration and director of the Comparative Development Studies Center at State University of New York at Albany. He received his Ph.D. in political science from the University of California at Berkeley in 1961 and has specialized in development administration, comparative politics, and organization theory. Dr. Heaphey has published articles in these areas, particularly with the Near East and Yugoslavia as focuses, resulting from research in those countries. He has also published on the theory of comparative and development administration. He has traveled widely in the Near East, Europe, and Latin America doing research and as a consultant with the U.S. State Department. He was born July 28, 1930 in Cleveland, Ohio.

Henry C. Hart is professor of political science at the University of Wisconsin. He is also chairman of the Department of Indian Studies. He has been in India three times for teaching and research over the last two decades. His books are *New India's Rivers*, 1965; *The Dark Missouri*, 1957; *Campus India: An Appraisal of American College Programs in India*, 1961; and *Administrative Aspects of River Valley Development*, 1960. His current research deals with the nation-building functions of the elective national legislature in India. The chapter published here was developed in the CAG Seminar at Pittsburgh in 1965, and refined at the East-West Center where the author was senior specialist in 1966. He was born November 17, 1916 in Lucknow, India.

Emmette S. Redford is Ashbel Smith Professor of Government and Public Affairs at the University of Texas. After receiving his B.A. and M.A. degrees from the University of Texas, Dr. Redford had his Ph.D. from Harvard in 1933. In addition to an extensive teaching experience in a number of universities, Dr. Redford has had several government appointments, both at the national and state levels. He is an active member in several academic and professional associations and has served in various administrative capacities including the president of the American Political Science Association, 1960–1961. His publications include numerous articles and books on national and field administration with particular reference to the American experience. With the increase in the regulatory activities of the national government, Dr. Redford's many publications include *Ideal and Practice in Public Administration,* 1958; *American Government and the Economy,* 1965; *Democracy in the Administrative State,* 1969; and, as co-author, *The Regulatory Process,* 1969. He was born September 23, 1904 in San Antonio, Texas.

Jerry F. Hough is an associate professor of political economy at the University of Toronto. In 1961 Dr. Hough received his Ph.D. from Harvard University. He taught for six years at the University of Illinois and spent one year at the Russian Research Center as a research associate. Dr. Hough's articles and research focus on the Russian and Yugoslav political systems. He is the author of *The Soviet Prefects,* 1968. He was born April 26, 1935 in Salina, Kansas.

John C. Shearer is professor of economics and director of the Manpower Research and Training Center at Oklahoma State University in Stillwater. After receiving a bachelor of science at Cornell University in 1952, he was a Fulbright Fellow at the University of Manchester, England. He received his Ph.D. in economics from Princeton University in 1960, and has specialized in labor economics, manpower, industrial relations, international economics, and economic development. Dr. Shearer has published numerous articles in these areas, particularly with Latin America as a focus, resulting from research and consulting experience in several Latin American countries, including a position as Professor/Economist, Latin American Institute of Economic and Social Planning (United Nations, Economic Commission for Latin America), Santiago, Chile, 1962–1963. He was born June 24, 1928 in Philadelphia, Pennsylvania.

Bertram M. Gross is Distinguished Professor of Urban Affairs and Planning, City University of New York. After receiving his M.A. degree in 1935 from the University of Pennsylvania, Professor Gross taught at a number of universities including Harvard Graduate School of Business Administration and the University of California at Berkeley. He has held numerous important governmental positions, including being executive secretary to the Council of Economic Advisors to the President, 1946–1952. His publications include *The Legislative Struggle,*

1953, *The Managing of Organizations,* 1964, *The State of the Nation,* 1966, and *Action Under Planning,* 1967. Professor Gross has traveled extensively in the Near East, Europe, and other areas of the world. He was born in 1912 in Philadelphia, Pennsylvania.

Contents

Spatial Dimensions of Development Administration

Chapter 1

Spatial Aspects of Development Administration

James J. Heaphey

Development of nation-states is one of the more demanding features of international and comparative economic, sociological, and political studies today. There are many dimensions to such development, but surely it is obvious that the spatial dimension is both crucial and regrettably understudied. In political science there has been far more concern with the capital division of powers (law-making, implementation of laws, and judicial review of laws) than with the areal division of powers. In one of the few books on the spatial dimension, Arthur Maass said in 1959 that he saw a "marked decline in interest and analysis by political scientists of factors related to the areal division of powers," and "a relative deterioration in the study and application of the several social sciences . . . to areas below the national level" during the twenty-five years preceding 1959.[1]

In another chapter of that book Stanley Hoffman suggested that we fail to realize the seriousness of the spatial dimension of the nation-state because our political language derives from the Platonic and Aristotelian age when the polis, a community of face-to-face political relationships, was the ideal political unit. "Our problem," Hoffman said, "begins where the *polis* ends: when the community becomes so large that the ideal of . . . a city where everyone knows or could know all the other members becomes im-

1. "Division of Powers: An Areal Analysis," in *Area and Power,* ed. Arthur Maass (Glencoe: The Free Press, 1959), p. 23.

practical." [2] This problem has been confronted since Alexander began building his political empire. Surprisingly, there is relatively little systematic theory about it. Franz Neumann noted in 1955 that although some prominent defenses of federalism are based on assumptions about the relation of territorial size to political structure, there are precious few studies of political geography.[3]

Accepting, with regrets, the limitations of political science in regard to the spatial dimension of nation-state development, one would expect to turn with pride to the field of public administration. Surely the continuing battles with spatial dimensions have affected the literature in that field, one thinks; at least we will find in the literature of public administration rigorous thinking about the questions of centralization and decentralization from which we can launch a consideration of more general spatial aspects. But an authority on this subject, James Fesler, told an international audience just a few years ago that "we appear to have neither a term that embraces the full continuum between the two poles nor a term that specifies the middle range where centralizing and decentralizing tendencies are substantially in balance." [4]

Economists must be credited with being spatially sensitive. You can hardly find "space" in political science or sociology, but you can find it in economics. There is the Regional Science Association, which publishes a journal. There is a spatial theory called "location theory," and there is a general understanding among economists that "regions and space are a neglected but necessary dimension of the theory and the practice of economic development." [5] Anthropologists and rural sociologists are spatially sensitive, but few of them deal with nation-state space. An exception is the work of Frank W. and Ruth C. Young, who have discussed

2. "The Areal Division of Powers in the Writings of French Political Thinkers," in ibid., p. 114.
3. *The Democratic and the Authoritarian State* (Glencoe: The Free Press, 1957), p. 224.
4. "Approaches to the Understanding of Decentralization," Paper delivered at Sixth World Congress, International Political Science Association, Geneva, September 21–25, 1964, p. 2.
5. John Friedman and Walter Alonso, eds., *Regional Development and Planning* (Cambridge: M.I.T. Press, 1964), p. 1.

propositions such as: "The direction of community growth is always toward greater participation in the national social structure." [6]

Planners, particularly urban planners, think a great deal about the spatial dimension. Most notable in this regard is C. A. Doxiadis, whose concept of *ekistics*—the science of human settlements—has sparked many social scientists throughout the world.[7] The use of scale models by urban planners indicates their intention to visualize what confronts them. Although ecology is a much-used word by social scientists nowadays, most social scientists do not go beyond analysis of the sociological environments, whereas urban planners probe into biophysical environments.[8]

Studies of resource development and use also deserve credit for bringing out the spatial dimension. This is due in part to the fact that regional economists have worked on the question of resources, and in part to the fact that political scientists working on resources are forced to take a functional view and such a view demands consideration of, for example, the spatial aspects of water, timber, land, and mineral deposits. This essay has three interrelated parts, in addition to these introductory comments on the study of space. First, we will discuss what appear to be the essential variable interrelationships between spatial aspects and development administration. Second, we will consider how the spatial dimension enters into, or results from, the ideologies of de-

6. "Toward a Theory of Community Development and Urbanization," United States Papers Prepared for the United Nations Conference on the Application of Science and Technology for the Benefit of the Less Developed Areas, Vol. XII, n. d., p. 27.

7. C. A. Doxiadis, *Ekistics—The Science of Human Settlements* (Southampton, England: Town and Country Planning Summer School, 1959). A good study along these lines is Jack C. Fisher, *Yugoslavia—A Multinational State* (San Francisco: Chandler Publishing Co., 1966).

8. Lynton K. Caldwell suggested as recently as 1963 that environment could be a new focus for public policy, meaning that though the concept has been much in vogue, the biophysical aspects of ecology are not being surveyed and analyzed. "Environment: A New Focus for Public Policy?" *Public Administration Review* 13, no. 3 (September 1963): 132–39. In a later piece on the comparative public administration movement, Caldwell says: "Although committed in principle to an ecological approach to comparative studies, surprisingly little interest in the biophysical aspects of administration or development has been evidenced in the comparative public administration movement." "Conjectures on Comparative Public Administration," in Roscoe C. Martin, ed., *Public Administration and Democracy* (Syracuse: Syracuse University Press, 1965), p. 239.

velopment elites; that is to say, how do the visions of Arab Socialism, Pan-Africanism, and so forth, interrelate with the spatial dimension. Third, we will look at strategies formulated to deal with
the spatial dimension—such as federalism, deconcentration, decentralization, regional economic development, and so forth—
with a view to explaining what the strengths and weaknesses of
these various approaches are.

Spatial Aspects and Development Administration

Government, economic development, and nation-building are
closely interwoven spatially, none being quite the cause of the
others, yet all three being inextricably bound together. "Only
where agricultural occupation of a region can be and has been
accomplished," wrote O. D. Von Engelin, a geographer, about
fifty years ago, "is nationality possible. Commercial and industrial
activities consolidate nationality further because they promote an
even wider possession and utilization of the resources of the land
than does agriculture." [9] Pursuing the thesis that nationality is a
social condition resulting from spatial settlements, Von Engelin
said that "as widely as there exists a willingness to co-operate,
without discrimination between individuals or communities, in
the development of the resources of lands, and as widely as the
feeling exists among the inhabitants of these lands that they are
co-partners in the possession of these lands—so far does nationality extend." [10] If cooperative development of the land is a corollary
to nationality, surely government of the land undergoing cooperative development is another necessary ingredient. Can economic
transactions take place in an area without government? Perhaps,
but surely it is not common. There must be some way in which
understandings are enforced. A clear recognition of this principle
inheres in the demand for Arab unity coming from Arabs in Egypt,
Syria, Jordan, and Saudi Arabia. Rupert Emerson observes that

9. O. D. Von Engelin, *Inheriting The Earth* (New York: Macmillan Co., 1922),
p. 45.
  10. Ibid., p. 47.

the last thing of which these countries could be accused is that they are, as they now exist, a coherent economic bloc. "They seek political unity in order to be able, among other things, to cut back on alien encroachment and to construct their own economic unity. For them as for others, political action is needed to tame the economy and bring it under national control." [11]

Pitirim Sorokin provides a sociological suggestion of similar implications. He noted that certain culture systems, particularly the artistic and sometimes the scientific, can flourish even when the authority of an empire is declining. Although, in the same context, Sorokin speaks of how economic growth can accompany growth in the effective control of an empire, he does not say that the economic culture system can grow during a time of decline of the empire's ability to control. [12] Sorokin seems to propose that growth in the culture system of economics is more closely tied to territorial control than is growth in any of the other culture systems.

We hope that we will not be accused of fostering what François Perroux, a distinguished regional scientist, calls "a banal sense of space location" which "creates the illusion of the coincidence of political space with economic and human space." [13] When we say that government, economic development, and nation-building are closely interwoven and stress the dependence of economic viability on territorial control, we are not denying that the repercussions of economic activity in a country can be felt far beyond the borders of that country, nor are we hinting that in some natural way economics and government are spatially the same. We are saying that most of the economic transactions taking place in the world today have a context of authority within which to operate and that, for the most part, this authority is geographically localized.

There are some recent examples that appear to bear upon these matters. The failure of the Federation of Rhodesia and

11. *From Empire To Nation* (Boston: Beacon Press, 1962), p. 171.
12. *Social and Cultural Mobility* (London: Free Press Paperback, 1959), pp. 601–603.
13. "Economic Space: Theory and Applications," *Quarterly Journal of Economics* 64 (February 1950): 64.

Nyasaland to contribute to economic development of the two countries is blamed, by more than one observer, on the federation's inability to establish control. Though successful in attracting money to build the Kariba Dam and Hydroelectricity Station the federation failed to attract investment in economic activity for use of the Kariba facility because of concern throughout the world for stability in the federation. There was a steady stream of investment going into areas of the federation, and most of those areas were in what appeared at the time to be under secure white control in Southern Rhodesia. "The lesson from this," Herbert W. Chitepo has said, "would appear to be that investors will invest, if only for short terms, if they have confidence in the ability of the government to retain control and ensure the safety of their investment."[14] Investment is not all there is to economic development, but it plays the critical role at certain stages.

The proposition that economics requires governmental control should not be construed to say that political control is required. Indeed, whether or not a polity is a necessary ingredient, or outcome, of the developmental process is a critical and unanswered question. If aid-giving countries supported a military dictatorship in an underdeveloped country, can we state categorically whether or not economic development and nation-building could take place there? Clearly, there is no answer. Whether or not a system of power need be, or in process of becoming, a political system in this context is a matter of confusion in the literature on development because so many writers equate politics with control. A control system is generally referred to as a "political system," and political system is usually conceived as embracing various typologies, such as "traditional-transitional-modern."

If one assumes that any system of territorial authority is the same thing as a political system, then, of course, it makes sense to classify developing countries as "transitional political systems," for example, just as it makes sense to talk about the "non-Western political process." But what is the point? What range of phenomena are we identifying by the word "political" that are not identi-

14. "Developments in Central Africa," in *Federalism and the New Nations,* ed. David P. Currie (Chicago: The University of Chicago Press, 1964), p. 9.

fied by the words "government," "control," "authority?" If, alter-
natively, we view politics as a type of government formulated by
the Greeks and later developed by the Western world to achieve
certain valued goals, it does not make sense to talk about any
"non-Western political process," because politics is one of the
behavior patterns by which we distinguish Western from other
civilizations. Carrying this on, we see that the fact that Western
man has thought of himself as living a political, as well as a religious and economic, life, that he has written abundantly about
politics, that he is, simply and certainly, conscious of being a
politikon zoon, indicates that politics is a Western cultural phenomenon. To refer to the "politics of Saudi Arabia" may be as
fatuous as referring to the "Islamism of France." This is not to
say that there are not power struggles, authority, "who gets what,
when, where, and how," and authoritative allocations of power
in Saudi Arabia; it is to say that such behavior does not necessarily indicate that people in that culture think of themselves as
acting politically.

Spatially, Western culture is distinctive in its orientation to
the territorial political community. You can find persons in Western culture who have their primary orientation to religious, folk,
and other communities. What is distinctive about Western culture, however, is the use of political community in a certain territory as a primary focus. Ancient Greek had no word for community other than "state."

Culture and Space in Developing Countries

Benjamin Lee Whorf has noted how man uses spatial metaphors as part of his scheme of objectifying.[15] Elites in developing
countries consider the emergence of identity with the territory
involved on the part of the people to be a sine qua non of their
goals. Peasants, merchants, laborers are induced to identify their
future with the future of Egypt, or India, or Tunisia, and so on.
Development is a concept normally connoting a country like one

15. *Language, Thought and Reality* (Cambridge: M.I.T. Press, 1956), p. 145.

of those; and because it is, it is foreign to vast numbers of people who are expected to be part of development programs. "Egypt," "India," and "Tunisia" are not operational aspects of the culture of many people within those countries. They do not employ the same spatial metaphors for objectification as do the development elites. In some cases life space does not extend beyond the village and marketing center; in other cases it does not extend beyond the village. For a peasant in some developing countries, setting foot outside his own village is a step onto completely foreign ground, even though the basic features of the environment and people are the same as those in his own village. Such a man simply does not see continuity, in environment and people, as he goes beyond the space of his village. What he sees is strange and fearsome, no matter how similar his village and the proximate place he goes to outside his village appears to those of us who have been conditioned to visualize in our particular way. Vidal de la Blanche quotes an Annamese official as saying: "Because there is so much variety of the communal institutions as soon as we set foot outside our own village we Annamese feel as though we were in China or America." [16] The situation, writes Koji Iizuka, has been well expressed in the Chinese proverb: "If one travels five *li* one will find that the manners of the people are different; if one travels ten *li* one will find that the standards of measurements are not the same."[17] For the native of French Africa, L. Gray Cowan says, "when one's horizon is bounded by the next village or at most by the nearest large town, Lagos is as far away as Paris." [18]

Thus the countrysides of developing countries have been referred to as "mosaics of unrelated parts," indicating that to the people of the individual communities composing what to us is the country, there is no relationship between the small village-type communities. J. Van Der Gelderen says that "even in territory such as Java, local differences are still very wide," and that "the many different territorial levels of economic development

16. As quoted by Koji Iizuka, "An Approach to Asian Studies from the Standpoint of Human Geography," *The Developing Economies* 2, no. 3 (September 1964): 241.
17. Ibid.
18. *Local Government in West Africa* (New York: Columbia University Press, 1958), p. viii.

might be compared to the unequal contents of a number of small vessels set side by side but unconnected." [19] Sociologists refer to this as "inorganic diversity." Egypt has had diversity, but it has been inorganic diversity. "The townspeople of Cairo and Alexandria," an observer said in 1938, "know the countryside only by glimpses caught through a train or car window. The fellaheen shut in by their fields and villages know nothing of the city except through the [village chief], the Greek grocer, or the landlord's agent. . . . Each [group] has its own mentality and its own Egypt." [20]

John Kautsky says that in these communities:

> [The peasant] is tied to the soil by the necessities of his work, if not by law, and mobility beyond a very small radius seems to him neither possible nor desirable. Engaged in a subsistence economy, he is dependent on neither imports nor exports from his small village community. In such a society communications between the village and the outside world are extremely limited, and so, therefore, are the peasant's knowledge of that world and his intellectual horizon. [21]

Strangeness prompts negative attitudes. Few Iranians, it has been observed, have a good word for people in other parts of the country. Villagers view townspeople, whom they never have seen, "with distrust and have them neatly categorized with epithets which are often uncomplimentary. Thus, the people of Kashan are regarded as cowardly and complaining, those of Isfahan are shrewd and grasping, those of Shiraz as more enlightened than most because of good climate, those of Meshed as tricky and untruthful, those of Semnan as frugal, and those of Tabriz as aggressive and brave." [22]

The inconsistencies of state boundaries and communities are

19. "An Approach to Asian Studies from the Standpoint of Human Geography," p. 241.
20. As quoted by James Heaphey in "The Organization of Egypt: Inadequacies of a Non-Political Model for Development," *World Politics* 18, no. 2 (January 1966): 178.
21. "The Politics of Underdevelopment and Industrialization," in *Political Change in Underdeveloped Countries*, ed. John H. Kautsky (New York: John Wiley & Sons, 1962), p. 15.
22. Donald N. Wilber, *Contemporary Iran* (New York: Frederick A. Praeger, 1963), pp. 44–45.

particularly striking in Africa. Tribes, the most cohesive social
structure in Africa, usually occupy territories smaller than the
territories of the states, and one often finds a tribe "cut up" by
state borders. Thus, Pan-Africanism has an appeal and those Africans conscious of current developments live, so to speak, in "spatial confusion." While pursuing a path to establish territory and
political space in the area bounded by the lines drawn for them
in the arbitrary partitioning of Africa, the political elites of that
continent cannot ignore the logic of Pan-Africanism. Neither alternative seems viable today, and the search for a "golden mean
in space" will be a source of African history during the next fifty
years, at least.[23]

Space is a cultural creation just as language is, and it is learned
through the same kinds of cultural processes. "Greenland was one
kind of country to the Vikings; it was another kind of country to
the Eskimos," a geographer has noted.[24] Some cultures are quite
conscious of the malleability of space. The Japanese move the
walls (i.e., the screens) in their homes to adapt to felt spatial
needs. Other cultures appear to believe that space is given in
some absolute sense, perhaps by a god or divine law. Some cultures cannot thrive in regions that are controlled politically by
another culture. Other cultures can, such as the Jewish. Some
cultures prefer to develop business in regions controlled by another culture. The Chinese, writes Von Engelin, "more than any
other group, would be content that the political control of a
region where they lived and worked should be in alien hands.
The Chinese could be a nation in a new home without also desir-
ing to constitute themselves a state."[25]

The variations one finds in man's visual world justifies James
Gibson's differentiation of "visual field" from "visual world." Gibson says that visual field is made up of constantly shifting light

23. See Immanuel Wallerstein, *Africa: The Politics of Independence* (New
York: Vintage, 1961); Rupert Emerson, "Nation-Building in Africa," in *Nation-
Building*, ed. Karl Deutsch and William Faltz (New York: Atherton Press, 1963);
and Gabriel d'Arboussier, "Le Problème de l'Etat et de la National en Afrique
Noire," *Syntheses*, December 1959–January 1960.

24. Isaiah Bowman, "Geography in the Creative Experience," *Geographical
Review* 28 (1937): 11.

25. *Inheriting the Earth*, p. 377.

patterns recorded by the retina. Man uses these to organize his visual world, but he uses other data as well, that come from his culture.[26] Gibson says that if we can accept the idea that the visual world is culturally created, we can reject the widespread notion that "a stable, uniform 'reality' is recorded on a passive visual receptor system, so that what is seen is the same for all men and therefore can be used as a universal reference point." [27]

Development is something that political elites and government officials talk about, not the man at the plow, although the attempt is made to get the man at the plow to do so. Such political elites and government officials tend to think in terms of the country included in the geographical limits of the state in which they are recognized by other sovereign states as having the right to rule. That is, they tend to think in terms of the same space that an American would think about when considering development. They are of a different culture than the villager in this respect; they have a different visual world than the man at the plow. Some national political leaders try to destroy cultures unlike their own. "In three or four years," Sékou Touré said more than once, "no one will remember the tribal, ethnic, and religious differences which have caused so much difficulty to the country and the people in the recent past. We are for a united people, a unitary state at the service of an indivisible nation." [28] Other national political leaders have tried to find a way to accommodate varieties of subcultures while thinking of the "whole country."

In either case, the task is to develop a national culture to match the territory of the state. For what we think of as "India," the task is to develop a national culture covering the same territory as the state of India, in the sense that people living in the place indicated by the geographical boundaries of the state must learn to "see" that space as being important to them. The visual world of the national leaders must become the visual world of the man at the plow. But whereas the Western concept of nation is closely tied to the idea of political space, land, property, and so on, non-

26. *The Perception of the Visual World* (Boston: Houghton-Mifflin, 1966).
27. Ibid., p. 64.
28. As quoted by Paul E. Sigmund, Jr., in *The Ideologies of the Developing Nations* (New York: Praeger, 1963), p. 7, n. 6.

Westerners do not do so, at least not as a natural outcome of their cultures. Arabs, for example, do not value land other than for its functional uses. The American's relationship to land ownership is equivalent to the Arab's relation to familial identity. The word currently in use to express the "nation" of Arabs is *qawmiyyah*, which means the union of hearts. Earlier words had been used which came much closer to implying land. At one time *watan*, meaning "dwelling place" or "home land," was used to designate the meaning of the Arab people, and later *wataniyyah* was used. This is not to say that all Arabs work exclusively with the concept of *qawmiyyah* rather than *wataniyyah*. Syrians stress *qawmiyyah*. Prior to 1952 the Egyptians stressed *wataniyyah*-nationalism. Saudi-Arabians utilize both concepts. Tunisians stress *wataniyyah*-nationalism.

Regional Economics

As leaders in developing countries foster spatial consciousness, they also foster economic development, and they find therein a problem. Economic development must deal with the concept of regional economic development. "Macroeconomics" is a term used to denote economic concepts relating to spatial units the size of countries. It has been said that "in the few years that nations have sought economic development as an explicit goal it has become clear that the arithmetic of macroeconomics has need of and is made more powerful by the geometry of regional considerations." [29]

Until recently, planning was either national or urban. But today the concept of regions is fundamental in economic development theory and regional planning is a field unto itself. Planning for subnational regions may mean one of three things, according to Benjamin Higgins: It may mean planning for a city, state, metropolitan area, or depressed part of a country as a separate economy. A special authority may be established to deal with a region, such as the Tennessee Valley Authority in the United

29. Friedmann and Alonso, *Regional Development and Planning*, p. 1.

States, or the Corporación Autónima del Valle del Cauca in the Cauca Valley of Colombia. Second, subnational regional planning may refer to utilization of regional plans covering the territory of one country in order to facilitate formulating the national plan. Socialized countries prepare regional plans for republics and subsidiary areas and compare their consistency with one another and with the national plan. Third, subnational regional planning can be a way of locating projects of a national plan in such a way as to reduce economic disparities among regions in the country and to guarantee rational location of the project in terms of what the project is intended to accomplish.[30]

Regional economics also means multinational cooperation. Though this is an important spatial aspect of development, it is not one that is used as focus for any of the chapters in this book; therefore we will not attempt to go into it in this introductory chapter. Our prevailing focus in this book is the country and its parts.

The regional question is problematical in all economies. In economies where industrialization is in the early stages, activity is usually concentrated in a few centers. These centers, it has been observed,

> not only grow so rapidly as to create problems of an entirely new order, but they also act as suction pumps, pulling in the more dynamic elements from the more static regions. The remainder of the country is thus relegated to a second-class, peripheral position. It is placed in a quasi-colonial relationship to the center, experiencing net outflows of people, capital, and resources, most of which redound to the advantage of the center where economic growth will tend to be rapid, sustained, and cumulative. As a result, income differences between center and periphery tend to widen.[31]

As these regional differences occur, they can become social differences which, in turn, reinforce the economic differences. Peo-

---

30. This paragraph is based on a few pages in Albert Waterston's *Development Planning: Lessons of Experience* (Baltimore: Johns Hopkins Press, 1965), pp. 22–23.

31. Friedmann and Alonso, *Regional Development and Planning*, p. 3.

ple in more developed regions begin to consider themselves superior to those in less developed regions and, according to Albert Hirschman, they "set themselves apart from the less progressive operators by creating a picture of the latter as lazy, bungling, intriguing, and generally hopeless." [32] In time this can become a political obstacle to development of underdeveloped regions because the people in developed regions are doubtful about government programs to encourage such development. As has been noted, there was more opposition from politicians and economic interests to transferring north Italian resources to the south than to transferring French resources to Africa. Similarly, despite their impressive pronouncements for balanced development, Yugoslavs must live with the fact that many persons in more developed regions resent the suggestion that part of their productivity should be invested in poorer parts of the country. Furthermore, Yugoslav development theory is replete with differing perspectives resulting from the opposition of "Danubian" to the "Adriatic" orientation; the former is Serbia's view that investment should be concentrated along the Danube River, and the latter is the Croatian and Slovenian view, promoting investment concentration in the Adriatic area.

Persons who live in the less developed parts of the country and have ambition may consider moving to the more developed centers of activity as the only way they can live a meaningful life. At best this is a "brain drain" which leaves the less developed regions without the talents peculiarly conducive to development. At worst, this creates a *lumpen proletariat,* unemployed transients in a city, and *lumpen intelligentsia,* unemployed intellectuals in a city.

Governments must organize concepts to deal with such movements of people. If the only problem appears to be a brain drain, that is, if persons who move from the village to the centers of economic activity are quickly employed, then government might take one of two positions vis-à-vis the areas from which the movements take place; something can be done to create viable eco-

32. *The Strategy of Economic Development* (New Haven: Yale University Press, 1958), pp. 190–95.

nomic life in those areas which will keep productive persons in that area, or the movement can be unaltered by public policy and subsidies can be given to the suffering areas. If, however, this movement results in large numbers of unemployed productive young people in the cities, then government must be concerned not only about rational use of productive people but also about maintaining order because when large numbers of persons with aspirations about a better future are lumped together in relatively small spaces, the potential for revolutionary acts is rather high. As one writer put it:

> Physical densities, communication, and other facilities make political organization relatively easier in cities [than in rural areas]. Groups with resources and tightly-knit organizations, like the Communists or the Rashtriya Swayam-Sewak Sangh are at a relative advantage in such situations. . . . Psychological densities—intense interchange of ideas, rumors, and stimulations in crowded situations—are conducive to demagoguery and crowd formations. Speakers and audiences tend to stimulate each other into states of irresponsibility and frenzy in situations of crowding and anonymity.[33]

Some countries must contend with still another situation that results from these movements. Even when the people are readily employed in the place to which they move, there is still a social problem of anomie. Will the government try to provide community in the new place in such cases? Perhaps the clearest reply comes from Communist and Socialist countries. The Chinese Communists, for example, tried unsuccessfully to turn urban organizations into communities in the hope that both production and social problems could be dealt with through one social strategy.[34]

33. Shanti Tangri, "Urbanization, Political Stability, and Economic Growth," in *India's Urban Future*, ed. Roy Turner (Berkeley: University of California Press, 1962), p. 199–200.
34. See Franz Schurmann, *Ideology and Organization in Communist China* (Berkeley: University of California Press, 1966), chap. 6.

Area and Social Philosophy

Still another significant spatial variable is the social and governmental philosophy of elites in developing countries. "Any preference for a certain scheme of areal division of powers," writes Stanley Hoffmann, "presupposes a decision on the ends for which power is to be exercized—a decision on the values power should serve and on the way in which these values will be served. It involves a whole philosophy of government and society." [35] Decisions regarding spatial aspects of development are affected by political ideology as well as by questions of regional economic advantage, demographic clusterings, and so forth. Development is a consciously pursued policy of socioeconomic change; developmental elites are not without vision as to what they want to change. As Norman S. Buchanen and Howard S. Ellis noted in one of the first American volumes on the subject,

> economic development now has much more explicit political and ethical objectives than inhered in the old tradition of economic progress. . . . The great drive toward economic development in most underdeveloped countries today either springs from or is intimately connected with movements of national independence and glory, internal political changes, and—generally speaking—equalitarian and social welfare sentiments. Ideological elements play a more conspicuous role in "development" than they did in the concept of "progress" a century ago. [36]

Many developmental elites have said that tribal, ethnic, and religious differences would have to give way to a unitary state at the service of an indivisible nation.

It is interesting to note in this regard the well-known difference between British and French administrative styles in their

35. "The Areal Division of Powers," p. 113.
36. *Approaches to Economic Development* (New York: The Twentieth Century Fund, 1955), p. 122.

so forth; but Egypt lacks organizations that the Yugoslavs take for granted, such as the League of Communists and the Socialist Alliance of Working People, organizations which operate throughout the country with singular purpose, and so long as Egypt lacks these things, it cannot hope to find the Yugoslav success by using the Yugoslav strategy of communal decision-making. And so it goes. Strategies are peculiar products of individual countries.

Nonetheless, there are features of these strategies that are common enough to warrant treatment as themes, for example, the strategy of federalism which has been tried, during the past twenty years or so, in Africa by the Central African Federation, Ethiopia, Libya, Mali, Nigeria, the Republic of Cameroon, and Uganda; in Asia by India, Indonesia, Malaya, Malaysia, and Pakistan; and in Europe by the German Federal Republic and Yugoslavia.

Federalism has not been a successful strategy in Africa and Asia. A possible reason for the failure is that federalism is a way of protecting particular segments of a country against the majority; it is a protective device rather than a means to increase something like the productive capacity of a nation. Development ideology is passionate about bettering productive capacities and it is usually articulated in terms of majority interests. In the vision of development ideology, federalism can be seen as an irresponsible thing in a day when, it appears, just the opposite is needed.[41] Various experts on Africa have noted, for example, that Africans usually mean majority rule when they refer to democracy.[42]

Furthermore, federalism can be an obstacle to economic planning models. In Yugoslavia, for example, economic planners are complaining increasingly about the inadequacy of republican borders for spatial planning. "It is understandable that the constituent republics should be an absolutely relevant factor in the make-up of the entire policy of faster development of the under-

41. For a discussion of this aspect of federalism, see William H. Riker, *Federalism: Origin, Operation, Significance* (Boston: Little, Brown, 1964), p. 142.
42. See James S. Coleman and Carl G. Rosberg, Jr., eds. *Political Parties and National Integration in Tropical Africa* (Berkeley and Los Angeles: University of California Press, 1964), and Claude E. Welch, Jr., *Dream of Unity: Pan-Africanism and Political Unification in West Africa* (Ithaca: Cornell University Press, 1966).

developed areas," writes a bank director general in Serbia, "but the method of defining development and the distribution of Federal resources exclusively from the republican aspect is not always entirely adequate. Many questions of development pertain to the border regions between the republics. . . ."[43] In a similar vein, the fact that federalism has as its purpose the curbing of power and is based upon a distrust of power cannot help but detract from its attractiveness in the developing countries. For the most part, the prevailing ideology in these countries is that the use of power by the Western colonial countries in holding down the emergence of nationalism in Afro-Asian areas was undesirable use of power and is to be avoided at all costs in the future. Use of power by indigenous elites, on the other hand, cannot be viewed as intrinsically dangerous; indeed, the only way that rapid development is possible is through the use of a concentrated power in the hands of a benevolent elite with the good of the country in mind.

Regionalization, an emerging strategy to deal with spatial aspects of development, provides a focus on an area smaller than the entire country. One region can be established for one kind of production or service, another for different purposes, and so forth. The calculus for rational selection of the boundaries of a region are elusive. It appears that one should take into account existing subnational political boundaries, resource location, resource use, management problems, nation-building factors, and political difficulties, and it would seem that one should be able to take such variables into account in such a way as to indicate what would happen if a boundary change were made in the model under consideration; these are formidable variables to behold. In some cases the "decision," so to speak, is made easier by the existence of what appears to be an overwhelming influence, as for example in Colombia where three regional planning bodies (Corporación Autónoma Regional del Cauca, Corporación Autónoma Regional de la Sabana de Bogotá y Valles de Chinqínquiray Ubate, and Corporación Autónoma Regional de los Valles de Magdelena y

43. *Development of the Underdeveloped Areas in Yugoslavia* (Belgrade: Medunarodna Politika, 1966), p. 22.

Sinú) were established to match three regions, each of which has prodigious local pride and geographic and climatic distinctiveness.

Regional strategies can mean one, or a combination of two ideas, one being that regional units pursue development in regional terms, the other that national planners consider regions as parts of national whole pictures. An example of the former is the Corporación Autónima Regional del Cauca; an example of the latter is in Turkey where the Ministry of Reconstruction tries to divide the national Turkish problem into parts of that problem by conceiving regions. A lack of qualified persons is a technical obstacle to the former; the latter apparently makes better use of scarce economists, administrators, physical planners, and so forth. Another apparent advantage of the latter is that it avoids the sin of localism, a condition in which subnational units elevate their own goals at the expense of national goals. The latter approach is not without its difficulties. In a definitive-type survey of regional and local planning Albert Waterston came to the conclusion that "planning for economic regions is uncommon and frequently unsuccessful in countries where it has been tried." [44] National bodies can conceive regions only with difficulty, and once conceived, the regions have been next to impossible to coordinate.

Another strategy being used today that is significant in terms of the spatial dimension is the attempt to promote participation in development at local levels. No country can be credited with inventing this strategy, though Yugoslavia is probably its best-known user. Faced with the problem of blending together Serb, Croat, Montenegrin, and Macedonian cultures, Yugoslav national development theory, strongly guided by Marxist perspectives, has formulated a strategy of "self-management" which, inter alia, is expected to deliver the country from the probable negative results of excessive nationalism on the part of the five cultures in Yugoslavia. President Tito has said that the nationalities in Yugoslavia tend to shut themselves up within their own borders

44. *Development Planning: Lessons of Experience* (Baltimore: Johns Hopkins Press, 1965), p. 564.

whereas workers in production know no boundaries "because their interests are identical with those of the entire social community." [45] Marxist theory interprets nation-states as communities resulting from capitalism. The territory covered by such a nation-state is a reservoir of resources under exploitation by capitalist doctrine to entice participation by the workers in a game at which they can only be losers. The nation-state, Lenin said, is "the typical, normal state for the capitalist period." [46]

The Yugoslavs are searching for a perspective in terms of which the Yugoslav economy can be integrated in some framework other than that of the nation or the state. They have formulated the idea that if the operations of production are managed by the persons involved in those operations, and if larger and larger organizations of interdependent production functions are formed on the basis of self-management (or self-administration), eventually there could be an economic system large enough to provide for meaningful development and yet not a capitalist, nation-state system. "Such a consolidation of the role of self-administration," the eminent Yugoslav theoretician Edvard Kardelj has said, "would offer new impetus to truly progressive integrational processes among the nationalities within the sphere of economic development, primarily because these processes would actually be based on and stimulated by the very working and economic interests of self-administration by the working people. Such integration is the present and future of mankind. It transcends all boundaries and languages." [47]

Yugoslav thought and practices in regard to local self-government are rather well-known among educated elites concerned with development throughout the Afro-Asian world. This is because the Yugoslavs exert considerable effort to distribute information about their ideas and also because intellectuals in countries

45. "The Role of the League of Communists in the Further Development of Socialist Social Relations and Current Problems in the International Workers Movement and in the Struggle for Peace and Socialism in the World," *Practice and Theory of Socialist Development in Yugoslavia: VIIIth Congress of The League of Communists of Yugoslavia* (Belgrade: Medunarodna Politika, 1965), p. 37.
46. *The Right of Nations to Self-Determination* (Moscow: Foreign Languages Publishing House, 1951), p. 10.
47. "Socio-Economic Aims of Economic Development in the Forthcoming Period," *Practice and Theory of Socialist Development in Yugoslavia*, p. 101.

like India and Egypt have a genuine interest in the Yugoslav approaches. The Yugoslav communal system, for example, is widely known and praised. What is emphasized in Afro-Asia are the functional aspects of Yugoslav ideas, with regard to spatial aspects of development, rather than the Marxist aspects of these ideas. As the first country with a highly centralized planning and administrative machinery to decentralize, Yugoslavia represents a significant model to many observers.

The attempt to promote participation in development at local levels is both a response to a classical administrative problem and a peculiar feature of nation-building. The classical administrative problem is that highly centralized systems lead to unnecessary delay, inappropriate action, and so on. The peculiar feature of nation-building is the need to foster identification with the nation through participation in the nation-building process. In many countries it appears that use of local participation is an ideal solution, both to the dangers of overcentralization and the need for nation-building.

Decentralization within government organizations is still another strategy to deal rationally with the spatial dimension. Overcentralization of authority and responsibility in ministry headquarters in capital cities is generally regarded as a formidable obstacle to development. It is a characteristic of administrative systems in developing countries that decisions are not made in the field, that all guidelines for action and all action itself emanates from central headquarters, and that administrators in the field accept very little responsibility for what they do. As sincerely as some governments try to decentralize their bureaucracies, they seldom succeed to the degree that they regard as minimal if administrative institutions are to facilitate rather than hinder development. This failure, and the problems in the strategies of federalism, regionalism, and local participation, may lie in the absence of "value integration" and "professionalism," both of which enable decentralization of systems.

Value integration in a system enables decentralization of that system because the delegators of authority can trust the delegatees to act as they would act. For example, Herbert Kaufman has noted how the United States forest ranger in the field uses criteria for decision-making that are almost precisely those that would be used by his superiors in the same situation.[48] In some organizations, as Bernard Baum has noted in the case of the United States Civil Service Commission, there can be value integration between some superiors and subordinates, but not between all.[49] The developing countries do not enjoy a high potential for value integration. Development is a process, not a precise set of goals around which everyone can mobilize their interests. Perhaps the most identifiable goal found within the many goals of development is production increases. This could be a means of value integration. Production is concrete enough, and the value of increasing production could be clear enough to establish agreement on terms and observations. But production increases are not viewed—in India, Egypt, Nigeria, Vietnam, and so many other developing countries—as the crucial, let alone the sole, goal of development. For example, the Indians based their struggle for freedom from British tutelage on the argument that self-government is preferable to efficient government. The sight of a defunct Suez Canal attests to the noncentrality of the ethic of production in Egypt. And so it goes.

In postcolonial developing countries experienced administrators have often been regarded with distrust because of their former loyalty to the colonial regimes. Furthermore, it was not unusual for those who learned administration from colonial tutors to look upon their jobs as nothing more than trading services and loyalty for more money. They were told what to do, given definite guidelines for that action, received pay in exchange, and managed what other emoluments were possible. What could have helped the developing countries work in value-integrated systems, but what did not happen, would have been socialization to administrative roles as purpose-oriented roles rather than as self-satisfying roles. What is needed, and is lacking, is an orientation to administration (or, indeed, to development) as purposeful activity involving numbers of persons with similar goals.

48. *The Forest Ranger* (Baltimore: Johns Hopkins, 1960).
49. *Decentralization of Authority in a Bureaucracy* (Englewood Cliffs: Prentice-Hall, 1961), pp. 152–53.

Even if the administrative systems of developing countries had had this orientation, their capacity to be value-integrated, decentralized systems would be under severe strain, given the flux and uncertainty of development processes, because under pressure of uncertainty, conflict, and turmoil decentralized systems tend toward centralization as administrators in the field hesitate to make decisions and turn to the central office for guidance. Furthermore, a developing country is a poor country in which the temptation of corruption is more difficult to resist than in a rich country. And just the knowledge of this alone, let alone experience with corruption, can dissuade an administrator from decentralizing by delegating authority to another.

Another way in which decentralization occurs is through professionalization. An organization is a set of tasks. Persons performing those tasks may become more knowledgeable about the tasks than their organizational superiors and they may develop loyalties to professional groups whose membership cuts across a number of organizations. When this happens, there may be a demand for independence in decision-making by the persons carrying out the tasks. If the society supports the legitimacy of such demands, there can be, as is very much the case in modern Western societies, a "professionally determined decentralization." Specialties are being learned in developing countries, but there is little sign of professions emerging. Furthermore, developing societies do not yet accept the idea that decisions should be made by persons technically expert in the matters concerned. Indeed, such acceptance might well be a crucial sign of development itself.

Nontransitivity: The Strategy of Flexibility

The spatial dimensions of development indicate a need for flexible strategies in dealing with them. There are various salient reasons why a monolithic and rigid model is quite improper as a strategy. From the development elites' viewpoint, even if they were to be agreed on their general and specific purposes, no one spatial pattern can be the basis for all developmental activity. The various technologies used in development activities do not share the same spatial dimension. A public health program has different areal requirements than a program to increase industrial coordination. The technology of rural agricultural development dictates smaller areal work units than the technology of rural electrification, though both are functionally interdependent. And so it goes. Furthermore, the spatial dimension is dynamic; as development takes place, new areal concerns emerge. This is particularly obvious in the growth of towns around new industry.

All of this points to the need for an administrative system which can adapt to spatial heterogeneity and flux, that is, a nontransitive as opposed to a transitive system.[50] A transitive relation, in logic and mathematics, is such that if A has a relationship of "greater than," "precedes," or "implies," to B, and if B has the same relationship to C, then A has that relationship to C. A nontransitive relation is one in which the relationship between A to B, and B to C, does not necessarily carry over to the relationship between A and C. The advantage of the nontransitive system is that it has the capacity to adapt to learning, whereas the transitive system must play by the same rules of the game no matter what is indicated by and learned through experience. Furthermore, a nontransitive system provides more opportunity for experimenting with various forms of action, which in itself sets up the possibility for learning about the spatial dimension and how to work within it.

Transitivity, however, is more often sought than nontransitivity. Models for local government, field administration, and so forth, are usually articulated in terms of specified powers under specified circumstances. The French classical prefecture system, for example, is a transitive one wherein the prefect is put in charge of virtually all government activity in his prefecture, and it has been far more copied than has the Italian prefecture system, which is less transitive, wherein the prefect is not the ultimate source of authority in the prefecture. The French-type prefect is the official representative for all the ministries that have

50. Karl Deutsch uses these concepts effectively in *The Nerves of Government* (New York: The Free Press of Glencoe, 1963).

programs in that prefecture, and he is chief administrator for all functions classified as "housekeeping," for all field offices in the prefecture. The Italian-type prefect does not have official control over such housekeeping functions, nor is he officially responsible for all ministries' programs in the prefecture. He is the agent of the minister of interior, only. Robert C. Fried refers to the French system as "integrated prefectures" and to the Italian system as "unintegrated prefectures." [51] He points out that the Italian prefect can be the center of considerable power though his official sphere of authority is delimited. Most important for our concerns here, the unintegrated prefecture is a flexible, nontransitive model in which "the authority of the Prefect can be adjusted to allow him to control or coordinate some programs or activities where the case for such coordination is particularly strong, rather than a general desideratum." [52] Furthermore, "the unintegrated system gives free rein to all the functional services . . . allowing for the necessary geographical adaptation within their respective services." [53]

Development depends upon transivity as well as nontransivity. Any change, if it is to be implemented, requires mobilization of energy, and mobilization of energy requires some degree of transitivity. Bureaucracy is a highly transitive system. It is both detrimental and vital to development. Development requires innovation and the power to innovate. It suggests a societal need to innovate and a societal ability to control, simultaneously. Development is an impossible model for action, in a number of ways, but mostly because it asks for the simultaneous maintenance of two contradictory ideas, the idea of change and the idea of control. Control is necessary for development, yet development is opposed to the current order. To clarify the point here, it might be helpful to note that the questions with which we are dealing are not the same as questions about the thermostat in your living room, if you are lucky enough to have one. Thus, a model of a closed system is not applicable here. We need a model of an open

51. *The Italian Prefects* (New Haven: Yale University Press, 1963), pp. 306–307.
52. Ibid., pp. 308–309.
53. Ibid., p. 309.

system that has the potential for control when it is needed. Which may be asking for more than social systems can deliver.

Conclusions

Recognizing the extreme difficulties posed by the spatial dimension in national development, those of us who have worked together on this book hope that we have made a contribution to better understanding of the difficulties and, perhaps, to better operational handling of these difficulties.

The following chapters do not rhyme, but I think they reason together. Each one searches a significant aspect of space and development, following the themes mentioned in this introductory chapter, that is, themes of:

1. How the nation-state must be spatially unified while allowing for spatial innovation.
2. How culture and space are intertwined.
3. How economic development has spatial aspects and implications within one country undergoing development.
4. How placement of people affects development.
5. How political ideology and space relate to one another.
6. How, and to what effect, political elites try spatial strategies.

Not every chapter deals with every theme, though some deal with most of the themes; our purpose is not to take a checklist and have each writer deal with it. In the final chapter of this book I will suggest how I view the ways in which the following five chapters relate to the themes, so it would be premature, or redundant, to do so here. This book is not based on any precise definitions of "space" and "development." Our purpose is to suggest how these terms can be defined in an interrelationship. Rather than seeing our task as one requiring first, a definition of "development," second, a definition of "space," and third, a series of propositions about those two definitions, we regarded it as something more empirical and phenomenological. Only judgments of this book can decide if we made a mistake in doing so. We deal with "development" and "space" not as scientific terms but as culturally created phenomena. In Yugoslavia these phenomena are talked about and dealt with in a manner different from the way they are talked about and dealt with in Pakistan. The Pakistan approach is different from the Russian approach. And so it goes. We are trying here to generalize, not to promulgate abstract generalizations.

Chapter 2

The Village and Development Administration

Henry C. Hart

Among the problems of administering change which confront the national leaders of the newly developing nations, rural development is emerging as at once the most imperative and the most opaque. Unanticipated takeoffs of national populations make agricultural productivity imperative now, as drawing the peasantry into national political life had seemed a decade earlier. A recent policy conference at M.I.T. indicated some reasons why administering agricultural development is even more difficult than launching industries in an industrially undisciplined society, or setting up national social services: "Farm decision-makers are widely scattered geographically, they vary enormously in economic status and potential, they cover a wide political spectrum, they are subject even in one country to a considerable variety of institutional connections, and they exhibit a widely varying pattern of attitudes and motivations."[1]

What We Can Learn From Community Development

Fifteen years ago, the path of rural development seemed to lie clear ahead—the approach of community development. We need

1. David Hapgood, ed., *Policies for Promoting Agricultural Development: Report of a Conference on Productivity and Innovation in the Underdeveloped Countries* (Cambridge: M.I.T. Center for International Studies, 1965), p. 16.

not trace its progress, save to point out that it gained the character of an international movement, and that its efficacy has now come into doubt. Analytically, its form varied in the thirty or so nations which applied it. But in the conscious attempt to learn lessons from one another's experience, strongly stimulated and helped by United Nations, United States AID, and British colonial advisers, the movement took a definite character capable of projection abroad.[2] The "principles," "model," or "methods" have been communicated in an extensive literature, part shop-talk, part analytical.[3] It is, in fact, remarkable that British, United Nations, and American technical assistance thinking should reflect a common denominator among programs worked out for extremely diverse societies. Carl Taylor, one of the most experienced American advisers, words it in the way we find clearest: "A community development program attempts to join the contributions of the leaders and servants of government and the contributions of energized, organized, local village groups."[4]

Immediately, we can make out three quite different elements or actors in such a program: leaders of government, servants of government, and local village groups. Community development is interaction among them. What kind of interaction becomes clearer as we draw out slightly more specific defining characteristics, this time characteristic methods:

1. Introduction of a wide spectrum of changes, reaching into agriculture, health, education, social organization, communications, and marketing. Agriculture may later be singled out, but by conversion of organization and methods designed for wider objectives.

2. Group self-help by the participating rural populace, the village being the unit defining most groups.

3. Extension to the village by the government of a stimulus or catalyst (typically, though not invariably organized via vil-

2. A classic statement is by the United Nations, Economic and Social Council, *Community Development and Related Services* (E/2931), 1956.

3. *Community Development Abstracts*, prepared for AID by Sociological Abstracts, Inc. (Washington, D.C.: AID, 1964), contains 1,108 abstracts of articles and books.

4. "Making a Community Development Program Work," *Community Development Review*, December 1958, p. 41.

lage extension workers) and of resources of technical assistance and material inputs.[5]

We can discover still more specific shape to the community
development experience if we examine the administrative scene
into which it is introduced. Peter du Sautoy has done this in his
"theory of rural vacuum." [6] By this he means the characteristic
lack of field services of development departments of government
beyond headquarters towns serving not less than 100,000 people
and 100 square miles. But as plans are made to extend services,
coordination among them becomes imperative partly for economy, partly because the traditional peasant and his village are
unable to cope with unintegrated specialized proposals from separate government departments. We can see a general administrative rationale justifying point 1, above, in the light of the difficulty
of point 3. Clearly, too, the rationale has a spatial logic.

There is a very different spatial consideration in the adoption
of community development programs for which we have to dig a
bit beneath the surface. Carl Taylor points out that these programs have not come in response to political demand in the villages, or even manifest unrest in the villages. They have been
decided, especially before they took on the character of an international movement, by eminent national leaders—Nehru, Mag-
saysay, Munoz Marin—seeking to mobilize the rural masses into
national political and economic life. Taylor calls them "democratic" leaders, which they were, but we can be more specific.
They were democratic leaders who knew that constitutions and
elections would not draw peasants into democratic life quickly
enough, and who sought economic and social participation to re-

5. To these characteristics there was agreement among U.N. Doc. E/2931,
Peter du Sautoy (see citation in n. 6, below), and Louis M. Miniclier, "Community Development Defined," *Community Development Review,* December 1956,
pp. 1–2. However, an analytical survey distinguishes among and within these
characteristics to give us a more accurate comparative view of any particular national application as a distinctively proportioned mix of them. For one of the
clearest such, see Arthur T. Mosher, *Varieties of Extension Education and Community Development* (Ithaca: Cornell University State College of Agriculture,
Comparative Extension Publication No. 2, 1958). Here we find that multi-subject-
matter extension (point 1, above) may be applied with little resort to local groups
(point 2). Our Etawah case, below, was of this nature. Our Comilla case dis-
penses with the village extension agent.

6. *The Organization of a Community Development Programme* (London: Oxford University Press, 1962), pp. 47ff.

inforce political. They were (as were the British colonial administrators, e.g., in West Africa in the postwar years) nation-builders.

Community development to these men was a means of underpinning new nations with local communities conscious of their two-way participation—receiving government assistance, producing vitally needed food and savings, choosing governments. This second spatial aspect came later to scrutiny, but we find it noticed by a group of experts appointed by Secretary General U. Thant in 1963: "Community development makes use of and even creates those units of local action which seem most appropriate to the objective of linking people in with the national framework." [7]

We can now see that the three "actors" in community development, political leaders, administrative systems, and peasant communities, stand in some order of transitivity. Community development is government programs happening to villagers, and their responses. This is true certainly of the initial stage. Then villagers will presumably make demands, but we note that even the units in which they articulate those demands may be created by governments. We cannot be sure, yet, of the transitive relation of political leaders and administrative systems.

After fifteen years, the movement does not seem to provide a clear solution to the problems of rural development. The report on the M.I.T. policy conference commented that "the record of recent years is one of general failure and only rare successes." [8] Rural development policy is moving in new directions based on different assumptions. For example, agricultural production per se is tackled. Yet the new assumptions are not based on verified knowledge of the potential interrelations of political leaders, administrative systems, and villages. [9]

7. United Nations, Secretary-General, *Community Development and National Development: Report by an ad hoc Group of Experts Appointed by the Secretary-General* (New York: United Nations, 1963), p. 8.

8. Hapgood, *Policies for Promoting Agricultural Development*, p. 3.

9. The president of the Rural Sociological Society said in 1963, "It is my feeling that we know relatively little about the structure and process of integrating the many diverse local interests as well as the roles of the many specialized agencies in attacking area problems. This seems to be the heart of the problem of community development the world over." Eugene Wilkening, "Some Perspectives on Change in Rural Societies," *Rural Sociology* 29 (March 1964): 11.

The empirical studies of community development consist chiefly of analyses of the village end of the transactions, taking the behavior of farmers, or village groups as dependent variables, and detailed program elements as independent variables. The rationale is to discover which program elements achieve intended results under which village conditions. Would it be possible to use this large body of recorded and conceptually comparable experience to throw light the other way—on the political elites and the administrative systems? Could we ask why they adopted or conducted community development as they did? Now that we can see it was not wholly functional in its announced aims and methods, can we study it for "latent" functions? If so, we might gain knowledge of an inherent complex of problems of development administration, spatially considered, for the three elements of the complex are all here:

1. Nation-building motives and policies of national leaders.
2. Norms and internal relations of administration, considered as a national system undergoing change.
3. Norms, and solidarity and leadership of peasant villages, considered in relation to the above.

Can we gain any theoretical perspective that would suggest relations among these three elements in which the transitivity might run in any direction?

What We Can Learn from the Indian and Pakistani Cases

This chapter exploits a great body of information, some of it in the form of independent empirical investigations, upon the community development programs and projects of India and Pakistan. The programs are revealing because they contain successes and failures. They exhibit slightly different uses of an essentially common national administrative apparatus and therefore give us roughly controlled observation of element 2 above. They afford us variants in the village context: caste in India, and a more cohesive community religion in Pakistan. Unfortunately, we cannot be very sure how neatly these differences sort out, since these factors interworked so many centuries in the same Indian matrix. Our more revealing contextual comparisons would be among known subcultures and subsocieties within each nation; we shall not have much time for this sort of analysis.

What is particularly illuminating for our purpose is that within India and within Pakistan we can compare the community development of national political decisions and the administrative system with the community development of a pilot project. Hopefully, we can thus isolate the impacts of national leaders and the nationwide administrative system from the standard characteristics of international community development. Previous studies have asked how the movement was received in a particular village context. We can try to find out how the movement was received and interpreted by the two main categories of governing elites: political and administrative. In the process we can seek a more rigorous understanding of their relations to the villages. We can try to specify what kind of explanatory theory would encompass these relations, viewed as reciprocal.

We should be clear that the very common characteristics which make India and Pakistan comparable also, unfortunately, distinguish them from many other nations which have tried community development. Each nation has emerged with an extraordinary (perhaps unequalled) gulf separating the political and administrative leaders from the village folk. The leaders were first drawn out for a century by English-language university training and the powerful Westernizing pull of gradually opening opportunities in business, professions, and government. They were drawn slowly and permanently into parties, leadership roles, elite services. All the constitutional form, the available scientific and technical personnel, and the inclination to plan and systematize come from this elite heritage. By contrast, the peasant populations are not only as miserable (by the external standards of calories, literacy, life expectancy) as any ever reached by development plans, but they are also in some ways uniquely enculturated in that condition.

But if the division between leadership and peasantry is deep and old and thoroughly structured, leaders and peasants are also powerfully drawn toward integration. That, too, is old.

The administrative elite served its apprenticeship looking after rural welfare. The political leadership did not suddenly gain power by championing an easy independence. It had to oust the British the hard way, which meant gaining some peasant following. Gandhi succeeded radically; Pakistan exists because Jinnah demonstrated that he could succeed. It is, of course, the dynamism generated by this old and vigorous search for the means to bridge their deep divisions that brought India and Pakistan so early and with such well considered plans to establish community development. India in 1952 and Pakistan in 1953–1954, followed by the Philippines in 1955, are generally regarded as the original large approximations to the international model.

So that, although these characteristics differentiate the nations we study from others to which we would like to gain predictive power, we can at least be sure that community development has engaged the energies and aspirations of leaders and has tapped important potentials of peasant motives and solidarities. These were nations community development advocates of a decade ago were glad to see the movement tested in; they are nations it significantly tested.

Community Development in India

Pilot Project, India

Among small-scale Indian development projects, some of which were begun in the 1920's and 1930's, we prefer for comparison the one which most directly tests relations to existing political and administrative environments. Fortunately the postindependence project which is most comparable to the national one is also best recorded: the pilot project in Etawah District of Uttar Pradesh.[10]

10. In rough chronological order, the seven projects are: (1) District Officer F. L. Brayne's work in Gurgaon, Punjab; (2) Tagore's Sriniketan in Bengal, developed by Leonard Elmhirst; (3) Spencer Hatch's YMCA project at Martandam (Kerala); (4) Sevagram and other model villages of Gandhi; (5) Albert Mayer's

The Etawah project had a six-year career; it was established in 1948 and absorbed into the nationwide program from 1954. It was controlled and paid for by the state government, though led by a remarkable American architect and planner, Albert Mayer. It did not seek to discover new, untried agricultural techniques. Its rationale was, rather, that the Indian agricultural experiment stations already had knowledge of techniques capable of increasing yields; the problem was to get them into use.[11] The project methods were to demonstrate the simplest of the changes, improved seeds, and take care that all facilities were available. As this change proved its value, demonstrations of more difficult techniques followed: fertilizer, line sowing, growing and turning under green manure. This is standard agricultural extension technique—Arthur T. Mosher called it "multi-subject-matter extension."

Some land reclamation was done—gully terracing with heavy tractors. Relatively few of the changes introduced required group or village action. Project staff, on realistic appraisal, found too little solidarity, generally, to sustain collective self-help, despite the fact that government-propagated cooperatives had long existed pro forma.[12] There were exceptions. Untouchables, united in adversity, worked together to build housing. To break a brick shortage for building, peasants cooperated in running village kilns.

The project's structural changes in administration were mainly

pilot project in Etawah District, U.P.; (6) Allahabad Agricultural Institute's three-year extension experiment; (7) Barpali, Orissa, village projects of Friends Service Committee.

Numbers 1, 3, 4, and 5 are summarized in Government of India, Ministry of Community Development, *Evolution of Community Development Programme in India* (Delhi: Mgr. of Publications, 1963). For 2, see Hashim Amir Ali, *The Environs of Tagore* (New York: Asia Publishing House, 1960); for 6, Allahabad Agricultural Institute, *Experiment in Extension: The Gaon Sathi* (Bombay: Oxford, 1957); for 7, T. M. Fraser, Jr., "Barpali Village Service: A Quaker Experiment in Community Development," *Journal of Human Relations* 9 (Spring 1961): 285–99. On Etawah we have the inside record, critically edited and commented upon: Albert Mayer, McKim Marriott, and Richard L. Park, *Pilot Project, India* (Berkeley: University of California Press, 1958).

11. Rudra Dutt Singh, "The Village Level: An Introduction of Green Manuring in Rural India," in Edward H. Spicer, ed., *Human Problems in Technological Change: A Casebook* (New York: Russell Sage Foundation, 1952), pp. 55–57.

12. Mayer, Marriott, and Park, *Pilot Project*, pp. 227–28, 279–81.

designed to fill the "rural vacuum." Village extension agents, one to every five villages, were backstopped by a small team of technicians, directed by four technician-administrators at the project level. Mayer was strategist; there were three or four Americans; and the remaining staff was transferred from existing government careers or more often recruited afresh. Selection was for personal qualities as well as skills. Appointees were trained only a few weeks before going to work; most learning took place in regular staff discussions of actual pending decisions and future strategies. There is no doubt that the resulting reorientation of administrative personnel was significant. Mayer reported on the case of a transferred officer: "Mirza is now a different man, anxious for the rough-and-tumble of real work and close contact with the people, instead of the . . . power and control and hierarchy which were the hallmarks of his former career."[13] Mayer refers to all these changes as "democratization." It is true that decision-making rules were transformed to include consultation. But commitments, once accepted in such a decision conference, had to be fulfilled. That, too, was a change.

The pilot project had been established by the highest state authority. It began to show results in production. Then it came in direct conflict with the established administrative system. Mayer likened project methods to a "little flower that happened to catch hold . . . in a minor crack of the rock face of hierarchical administrative relationships. . . . Either the plant would grow strong enough to crack the rock face, or the rock face would crush the little plant."[14] We can make out reasons for the clash. Project administration looked to results. Its decisions were commitments to its own workers (who would be held to them, too) and to villagers. ("We cannot fall down on a promise. That is the absolutely unforgivable sin."[15]) The project would not accept changes for administrative convenience if they interfered with these commitments.

13. Ibid., p. 91.
14. Ibid., pp. 63ff.
15. Ibid., p. 134.

The project won direct access to the state development commissioner, skipping less result-oriented echelons of administration. The rock face gave way. We must recognize, however, that the conflict was posed by a going concern blocked by the system —the little plant had three years to take root. It was carried, second, to the top political authority in the state, and to Prime Minister Nehru. Mayer was not contained by the hierarchy.

What were the overall results? We have corroborating evidence supplementing Mayer's own records: an appraisal published by the national ministry of community development by a former Etawah administrator, and a report by a skeptical observer of rural development throughout India, Kusum Nair.[16] Wheat yields are up 50 to 100 percent compared to nonproject areas of the district. Barley yields are up less, grain more. Green manuring remains a farming practice years after pilot project staff departed. Peasants retain old attitudes, according to Mrs. Nair's account, but with unreconciled new ones added. They say: "Only four or five families would be prosperous, while the rest starve." They acknowledge increased yields, but attribute them to merit in former incarnations (*karma*). Yet they also believe that "those who work hard earn more." Another tender plant has perhaps taken root.

Etawah might appear to have set the administrative pattern for India's nationwide effort. Yet Mayer was convinced that the nation was making all the mistakes he had learned to avoid—remote and rigid control, paper results, overrapid expansion. Certainly the national program did not follow the pilot in one vital respect: it did not generate result-oriented local leaders capable of fighting the administrative system when blocked by it.

Why a pilot project is now used as pilot is for our comparison to reveal. We can, at this point, discern a limitation of Etawah itself. It did not, in the strict sense, experiment, whether with agronomy or extension methods. This is evident when we com-

16. *Evolution of Community Development Programme in India*, p. 61 and Table I; *Blossoms in the Dust, The Human Factor in Indian Development* (New York: Praeger, 1962), pp. 73, 79.

pare the experimentation done during the same years by Allahabad Agricultural Institute.[17] Allahabad showed the differing
results of different kinds of staff, different training methods, different extension techniques. Etawah produced ample feedback
to its own staff, immediately through staff conferences, on more
basic questions through researches by its own rural life analyst.
But since alternatives were not tried, outsiders could content
themselves that they knew better methods, or that Etawah results were due to Mayer's personal qualities. It is perhaps significant that the Etawah innovation which has extended and renewed
itself is the U.P. Planning Research and Action Institute, which
joins field research to program and process innovation. Is an experiment and research component required to render pilot demonstrations extensible?

Nationwide Community Development, India

India's experience with national community development provides us with a giant, complex, and yet, for our purposes, particularly apposite case. The program started in October 1952. Very
quickly national plans called for extending it nationwide, and by
December 1963, the responsible ministry reported that 99 percent of the 400 million people were covered.[18] It was by far the
world's largest program. Moreover, there could be no doubt of the
seriousness of the Indian government's commitment: "Community development is the method and Rural Extension the agency
through which the Five Year Plan seeks to initiate the process of
transformation of the social and economic life of the villages." [19]
As the capital letters in this statement suggest, commitment was
to a well-defined model, the very international model presented
in our introductory paragraphs. Indeed, because India's adoption
came so early, Indian experience was often taken to be the realization of the model.

Even before the nation had been covered, shortcomings had

17. *Experiment in Extension.*
18. Ministry of Community Development and Cooperation, *Report, 1963–64*
(New Delhi: Government of India, 1964), p. 10.
19. Planning Commission, *First Five Year Plan* (New Delhi: Government of
India, 1952), p. 223. Repeated in the second plan document.

been recognized by the government. A drastic change, involving some measures of control by representative councils, began to be introduced in the seventh year. From the mixed record of achievement and frustration we gain data to test explanatory theories. The new phase of the program, called *panchayati raj*, gives us a partial cross-check upon these theories, centering as it does upon government relations. We take this as warrant for a summary and incomplete analysis of an experience which can only be a mosaic of local differences.

Survival of the national program has turned on results in food production. During the critical shortage of food supply in 1965–1966, the Ministry of Community Development, independent for ten years, was absorbed into the food and agricultural portfolio, and Mr. S. K. Dey, ten years its minister, transferred. The food production test is not unfair, for this has been the "first claim" on community development staff from the start. But it is not an easy test to score with precision; rainfall still alters harvests more than development efforts do, even over periods of several years. What we can say is that with population growing 2¼ percent a year, and real demand faster, increases in yields per acre of food grains have not kept pace, being of the order of 1.8 percent over the whole period of community development. To be sure, additions to acreage have resulted in a per capita gain. But this is creditable more to irrigation than to community development.[20] Secondly, those planned agricultural inputs which lay within the powers of extension programs to introduce (not chemical fertilizers, but improved seeds, green manuring, and minor irrigation works) have lagged dismally and increasingly behind targets. The nation had to, and did, turn to other means to meet its target for the 1966–1971 plan —a yearly increase of 5 percent in food grain output.

Community development evaluated itself thoroughly and objectively. From the seven yearly reports of the semiautonomous program-evaluation organization we can derive a sort of profile of

20. C. H. Hanumantha Rao, "Agricultural Growth and Stagnation in India," *Economic Weekly* (Bombay) 17 (February 27, 1965): 408. Corroborated in *Indian Journal of Agricultural Economics* 20 (January–March 1965): 7. Hanumantha Rao finds a more rapid productivity rise in the six years 1955–1961; unfortunately they are years of good monsoons.

greater or lesser achievements of intended effects that will help us understand the shortage on the agricultural development front.[21]

1. Participation of villagers was invoked, but less than intended.
2. Contributions to village amenities, especially roads and schools, far surpassed contributions to directly productive works of formation of community organizations.
3. Agricultural improvements were taken up when individual effort sufficed to do so, economically stronger and more commercial cultivators doing the innovating.
4. New attitudes toward government developed. Village workers were accepted as trying to be helpful. Demands upon government for assistance and investment grew faster than attitudes of village self-reliance.
5. Participation of village people did not reach a self-sustaining momentum. In the words of the fifth program-evaluation organization report: "The proportion of people's participation to block expenditure has a tendency to decline in the later years . . . it only means that benefits from educational effort and radiational effect are not being obtained." [22]

The whole picture is one of progress that might have been achieved by other means, failure at the central community development mission of evoking self-sustaining self-help. We are confirmed in this diagnosis and given a clear explanation of it by a comprehensive study of Indian community development by its closest American advisers, Douglas Ensminger, Carl Taylor, and two associates.[23] Their explanation is a dysfunctional administrative system. They show the symptoms at each level of work.

21. These are listed and their contents summarized in Howard W. Beers, "Program Evaluation in India," *Rural Sociology* 25 (1960): 431–41. See also an evaluation done by the U. P. Planning Research and Action Institute: United Nations, Economic Commission for Asia and the Far East, *Community Development and Economic Development, Part IIA, A Case Study of the Ghosi Community Development Block, Uttar Pradesh, India* (Bangkok: ECAFE, 1960).

22. Planning Commission Programme Evaluation Organization, *Fifth Evaluation Report on the Working of Community Development and N.E.S. Blocks* (New Delhi: Government of India, 1958), p. 21.

23. Carl C. Taylor, Douglas Ensminger, Helen W. Johnson, and Jean Joyce, *India's Roots of Democracy, A Sociological Analysis of Rural India's Experience in Planned Development Since Independence* (Calcutta: Orient Longmans, 1965).

The 50,000 village-level workers (VLW's), each moving among his five to ten villages on his bicycle, they find to be motivated to the task and soundly related to the main strata of owning-cultivating villagers. Most are village-reared; their two-year training is effective. But they encounter two serious obstacles. They are not wise enough, nor authoritative enough, to mediate conflicts over village leadership or group formation. And they encounter from their superiors at the next higher administrative level, the development block, precisely the kind of arbitrary demands that produced conflict at Etawah. Here the conflict is bottled up. The VLW's fill in an average of two and a half reports per day, reports concerned with formal quotas and procedures, not village attitudes and relationships. They dance attendance when block officers tour. They are told, not asked, what their villages can do.[24]

Looking upward from the VLW to the block staff, the Taylor-Ensminger analysis comes across a kind of administrative fault line. At the block level (averaging 100 villages) and above targets are expected to be sent down from above, and sent down as directives below. The block development officer (BDO) is called a team captain, but as a rising young (perhaps twenty-eight years old) member of the elite Indian Administrative Service he feels superior to the agriculture or engineering technicians on his team. Technicians, for their part, look to their own departments—animal husbandry, agriculture, cooperatives—for advancement; they would not even under more sensitive leadership desire to integrate their programs. Probing further upward in the higher echelons: Why were not the intermediate levels of administration as thoroughly trained and retrained as the VLW's? They point to the "belief on the part of development leaders that they already know the ideas of villagers. . . ."[25] Why does planning from the village up remain a cliché in the plan documents, why the recurring stress on numbers of compost pits dug, not on effective village leadership? It is the rank-stressed, downward-acting pattern of bureaucratic relationships that is dysfunctional to gener-

24. See, in addition to the summary in ibid., pp. 560–62, 564, the revealing diary of a village worker included as an appendix in S. C. Dube, *India's Changing Villages* (London: Routledge and Kegan Paul, 1958).
25. Taylor and Ensminger, *India's Roots of Democracy*, p. 538.

ating self-help. The sociological analysis attains its greatest penetration when it shows that all who work together in community development (BDO–VLW, VLW–block technician, BDO–block technician, BDO–district officer, VLW–villager) "must have fluid, that is uninhibited, interpersonal relations" analogous to those in a primary group. But India's "splendid, rationally designed programme" was "in some ways sabotaged" by "administrative procedures and attitudes." [26]

In our scheme of inquiry, this diagnosis takes on a clear meaning. National political leaders understood village requirements; the administrators thought they did, but were wrong. They were wrong because of their institutional heritage. (We must modify the "rural vacuum" metaphor; community development encounters administrative patterns as a going concern.) The elite administration of empire, the Indian Civil Service, though alien in its tasks and law, was thoroughly rooted in the status-ordered Indian countryside. Reincarnated as the Indian Administrative Service, it unwittingly distorted the national political goals. Of course, the question is: Why was community development entrusted to it, since Etawah had demonstrated the inherent conflict? The Taylor-Ensminger answer turns to political considerations we can examine later: "There were widespread expectations, even among the masses, that something would be done to improve their conditions . . . there was no alternative to launching a programme of giant proportions . . . since the programme was to be nationwide, it was necessary that she make maximum use of this efficient bureaucracy." [27]

This judgment of efficiency seems to be irreconcilable (at least in hindsight) with the diagnosis of "sabotage." But the Taylor-Ensminger analysis points out that the turnover to elitist administration was not complete: the block was deliberately new-modeled separate from the old administrative unit, the *taluk* and *tehsil*, and the VLW's were wholly new. In our terms, we can now see the administrative strategy, and its dilemma. A prestige-ordered administrative system was to be supplemented at the

26. Ibid., pp. 577–80, 190, 637.
27. Ibid., pp. 190, 570.

bottom by a new service identified with villagers. The question was: Can a prestige-ordered system be changed from the bottom up?

The strategy of relying on the ICS-IAS gains further plausibility if we move beyond the sociological diagnosis to one attuned directly to national administrative problems. In 1953, Paul Appleby punctured a myth of Indian federalism by pointing out that national ministries (he referred explicitly to the community development organization) were administratively impotent, for they relied on hierarchies politically controlled by elective state ministries for execution of programs.[28] Between the national ministry of community development and the state ministry is a genuine, and growing, gap in accountability. The national ministry can call conferences, issue circulars, propound ideologies; it cannot command. Yet it makes the design, the policies, the plans. Across this gap the ICS-IAS is the most reliable bridge: the ICS secretary to the national ministry can make his decisions effective in the states via the ICS or IAS development commissioners, although Mr. S. K. Dey may not get genuine compliance from their state ministers. This is a sharp modification of the Taylor-Ensminger top-down hierarchical explanation, for we see an elite service useful to bridge a federal gap in the chain of command. But we arrive at our second question, this one peculiar to federal nations: Can a self-help program be conveyed to governments of separate political responsibility by a prestige-ordered service?

Panchayati Raj

Indian community development has more to teach us than why it fell short of its central objective. In a remarkable self-analysis, the planning authorities detected the shortcoming in 1957, instituted a searching inquiry, and recommended a radical cure.[29] The cure was *panchayati raj*. For our purposes, this highly diverse reform can be understood simply as a three-level representative

28. *Public Administration in India, Report of a Survey* (Delhi: Manager of Publications, 1953).
29. Committee on Plan Projects, *Report of the Team for the Study of Community Projects and National Extension Service*, 3 vols. (New Delhi: Planning Commission, 1957), vol. 3 in two parts.

government of rural development. Villages elect *panchayats* by adult suffrage, *panchayats* are in various ways represented on block councils (*samitis*), and district councils (*parishads*). In 1957 recommendations have now been effected, with modifications, in all states, starting with Rajasthan and Andhra in 1959. In our inquiry, the reform means that national political leaders, finding community development frustrated by a status-oriented administrative system, found a solution by placing local policy in the hands of village representatives. Thus would self-help be revived by self-government. It was a cure which fully satisfied the Taylor-Ensminger diagnosis.[30]

There is already a rich store of empirical knowledge concerning the early working of *panchayati raj*. We need be concerned only with the question whether direct and indirect effective control of community development by villages can, from the perspective of national leadership and policy, dispense with the dysfunctional administrative linkage. We can get to the heart of this question by examining the demarcation of the representative units, and the procedure for initiating the "revolution."

The 1961 census counted 567,338 villages in India.[31] By 1964, 99 percent of them were covered by elected *panchayats,* but there were less than 220,000 *panchayats*. Clearly, the way in which villages were grouped into *panchayats* could lay the basis for participative planning and trusted leadership, or for factional division and popular indifference. We note, first, that some states (Madras, Delhi Union Territory) constituted a *panychayat* for almost every census village; at the other extreme, Bihar averaged six or seven and Orissa twenty villages in a *panchayat*. These latter states are cautious about devolving responsibility.

Second, we find very little attempt to set national policy by gathering evidence on the conditions under which a traditional village, or a cluster of small villages, might form the stronger unit of local leadership and decision. National policy, on the contrary, came as a sort of diagonal of two conflicting cultural perspectives.

30. India "has recently taken revolutionary steps to correct these shortcomings [of administrative sabotage]. . . . The whole rural development programme is evolving back toward the well-conceived plan with which it started." Ibid., p. 637.
31. *Census of India, 1961, Vol. I, Part II-A (i) General Population Tables* (Delhi: Manager of Publications, 1964), p. 57.

Planners wanted areas large enough to warrant specialized staff, and to throw up talented leaders. Gandhians and "small community" devotees valued intimacy and trusted leadership. The former inclined to multivillage, the latter to one-village *panchayats.* The direction of compromise can be seen in the remarks of the leading community development planner, V. T. Krishnamachari. In principle, he sided with the one-village school, but to attain "convenient units" he thought villages of less than 1,000 people should be merged.[32] This would mean, in practice, redefining 83 percent of the villages, inhabited by 44 percent of the rural people. The community development manual said these villages "should be encouraged to group themselves into clusters . . . in electing a panchayat. . . ." [33] Could a prestige-ordered administration be expected to approach the task this way? Or did the policy of merger, given the shortcomings of administration which *panchayati raj* was supposed to correct, mean that something approaching half of *panchayat* units would be creations of administration?

The development block, with its indirectly elected *samiti,* gained more power in *panchayati raj* than the *panchayat* below or (save in Maharashtra state) the district *parishad* above. But whereas *panchayats* followed some village boundaries and changed others, development blocks were deliberately created de novo as service areas for community development. Demarcation ignored "sociologically natural" units; ten years of development work in the blocks did not attempt to make their people "self-conscious local area groups." [34]

Panchayati raj opens the *samiti,* with its budget and supervision of block personnel, to political party contest in a territorial unit in which people do not yet sense interdependence, to which they do not sense loyalty. One can foresee two dangers: party

32. V. T. Krishnamachari, *Community Development in India* (New Delhi: Government of India Publications Division, 1962), pp. 71, 77. This was the policy of the Planning Commission, *Second Five Year Plan* (New Delhi: Government of India, 1956), pp. 152, 205.
33. Ministry of Community Development and Cooperation, *A Guide to Community Development,* rev. ed. (Delhi: Manager of Publications, 1962), pp. 6, 8.
34. Howard W. Beers and Douglas Ensminger, "The Development Block as a Social System," *Indian Journal of Public Administration* 5 (1959): 149. Taylor and Ensminger, *India's Roots of Democracy,* p. 632.

divisiveness, and leadership too weak to raise local funds for development. If they materialize, not less but more administrative
prestige may be required to sustain development.

The Etawah project enunciated a finding which is a cardinal
principle of extension technique: assumption of collective responsibility (in cooperatives or local self-government) will grow if
villagers are confronted with decisions matched to their social
capabilities. States observed this principle in some of the variations they made in *panchayati raj* structure; they did not observe
it in their phasing. Within five years of the initial *panchayati raj*
legislation, the national Ministry of Community Development reported full coverage in eleven states and declared that establishment in the remaining four states "assumes urgency." [35] What we
know of villages and districts suggests the extraordinary differences in their states of readiness, as indicated by their differences
in urbanization, literacy, commercial farming, linguistic, tribal
and religious divisions, communications, previous developmental
history. Armed with much data on each community development
block and a good research organization, the ministry did not seek
to identify conditions of readiness for elective control of development institutions.

The Committee on Plan Projects, proposing *panchayati raj*,
called it "an act of faith—faith in democracy." [36] It is not the magnitude of the leap beyond the known we are questioning. It is the
disregard of the known, which might have indicated more precisely the direction of the leap. Blanket coverage of centrally designed institutions for rural self-government certainly showed
faith that national democracy could dispense local democracy,
perhaps also that it could do so by administrative tutelage.

Community Development in Pakistan

Village-AID, Pakistan

Pakistan launched Village Agricultural and Industrial Development (called Village-AID) within eighteen months of India's

---

35. Ministry of Community Development, *Annual Report 1964–65*, pp. 1, 6.
36. *Report of the Team for the Study of Community Projects . . .* , p. 21.

community development; the decision was shaped even more than in India's case by outside considerations. Full use was made of the Indian model, United States technical assistance gave a "strong impetus," and the Ford Foundation initially supported staff training institute salaries.[37] The strongest governmental champion of the program, Chauduri Mohamad Ali, then minister of Finance and Economic Affairs, and later prime minister. (Like India's V. T. Krishnamachari, he had been a brillant career administrator, but outside the conventional ICS career.[38]) Antedating Pakistan's economic planning, the decision may not have been thoroughly considered and accepted government-wide.

As in India, the initial decision was to concentrate development on selected areas. But the second five-year plan (1960–1965) contained the commitment to extend Village-AID nationwide to 85 percent of the rural population. The timetable matched the Indian one. In the event, Village-AID was terminated as a distinct program in 1961. By that time more than one-fourth of the countryside had been included in the 207 development areas.

The Village-AID worker (VAW) was the same sort of young man, with the same mission, as his Indian counterpart. He had seven or eight villages to look after in East Pakistan, usually five in West Pakistan[39] where villages are larger. Twenty to thirty VAW's, serving about 150 villages, staffed a development area, headed by a development officer, assisted by two supervisors. As in India, the plan called for a staff of technicians helping the development officer. In fact, they were not made available by their home departments (agriculture, animal husbandry, etc.). The state or provincial head of the program was a special Village-AID administrator, not a broad-functioned development commissioner ranking as chief secretary to the state government. Thus, we can conceive of Pakistan's organizational strategy as approaching the

37. Training of workers began July 1953; first projects opened February 1954. James W. Green, "Rural Community Development in Pakistan: The Village-AID Program," *Community Development Review* 6 (September 1957): 45, 56.
38. Ralph Braibanti, "Public Bureaucracy and Judiciary in Pakistan," in Joseph LaPalombara, ed., *Bureaucracy and Political Development* (Princeton: Princeton University Press, 1963), pp. 373, 377.
39. Consolidation of former provinces and states in West Pakistan into one occurred in 1955.

other horn of the dilemmas we identified in the Indian case. Village-AID tended more toward duplication of, less toward dependence upon, existing national elite civil service.[40] Second, directives could go down the program hierarchy from nation to state to village with less interruption by separate political accountability. The differences, though incomplete, do partly test whether the shortcomings we discovered in India are due to particular organizational strategies, or to characteristics of the national decisional and administrative systems.

Save the progress reports coming up the hierarchy, there is much less information about results of Village-AID than of Indian community development.[41] Findings upon which independent judgments agree are that the VAW's were slowly accepted by landowners as bona fide aides, not agents of the rulers, that techniques applicable on individual holdings were successfully demonstrated to owner-cultivators, that cooperative efforts were not engendered, and the VAW's had not the ability nor position to deal with the factional rifts and threats to establish power positions involved in attempts to obtain village-wide self-help decisions.[42] Again we find the disjunction between the zealous VAW and his bureaucratic superiors, between the technical field men and the multipurpose development administrators. But Village-AID worked under an extra handicap. The department of agriculture never accepted its "claim" to constitute the extension channel to the villages for all rural development departments and programs. This denied Village-AID the technicians who could be had only by transfer from that department; it heightened the vulnerability of the new agency as being a duplication and tem-

40. Akhter Hameed Khan, *Rural Development in East Pakistan, Speeches of Akhter Hameed Khan* (East Lansing: Michigan State University, Asian Studies Center, 1964?), p. 11, puts it more flatly than this. "They made an attempt at bypassing the civil administration . . ."

41. John J. Honigmann, "A Case Study of Community Development in Pakistan," *Economic Development and Cultural Change* 8 (1960): 303. For one critical judgment of Village-AID, see A. K. M. Mohsen, *The Comilla Rural Administration Experiment, History and Annual Report, 1962–63* (Comilla: Pakistan Academy for Rural Development, 1963), pp. 1–6 (cited hereafter as PARD, 1963).

42. Ministry of Food and Agriculture, *Report of the Food and Agriculture Commission* (Karachi: Pakistan, Manager of Publications, 1960), pp. 188–89; Honigmann, "A Case Study," p. 302; Inayatullah and Q. M. Shafi, *Dynamics of Development in a Pakistani Village* (Peshawar: Pakistan Academy for Rural Development, 1963), pp. 160–61, 170–72.

porary.[43] We have here strong evidence that the difficulties encountered by nationwide community development in India are the products merely of the strategy of relying heavily on the existing elite administrative service, rather than on new hierarchies within each state. Pakistan came nearer the latter strategy with less satisfactory results.

Unfortunately for the rigor of our comparison, Pakistan's rural development situation differed in other than administrative terms. There was a greater dependence on water control works—second-crop irrigation and coastal embankments in East Pakistan, in the West wing vast canal systems covering 24 million acres of which 3 million were out of production due to waterlogging and salinity.[44] Land reform came in West Pakistan only five years after the initiation of Village-AID and left much larger inequalities than did Indian laws. Both factors made it more difficult for village extension workers to cope with the determinants of farm production or village leadership. Nevertheless, the conclusion stands that a serious attempt, carried forward over seven years and a considerable part of the nation, to evoke village self-help and increase yields by community development methods was judged by a vigorous development-minded leadership to be inadequate to those missions. In 1959 President Ayub Khan instituted Basic Democracies, bearing the same relation to Village-AID that *panchayati raj* did to Indian community development. Initially Village-AID was reoriented to train the new elected rural leaders. Pakistan also created instrumentalities for which there is no Indian counterpart, agricultural development corporations for each province to handle the supply of materials (seed, fertilizer, insecticides, tools, etc.) for which there was no commercial market. In 1961, Village-AID was terminated.

Pakistan Pilot Project, Comilla

Institutes to train village workers operated effectively from the start, but in Village-AID, as in its Indian counterpart, the train-

43. The point is made from different perspectives in *Report of the Food and Agriculture Commission*, pp. 189–90, 208; Green, "Rural Community Development in Pakistan," p. 63.

44. Stuart Lerner, *Agricultural Policy in Pakistan*, U.S. Department of Agriculture, Foreign Agriculture, no. 16, October 1961, pp. 5–9.

ing of administrators lagged behind. In 1959 the East Pakistan Academy for Rural Development opened in Comilla, a rather rustic town at the eastern edge of deltaic Bengal. (West Pakistan's counterpart is in Peshawar.[45]) The academy asked for, and was allotted for development under Village-AID, the surrounding *thana* (literally, police station) of 107 square miles and some 350 villages. This was to be the testing ground for any new development methods which might be incorporated in the training. The new academy had a regular staff of ten (eight with M.A. degrees, two with Ph.D.'s) all of whom received nine months of special training at Michigan State University before starting work. It has ordinarily had as many more foreign specialists or advisers (Japanese rice-cultivation experts, Peace Corps advisers, advisers on Harvard or Michigan State contracts).[46]

The academy's director, however, accounts for much of its distinctive development. Starting this institution at the age of forty-four, Akhter Hameed Khan had already combined achievements and commitments normally reserved for separate lives. Growing up in Agra, India, he won a coveted place in the ICS, studied the conventional two years at Cambridge, and served seven years as magistrate and rural administrator in Bengal. He thus acquired the judge's and officer's perspectives on village Bengal and the lasting regard which ICS officers reserve for members of the cadre. But he was far from a careerist. He read seriously in Muslim texts and became interested in a militant sect of Islam, the Khaksar movement. Before Independence he resigned from the ICS and taught for a few years at Jammia Millia Islamia, Delhi, an institute of Indian nationalist Muslims warmly supported by Gandhi. After partition, he chose Pakistan, East Pakistan, but it was some years before he found a vocation. In 1954, he directed the new Village-AID program in East Pakistan. At the end of the year, he quit.

45. The entire literature by and about the academies is listed in Edgar A. Schuler and Raghu Singh, *The Pakistan Academies for Rural Development, Comilla and Peshawar, 1959–64* (East Lansing: Michigan State University, Asian Studies Center, 1965).
46. There are several short general accounts of the history and methods of the academy: Mohsen, *The Comilla Rural Administration Experiment*, pp. 1–33: Akhter Hameed Khan, *Rural Development in East Pakistan*. A Michigan State University group has a full account in preparation.

I was convinced that the assumptions on which the program was based were only partially valid and that it was
necessary to have experimental areas. . . . But I realized
that as Director I would not be able to do any experimental
work. In the first place, all the answers seemed to be known.
. . . In the second place, in order to experiment, I would
need a very limited area.[47]

Akhter Hameed went back to a small college in Comilla where he
had been teaching; when the academy was established, he was an
honorary assistant to the local Village-AID area administrator.

What could be done at Comilla was conditioned by the ecology
and the social history of the *thana*. This eastern edge of the
Ganges-Brahmaputra delta lies only 15 to 18 feet above sea level.
The entire plain may be flooded during the monsoon. The people
survive on embankments and raised village sites, but the short
summer rice crop is lost. A later-maturing monsoon rice may survive. From December to April, the plain is brick-hard, too hard
for bullock-drawn plows, and too dry to yield a winter crop.
Crowding on the land had reached, probably surpassed, the den-
sity sustainable by low-yield, monsoon agriculture. Farms (not
per capita holdings) averaged 1.7 acres, shrunk to one-half or
one-third their former size as more sons survived. Land reform in
1951 had turned nominal tenants into owners, but withdrawn
from the countryside much of the traditional leadership and capital reserves. More and more frequently, especially after floods
and cyclones, farmers had to borrow to survive; in one village interest payments alone took a little over half the rice harvest.[48]

This was the rather grim picture the academy staff gathered
from many informal talks with peasants in 1959. Their task was
training administrators, but Akhter Hameed Khan was going to
train by involving administrators in development. That required
a strategy by which villagers could extricate themselves from their
downward spiral. Since water was available if it could be lifted a

47. *Speeches of Akhter Hameed Khan*, p. 24.
48. Henry W. Fairchild and Shamshul Haq, *A New Rural Cooperative System
for Comilla Thana—First Annual Report, Rural Cooperative Pilot Experiment*
(Comilla: The Academy, 1961); and Henry W. Fairchild and Shamshul Haq,
"Cooperative vs. Commune," in Gove Hambidge, ed., *Dynamics of Development*
(New York: Frederick A. Praeger, 1964), pp. 312–34.

few feet from rivers, village ponds, or wells, the readiest big gains
in income could come from irrigated winter crops. This meant
pumps. They would only pay if proprietors of many adjoining
half-acre plots used them jointly. The institutional requirement
seemed to be cooperatives. But cooperatives had failed to put
down roots in Comilla *thana* just as in other parts of the subcontinent. Could a new and workable approach to cooperatives be devised? To find the answer, the academy brought in two of the
most experienced cooperative organizers in the East Pakistan
government, and kept one on to apply the solution they found.

The academy's new approach began, not with government
agents going out to the villages, but with respected villagers who
were convinced of the feasibility of cooperatives spreading the
word to adjacent villages. By the end of the first year, no promotion was required. The example of functioning cooperatives was
enough. Functioning societies were found to consist of only forty
to sixty members, often from a single hamlet of a village, and
homogeneous as to class. Neither landlords nor landless tenants
had the need and ability to save. Small peasants, on the other
hand, were being compelled to forego consumption—often half
their harvest was taken by the moneylender as interest—and
could readily see the point of low interest credit. At this point in
the strategy, the conventional wisdom would have called for government credit resources to get the new cooperators on their feet.
Akhter Hameed Khan insisted that they themselves begin saving; the enterprise and the motivation had to be theirs. Each
week they had to bring at least a few *annas* (slightly more than
one cent) for deposit in the new society. The deposit took place
at the weekly society membership meeting, where attendance
was compulsory, and where the names of all depositors were read
out, along with the amounts of their deposits. In this way the hamlet's existing social controls served to reinforce a cooperator's initial resolve to lift himself out of the downward debt spiral. The
public, oral accounting also gave assurance against the few liter-
ate leaders of the cooperative society misappropriating the funds.

Leadership in the society was functional, not a matter of recognizing status. Normally the peasant who gathered the mem-

bers in the beginning remained in the key position of organizer. He conducted the meetings and represented the society to the Central Cooperative Association at Comilla. The accountant was an educated village youth, trained continually at the academy, keeping the books for four or five societies on full-time basis.

Every week the organizers of all societies gathered at Comilla. They deposited the week's savings in the Central Cooperative Association, attended a training session of several hours, and observed the demonstrations of the kinds of investments the societies' credit might allow—pumps, tractors, grain storage buildings, fertilizer. One distinctive feature of the Comilla system was that this training of organizers (and accountants), and their training of society members when they returned to the villages, continued week after week, month after month, year after year. Hand in hand with the training went control of policy. The academy term was "supervised" credit. The Central Association fixed rules for all loans made by primary societies, banked their deposits, acted as entrepreneur for the supplies and equipment societies were encouraged to buy or rent. Thus, the whole business of keeping tractors and pumps in running order, and keeping them producing as many days a year as possible, was managed by the Central Association. Member societies proposing to make loans to pay for feasts or weddings had their applications denied. At present a majority of the board of the Comilla Central Cooperative Association is elected by member societies; at the outset all were appointed by the academy director, Akhter Hameed Khan.

Now we can make out the strategy. There was a firm division of responsibility. Villagers were set the tasks they could do: keeping members united and effectively led, motivating saving, undertaking and assigning tasks in joint projects such as pump irrigation. The academy controlled those functions alien to the villagers: business, management, and economic development. But there was also a continual and direct learning from one another: the villagers learning through their own leaders what business management, mechanical maintenance, and productive investment meant, the academy staff learning what would work, or fail, in the villages. The communication was mainly oral, focused on

concrete situations that had arisen, always two-way. But it conveyed meanings intact only because each party had to act in ac-
cord with it. The academy had to set policies that would take
hold among peasants, peasants could only get help if they kept to
those policies. Note that the relationship, while complementary,
was not symmetrical. The academy was introducing national objectives, "by the spoken work and the sanction." [49] The task of re-
working village culture to include those objectives was never completed. For instance, members of the earliest societies, now out of
debt to the moneylenders and enjoying the old living standards,
no longer save as much as the more desperate members of the new
societies. [50]

The size and variety of the cooperative enterprises which have
grown in the *thana* in five years can only be understood from the
academy's reports and studies. In the first year and a half, 1960–
1961, forty-six societies were accepted with new groups waiting
to qualify. Cooperative saving and investment had spread from
the villages to Comilla town, where cycle rickshaw drivers had
purchased their own vehicles; later they put their profits into a
truck. By May 1965, there were in the villages of Comilla *thana*
139 societies with 4,424 members. Net worth of the whole cooperative system was 9 million *rupees.* [51]

At the end of the three years, Akhter Hameed Khan, reporting
as chairman of the Central Association, stressed these results, this
need:

> The villagers are learning to do all sorts of new things,
> conduct the weekly meeting of their society, keep the ac-
> counts in order, adopt improved arming practices . . . build
> a village godown and store rice in it for later sale at better
> prices, drive the new tractors and operate the new pumps
> . . . support the setting up of a cold storage plant and a rice
> hulling mill through their Central Association.

49. Fairchild and Haq, "Cooperative vs. Commune," p. 329.
50. *A New Rural Cooperative System for Comilla Thana, Third Annual Report,
1963* (Comilla: The Academy, 1963), pp. 54–55.
51. Advance figures from the 1965 annual report kindly furnished by Richard
Wheeler.

. . . an institution of great social and economic power has arisen—the village cooperative. . . . On all sides, too, we see traditional values remaining strong. . . . We need to understand the villagers better, and somehow find organizational approaches that elicit deeper responses from them. . . .[52]

In 1961, just after the academy's approach to cooperatives had begun to show effectiveness, a national planning commission official asked the director whether the academy might undertake the second experiment.[53] Could large numbers of idle agricultural laborers be put to work during the winter months, building simple productive structures, and be paid partly in American wheat? The proposal promised to complement the cooperatives in two respects. As the cooperatives introduced winter cropping and produced marketable surpluses, they uncovered needs for roads to get rice to market, ditches and ponds to provide water. Peasants who two years before would have resisted such works crossing their tiny plots now favored them. Second, employment on rural works would benefit the landless villagers who had proved to have little stake in cooperatives. There was a larger complementarity: the academy was being put to its national use—to find a way to do a job needed nationwide.

In 1961 Comilla *thana,* like all other rural areas in Pakistan, had a new system of local self-governing bodies, called Basic Democracies. To be sure, councils governing "unions" of twelve to fifteen villages had functioned lethargically for forty years. But the *thana* council, the next higher level, was new and largely unsure what it would do. The Comilla plan was to make this new *thana* council (of which the academy's Comilla *thana* could be a prototype) the deciding and controlling agency for the rural works, and to use committees of the union boards to supervise the work.

Within two months from the planning commission query, union conflicts in Comilla *thana* had decided on and drawn up

52. *Third Annual Report,* pp. 1–2.
53. For a full account, see PARD, Comilla, *Report on a Rural Public Works Programme in Comilla Kotwali Thana* (Comilla: The Academy, 1962).

twenty-one simple plans and budgets for drainage and irrigation works, and five large flood embankment schemes. The *thana* council had consolidated these, required revision of some, rejected others mainly because landowners would not give rights-of-way. By the end of December, the surviving twenty-four projects had been approved by the provincial engineering organization (Robert Burns, of the Peace Corps, served as project engineer), the district administration, and the state government. By mid-June, nine months after the question was broached, 8 million cubic feet of earth had been moved, employing the 45,000 mandays of labor. Of the twenty-four original projects, sixteen had been completed, six dropped, two were still underway in the monsoon.

To get this much done in one South Asian dry season was a feat. To get it done at rates (14 *rupees* per 1,000 cubic feet of earth moved) below both government estimates and the sanctioned budgets was still more extraordinary. To get rice-accustomed villagers to take part of their wage in wheat was not easy. (A below-cost lunch prepared of wheat served as a demonstration.) The real accomplishment was to do these things honestly under the management of village leaders who expected public works to be corrupt.

In Pakistan, as in Indian community development, a 50 percent "local contribution" was conventionally required. In practice, the contribution was made this way. Villager leaders submitted budgets showing earthwork costs at the government rate (in Comilla initial budgets in fact showed Rs. 18 per 1,000 cubic feet). Then village laborers, needing work in order to eat, were recruited at half the official rate (Rs. 9) and asked to place their thumbprint on the payroll for the full amount of which the government paid half. When union council chairmen were confronted with the evidence that they were starting to do this in Comilla *thana*, they were astonished to hear it called cheating. "How else," they asked innocently, "has the local contribution even been raised?" [54] Straight talk convinced these same chairmen that though laborers might be paid 10 or 12 *rupees*, the unions would receive from the

54. Ibid., p. 13.

government exactly what they paid the laborers. The academy had already learned that to stipulate a cash input from village sources was to invite dissembling. Instead, the unions and the villagers made three genuine contributions: owners contributed rights-of-way, project committees contributed the whole cost of planning, supervising, and keeping accounts of the work, laborers worked at 60 percent of contractors' rates.

Out of this 1961–1962 experiment has grown one of the principal and most effective features of Pakistan's third five-year plan (1965–1970). The nationwide rural public works program which began in Comilla *thana* four years earlier with an expenditure of Rs. 195,000 (money not even in the five-year plan) is now scheduled for Rs. 300 million annually in East Pakistan, and Rs. 200 million in West. "The programme generated unprecedented enthusiasm in both wings," explained the national Budget.[55] The academy had demonstrated a solution for one of the most common and most stubborn problems of economic development: how to engage the rural underemployed on works of economic value.[56] It had also demonstrated the flexible linkages with provincial administration and national economic planning which alone can employ a pilot project to steer a nation. A summary of these linkages in the three years after the initial 1961–1962 demonstration will show that the academy was putting into provincial use its three functions of training, evaluation-diagnosis, and further innovation.

During 1962–1963, a dynamic secretary of the East Pakistan Department of Basic Democracies and Local Government took up the academy's proposal to apply the public works plan to fifty-four selected *thanas* throughout the province. He sent their administrators (circle officers) to Comilla for training. Then, at a stroke, the national leaders decided to spend Rs. 100,000,000 to cover the remaining *thanas*—a development the academy had proposed take eight years. Now 284 more circle officers came to the academy for three days of training each. The Comilla manual

55. Ministry of Finance, *The Budget in Brief, 1964–65* (Rawalpindi: Government of Pakistan, 1965), p. 81.
56. Richard V. Gilbert, "The Works Programme in East Pakistan," *International Labor Review* 39: 213–26.

was the procedural bible for the crash program. President Ayub assembled the elected councilors, challenging them to play their parts. Inevitably the program deteriorated as it spread. But here the academy's evaluation and innovation roles took hold. In a quick but empirical survey of the 1962–1963 results, the academy found that too much of the works budget went into roads.[57] The academy found out why: circle officers needed roads to keep in communication with outlying unions; union and *thana* councils could not plan irrigation and flood embankment projects, without more engineering help. In the third year's program, 1964–1965, the imbalance was corrected.

Meanwhile, the academy had worked out, in its own pilot *thana,* solutions to more basic difficulties revealed by its 1962–1963 evaluation.[58] Training of local leadership could be "spun off" to each of the 411 *thanas* by establishing there a training and development center. Comilla could train the trainers, both circle officers and technical staff.

At the same time, the academy opened a new frontier for local public works—a *thana*-wide irrigation and rural electrification program. The simplified engineering, new techniques of local planning, and new relationships of financial responsibility required were demonstrated on the ground in Comilla *thana.*[59] The progression is endless. A year later, 1964–1965, the academy demonstrated how school teachers, students, and village parents could be mobilized to build new schools and repair existing ones —an extension of rural public works that tapped new motivations.

The academy's six-year accomplishments go beyond this account: reconstruction of the whole administrative pattern of the district, a variety of adult education programs bringing a thousand villagers to Comilla every week, a way of spreading birth control information, an effective technique to keep mechanical equip-

57. PARD, Comilla, *An Evaluation of the Rural Public Works Programme, East Pakistan, 1962–63* (Comilla: The Academy, 1963), esp. p. 92.
58. For independent evidence of the feedback of Comilla evaluations and demonstrations into provincewide administration, see East Pakistan Government, Department of Basic Democracies and Local Government, *Works Programme for 1964–65* (Dacca: East Pakistan Government Press, 1965), pp. 1, 5, 7.
59. PARD, Comilla, *The Comilla Pilot Project in Irrigation and Rural Electrification* (Comilla: The Academy, 1963).

ment running in scattered villages, a good deal of applied and some basic research.

The soundness of each demonstration, the ever-widening frontiers, call for dramatic explanations of success. Each strategy seems inevitable. But we find, when we look closer, that it is as sharp a break from previous approaches to the villages as are the results which follow. Outsiders who know him, as well as those searching for explanations, point to Akhter Hameed Khan's charismatic qualities. And the academy did not move so rapidly during 1965 when he withdrew from the directorship. But there are other explanations which must be credited at least with successfully institutionalizing these personal qualities.

Akhter Hameed Khan dressed in homespun, interpreting the Koran or developmental economics as need be, personified the depth of moral challenge for which Comilla has taken responsibility. But the daily routines show how profoundly the responsibility has been institutionalized. Villagers who have to learn not only new techniques and skills but new images of the good life relevant to those techniques are appropriately drawn into an unending training relationship. All of their culture-carriers are enlisted—not only the "good farmers," the organizers trusted with savings, the mothers, the schoolteachers, but even, as we shall see, the *imams* who conduct prayers at the village mosques. The academy operates also on the unconventional premise that administrators and technicians also need to be acculturated: their contemporary tasks cannot be contained by the old service morality, nor by transplanting inevitably alien "modern methods." Their mission while they are posted to the academy is to discover their own new norms while they are inculcating the villagers'.

Spatially, we can glimpse a new pattern at two levels. Agents of the new culture do not go to the village to plant it there. Instead, villagers send their own functional leader-learners to the academy to bring back answers. The academy's area of operation is large enough to warrant a diverse complement of both administrator-trainees and specialist-researchers, i.e., large enough to assemble the maximum feasible groups of village learners, and the limit of feasibility is the radius from which a villager can come to the academy and get back home in the same long day. There is a second, larger spatial lesson here. The academy is continually exhibiting, in operation, new development opportunities, which commend themselves to economic planners as well as to leaders concerned with public demands. The pressure to extend pilot demonstrations provincewide or nationwide therefore exceeds the academy's ability confidently to recommend extension.[60] Such recommendation is based upon two functions integral to the academy's work as a pilot institution. Its work is genuinely experimental enough so that it can to some degree isolate the conditions of feasibility that are capable of extension, and those that are not. Thus, it could recommend a rural public works program in every district the second year, but even after several years could recommend replication of the cooperative program only to a limit of a particular administrator-leader's (discovered in the elite service and trained at Comilla) ability to supervise them. The outsider can speculate that Comilla is a pilot project trying to deduce reproducable conditions of nationwide extension. Secondly, the academy, by providing its capability of training the administrators who will do the extending either in depth (for key leaders) or in great numbers (e.g., for all *thana* officers in the province), is able to create a basic condition of extensibility.

Both the cultural and the spatial powers of the academy rely on the searching, evaluating and explanatory power of its research. No new trial is instituted without considering what many village spokesmen say about what will work. Results are analyzed discriminatingly. At a few sensitive points, social-science studies are made to determine why changes came, or did not. As at Etawah, even the most shrewdly devised approaches have, in the first few months of trial, shown difficulties that would be corrected during the demonstration period: accountants for each cooperative society could be replaced by multivillage accountants, fictitious village contribution of labor costs to public works eliminated, etc. Akhter Hameed Khan's attitude of now knowing the answers had had this practical meaning. Secondly, when the Comilla academy

60. Hapgood, *Policies for Promoting Agricultural Development*, pp. 248–49.

recommended a change in province or national programs, it was a change already tested operationally at Comilla, not deduced from defects found in evaluating existing programs. These are, of course, values of research integrated with prototype action programs; they could not be had in the nationwide Indian program with its competent, but separate, program evaluation unit.

Community Development in the Peasant Society

The Nation-Builders and Peasant Society

At the beginning of this study, we segregated three elements whose interrelationships in some kind of pattern constitute community development:

1. Nation-building motives and policies of nation leaders.
2. Norms and internal relations of administration, considered as a national system undergoing change.
3. Norms, and solidarity and leadership of peasant villages, considered in relation to the above.

Taking the perspective of the developers, 1 and 2, we have been looking for the conditions under which intended changes occurred in 3. Already, this search has turned up an anomaly in the relations between 1 and 2: Why did both India and Pakistan keep their costly (and politically vital) community development efforts in administrative hands which were coming to be known as dysfunctional? Why, when a drastic change was made (at the end of seven years in both countries), had no alternatives been pretested? Our curiosity is reinforced by awareness that we are entering terra incognita of comparative administration. Not only in the present case, we know much more about why programs fell short than about why programs which fell short took the form they did.[61] Our interest expands, therefore, from the analysis of village results as dependent on administrative action, to administrative behavior as a set of dependent variables, interacting with village conditions on the one side and national political leadership on the other.

61. Martin Landau has, in conversation, suggested the need to study administrative behavior as dependent variable(s).

(We would consider our schema an interaction model among 1, 2, and 3, save that we have come upon so little action of 3 upon 1.) What we need to complete our theoretical framework is a perspective, based in the villages, that will look outward on the larger national institutional and decisional elements as parts of some whole.

A body of concepts from which we can begin was propounded fifteen years ago by Robert Redfield in his book, *Peasant Society and Culture*.[62] Peasant societies seem to include those of India and Pakistan by Redfield's two criteria: "agriculture is a livelihood and a way of life, not a business for profit" (p. 18), and "peasants are the rural dimension of old civilizations" (p. 20). (Situations in which the elite culture is imported, as in Latin America, may constitute a different category.) The peasantry in such societies constitutes a part-society and a part-culture (p. 21). In the cities, courts, temples, we find the "great traditions," to which the "little traditions" of the villages are thinly and distantly related. These "great traditions" as of China, classical India, or of Islam, have been flowing into the villages for centuries, "from teachers and exemplars who never saw the village, who did their work in intellectual circles far away in space and time" (p. 42). There is also a reverse flow—the absorption of elements of village tradition into the great tradition. Are these two flows analytically reciprocal? Redfield does not answer categorically, but his implication is that they are not. Roles are culturally defined for carriers of the great tradition into the villages (the *maulvi* and *imam*, the *brahmin*, the *nawab* or landlord-ruler). The reverse influences, save when an extraordinary saint or prophet suddenly raises some village practice to the larger sacredness, takes place at the pace of centuries, as Redfield observes, "without anyone's intention" (p. 58). We can understand this asymmetrical relation, for while "great and little traditions are dimensions of one another, those people who carry on the lower layers and those who maintain the high alike recognize the same order of 'highness' and 'lowness'" (p. 50).

Redfield's theory is useful in sensitizing us, and providing us

62. (Chicago: University of Chicago Press, 1956). The edition cited here was republished, 1960, together with *The Little Community*.

terms to express propositions relating the three elements with which we began. We begin with the first element, the nation-building motives and policies of national leaders. Proposition I: *In conceiving community development, the leaders of new nations behave as carriers of great traditions toward peasant society and culture.* Specifically, they feel the responsibility to define for the peasantry the values which village life will conserve for the nation. They create roles for the transmission of those values to the villages. They do not perceive a need for integrating those values with the villagers', nor think of link roles as having an integrating function. If the little traditions of the villages take effect, it is "without anyone's intention."

Has this proposition power to suggest new meaning for any of the community development experience we have noted? Let us consider the question of the spatial unit which would be the object of development in India. Both with regard to *panchayats,* as we have observed, and primary cooperative societies, policy controversy has remained fundamentally unresolved. The authoritative National Development Council took the position in 1958 that the *panchayat* and the cooperative should be coterminous. Ideology was, of course, involved. Gandhians, adherents to the European-American sympathy for small communities, civil servants whose work has been with solidary villages favored one-village units. "The village, consisting of families that know one another and have a feeling of identity of interests, is the natural primary unit." [63] Those concerned with introducing new skills in the village, breaking through crusted caste and landed control, and aggregating a sizable tax or credit base favored multivillage units. "[T]he formula, 'one society to one village and one village to one society' has failed as the basis for the organization of cooperative rural credit. It has failed because its underlying assumptions have proved incorrect." [64] One would suppose that, endowed with a federal constitution, and facing in any event enormous regional variation in all the significant determinants, the government of

63. V. T. Krishnamachari, *Community Development in India,* p. 70.
64. Reserve Bank of India, *All-India Rural Credit Survey, Vol. II, Report of the Committee of Direction* (Bombay: Reserve Bank of India, 1954), p. 450.

India would leave the states, and in the case of cooperatives, the societies themselves, to try their own ideas. The program-evaluation organization could then seek to distinguish the conditions under which a given sized society or *panchayat* attained various objectives.[65] Preoccupied with enunciating a nationwide policy, however, the planning commission and the ministry of community development had to resort to ambiguities and contradictions: "The block samiti staff should therefore strive for the development in each village of a panchayat, a village school, a cooperative" but, in the same official guide, "the conclusion is clear that each and every village cannot and should not have its own cooperative. What will be required is the grouping of villages. . . ."[66]

The Etawah project readily discovered which objectives villagers would pursue cooperatively. The Comilla project in a few months hit upon a design that preserved both the value of intimate primary relationships in the village and the managerial and policy strength of the *thana* Central Cooperative Association. Why should the Indian planning commission and ministry of community development, on other occasions pragmatic, have remained transfixed by an ideological controversy about the potential of half a million villages?

We can get some hints if we examine the thinking of Jawaharlal Nehru on the objectives of community development. He was the most eloquent and enthusiastic champion of the movement. He clearly understood its spirit. "Obviously it is necessary to plan, to direct, to organize and to coordinate; but it is even more necessary to create conditions in which a spontaneous growth from below is possible."[67] But in the same mind was a commitment completely to change the village. "To speak for myself frankly, I am not really enamoured of the Indian village, as it is" (p. 49). "The

65. Some such research was in fact conducted by the program evaluation organization. It pointed to the conclusion that small, intimate societies engender personal trust, large ones enforce uniform standards. If followed up, it might have led on to the innovation of some organization to gain both values. Taylor and Ensminger, *India's Roots of Democracy*, chap. 13.

66. *A Guide to Community Development*, pp. 8, 133.

67. Government of India, Ministry of Community Development . . . , *Jawaharlal Nehru on Community Development and Panchayati Raj* (Delhi: Government of India, Publications Division, 1963), pp. 7–8. Quotations in this and the following paragraphs are from this edition.

people in this country are good, but in certain respects they are backward. . . . They are not quite conscious of the strength which cooperation gives" (p. 16). "We in India . . . have not yet developed that emotional unity" (p. 47).

It seems a non sequitur when Nehru goes on with: "I have no doubt that the only way of work will be of cooperative farming" (pp. 47–48). The reasoning is not that India's peasants are ready to make it work. On the contrary, large-scale technology requires it. But, what is more fundamental, "A society changes as a result of the methods of production" (p. 94). Cooperative farming is required, not to fit, but to reconstruct the attitudes of the peasantry and their place in the nation. Nehru's reasoning was incorporated directly into the first five-year plan, which called for cooperative management of the village lands "so that the village may become a vital, progressive and largely self-governing base on the structure of national planning and the existing social and economic disparities resulting from property, caste, and status may be removed." [68]

The argument is a modern one, pivoting on Marxist determinism. And the prescription is not too different from the cooperative program in Comilla *thana*. What is totally different is derivation of the prescription. Comilla used cooperatives to solve the most serious problem small landowning peasants confronted; cooperatives seemed the only solution. (For nonowners, there was another solution—public works.) Nehru perceived solidary villages as the necessary building blocks of an Indian nation whose high purposes villagers would have to be trained (not compelled) to share. So while the argument was new, the role seems characteristic of the enunciators of the great tradition in peasant society: close to that of the *pandit*, the *acharya*, interpreting the meaning of the norms of the high culture for the interaction of the villagers among themselves.

But that suggestion is not fair to the drive and sense of specific purpose which animated a man like Nehru. We need also to consider the theory set forth in an article entitled "Indian Intellec-

68. *First Five Year Plan, A Summary* (1952), pp. 53–54. Repeated in *Second Five Year Plan* (1956), p. 206.

tuals and Rural Problems," by a Bombay professor of English named Sibnarayan Ray:

> Here is a vast subcontinent where for centuries the . . . people have lived in virtually self-contained villages. . . . It is a country of many languages and cultures, communities and religious sects, each with its own long history, and with little traffic from one to the other. But the strongest aspiration of the new Indian elite is for the accomplishment of national unity. The stronger the diversive back-pull of history, the more ardent is the demand for solidarity and unification. . . . Thus the intellectuals were confronted with a cruel dilemma. To be accomplished, their aims required support from the general community. But the very outlook which had given rise to those aims and aspirations tended to isolate them from the community.[69]

We cannot here elaborate nation-building theory. But we cannot neglect the impact of this tension in the minds of those charged with the nation-building mission upon their community development decisions. We need to refine our first proposition by adding a specification. Proposition I.A: *National leaders planning nationwide community development act as members of an intelligentsia needing to connect itself with the peasantry in order to achieve nationhood, but also as members of the cultural elite of peasant society. They seek, therefore, to work out in the life of the villages the challenges posed by ideologies at the elite level.* Planners of pilot projects are not involved in this nation-building tension.

The Administrative Systems of Peasant Society

Asking Redfield's question—what are the links between the two halves of peasant society?—we appreciate the importance in India and Pakistan of the civil service administrative system. It was entrusted with the tasks of community development beyond what the planners conceived to be its capability to innovate peasant participation. In the critical analyses which resulted we

---

69. In Leopold Labetz, ed., *Revisionism: Essays on the History of Marxist Ideas* (New York: Frederick A. Praeger, 1962), pp. 374, 377.

can find specifications of its shortcomings. Its critics hope it will change. We need, viewing the manner of its linkage, to think more clearly about the conditions under which that hope can materialize.

The sociological criticism of Taylor and Ensminger gives us a perceptive characterization of the administrative system. It is ordered almost entirely by status. A person of higher status dominates those of lower. This defeats community development which requires free communication among all personnel, and interpersonal relations among coworkers resembling those of primary groups.[70] Taylor and Ensminger fit Indian elitist administration to Weber's type, rational-legal bureaucracy. We would begin at once to distinguish within bureaucracies those that define roles in terms of functional expertise [71] and program assignments [72] from those that define roles in terms mainly of status. We would class the Indian and Pakistani systems as status-ordered, challenged to accept roles of expertise and program, and resisting the challenge.

The resistance becomes clear and specific in the critique of rural development administration presented by the Pakistan Food and Agriculture Commission. The district officer is still, for most people, they said, the government. Specialists, even of scientific training, are subordinated to him. Yet his brief tenure in a particular district (too short a time to see agricultural development through to success), his promotion upon seniority and for his own career rather than for program results, and the difficulty of disciplining him if he fails to produce program results, all heighten the stratifying effect introduced by recruitment from university graduates, with its implications for both class and English language culture. Financial controls designed to stop officials at the periphery from making mistakes further inhibit the responsiveness of the system to farmer needs or village initiatives.

The commission, itself staffed by experienced members of the

70. Taylor and Ensminger, *India's Roots of Democracy*, pp. 568, 576, 582.

71. Morstein-Marx, "The Higher Civil Service as an Action Group in Western Political Development," in Joseph LaPalombara, ed., *Bureaucracy and Political Development* (Princeton: Princeton University Press, 1963), pp. 67–70.

72. For a review that agricultural development organization should be thought of not as administrative boxes, but as "disposable plastic bags," see Hapgood, *Policies for Promoting Agricultural Development*, p. 118.

elite Civil Service of Pakistan, recommended, on these considerations, that agricultural extension and the supply of material to
agriculture be devolved upon government corporations, not the
existing status-role field administration.[73] Pakistan has, in fact,
created agricultural development corporations in both provinces,
but we may be skeptical concerning their role beyond the supply
of fertilizer, seeds, and other material inputs.

As in India, the prestige-ordered service of the traditional field
administration is functional in peasant society in ways not com-
prehended by its critics. The district officer earned his prestige, in
British times, by maintaining order in a vast area beyond the
capacity of the force he commanded to subdue. His prestige is
still needed to keep the peace and to deal with emergencies. Not
only that. Peasant society accords a thoroughly traditional legitimacy to the power of the educated and urban man, the representative of the great culture, who comes to govern, and who does not
affront the traditional peasant notions of the good life. The elite
civil service of the subcontinent, unlike those of developing nations in the Middle East and Latin America, grew in the countryside. It is enculturated in peasant society.[74]

Yet the ironic aspect of it is that the district officer, drawn from
the high culture and planted in the countryside, maintains his
working (as against his symbolic) relations with peasant society
only through layers of intermediary officers drawn from contrast-
ing cultural strata. At district headquarters the clerks keep the
door, sometimes at a price. Out in the lesser headquarters, the
subdivision, the *tehsil, taluk,* or *thana,* his subordinate is a college
graduate but identified more with a language state than with a
cosmopolitan English language culture. Each culture layer com-
prises a separate life career. The result was highlighted for us by
Akhter Hameed Khan's account of the initial attitudes of officers
sent for training to Comilla.

73. Pakistan Ministry of Food and Agriculture, *Report of the Food and Agriculture Commission* (Karachi: Manager of Publications, 1960), pp. 196–97,
202–204.
74. Akhter Hameed Khan, though he resigned from the ICS, argues staunchly
for its necessary leadership in rural development. *Rural Development in East
Pakistan,* pp. 11, 24.

When the officers came they said, "This is all talk. This cannot be done. . . . Even if we tried they (the officers at the top) would stop us." It was very funny for us because when we talked with the officers at the top, the District Commissioner or the Subdivisional Officer, they said, "This is all right but the officers at the thana level are all incompetent and dishonest and they would not do anything." [75]

Ralph Braibanti argues that the insulation of the higher strata is not a mere historical vestige, but that it has a necessary function: "This detachment (called 'aloofness' and 'snobbery' by detractors of the CSP) is an essential posture for whomever wields power in Pakistan. . . . To be close to the people is to place oneself in a web of loyalty to kin and caste (biradri) from which there is no escape." [76]

Now we can appreciate now intricately the status-role, culture-strata system is enculturated in peasant society. Each status layer of the society has its part. Each is subordinate to one of broader horizons and more respected learning. It is not the power to command specific performance (likely to be attenuated by the barriers to understanding and partially discreet values of the strata) but the general prestige of the higher level which maintains the system. We can begin to comprehend from this perspective what is obscure in the Taylor-Ensminger critique: why the system is not displaced in the Indian or Pakistani countryside; we understand, too, why it is not apt to be made to run without benefit of status by any reform which takes effect upon the bottom layers— whether the village level workers, or even the elected block councils.

We can also understand why the approach of the Comilla academy might moderately but surely change the system (given the presence of modern technology and elected councils). The Comilla approach is not bottom-up, but lateral. The officers of the Civil Service of Pakistan are training there along with officers of the provincial service, specialized extension agents, and the vil-

75. Ibid., p. 50.
76. "Pakistan" in LaPalombara, *Bureaucracy and Political Development*, pp. 393–94.

lage leaders with whom they work. The training is resident, continuing, actual. Men of different culture layers, examining the same development situation, are asked to understand not only the reality of the situation, but the difference of their perspectives.

There may also be a less obvious explanation for the innovative power of the academy. District officers must, for a long time to come, keep their prestige at least in reserve for emergencies. They cannot afford to fail. They cannot, therefore, afford genuinely to experiment. Posted for a year or more to a pilot academy whose mission is to learn by identifying its mistakes, they can innovate and err without failing. They can carry back to their posts a solution they have found workable in pilot application. They can prudently stake their prestige on its success. This may come closer to making change safe for a prestige-ordered administration than pre-entry training, or independent evaluative studies, which expect an officer to risk another's understanding of his problem.

Proposition II: *An extensive administrative system ordered by the prestige-ranking of culturally distinct careers and enculturated in peasant society cannot be reformed by eliminating prestige in the relation of ranks without the development of a specialized or program culture common to all ranks and to the peasantry.*

Preposition II.A: *Such a system resists reform from the top alone, or from the bottom alone. Reform may be instituted laterally, developing confidence in all layers that all are changing.*

The Village as Intersection of Social Fields

We set out by comparing two well-recorded programs, pilot and nationwide, to identify the governmental conditions under which self-help is evoked in peasant villages. In our Indian comparison the pilot project quickly gave way to the national; Pakistan offered a check upon our conclusions, its imperfect comparability strengthened by its reverse sequence—there it is the pilot scheme that lives and grows. The comparisons turned up the puzzling finding that nationwide community development plans produce unanticipated consequences, while pilot projects establish the intended relationships with the villages. A general theory of peasant society and culture led us toward one explanation. We might call it the latent function of elites in peasant societies. The heroic nation-builders, filling their modern roles as planners and politically responsible policy-makers, may inadvertently fill traditional roles as carriers of the high culture: to define the good life for the inarticulate millions in the villages. They do not, from this perspective, appreciate the revolutionary administrative and political demands of the mission they have undertaken. The senior civil servants blueprint a comprehensive administrative program —new roles for the old field hierarchy, a new cadre at the bottom. Still, prestige works through the culturally layered services more powerfully than specific instructions. Status, more than function, reaches the village-level workers, status unreconciled with function reaches the villagers. Again, the impact is unintended.

Conversely, we could see why Etawah in a minimal way, and Comilla comprehensively, might reach through the layers of culturally diverse careers to engage villagers in a direct encounter with selected national goals. Elites are not engaged as elites. The local effort is, in one sense, the more national one.

Elite theories are, in peasant society and culture, part theories. We need ways of thinking about differences between Etawah and Comilla villages as well as Etawah and Comilla programs and organizations. We need eventually to relate Indian and Pakistani concepts to the growing body of comparative concepts about culture change, adoption of new practices, community formation. More immediately we need to conceive how villages might receive, react to, influence government approaches. Taking a perspective which puts the village in the center and government on the periphery, we need to search for complementary processes to the political and administrative ones.

Again, it is Redfield who provides the relevant initial formulation. He did not propose his generalization specifically to explain development, nor derive it initially from South Asian ethnography; we are fitting it to our phenomena theory which can lay a claim to universality. Drawing on an account of a Norwegian fishing community, Redfield called attention to "systems of social relations . . . that connect the small community with other such communities, with the Norwegian nation, and with industrial systems wider than the nation." Redfield called these "fields" of social relations.[77] The Norwegian fishing community was on the way to becoming integrated into urban-rural national society. We can speculate that as its transactions with the larger society, even the world market, become more frequent, functionally specific, as each thus commits less of the life of the individual or the small community, the anthropologist would cease writing of them as fields, substituting reference groups, roles, interests, institutional memberships, interdependencies. But in the less integrated peasant village there is much latency about fields of outside relationships. There are ways in which the culture and interpersonal relationships within the village build expectations of encounters outside. We find Redfield's term useful to consider latent but patterned links between villages as semi-isolated sociocultural fragments and their civilizational matrix.

Redfield distinguishes fields of three kinds: the governmental-political (which he calls the "territorially-based"), the market, and a residual "country-wide network." Writing in general terms about "The Extensions of an Indian Village," Morris Opler considered ties of historical identity, as well as these present-day links: market, employment, caste, marriage, and religion.[78] For our own purposes, Redfield's government-territorial field must be broken down into: (1) the old revenue-law and order field, (2) the new community development (VLW, block officers) field, and (3) the new field of elective politics.

Tracing certain fields across the social-cultural juncture between the village and the town or nation, Redfield came upon a characteristic role. It might be in Guatemala the parish priest or shopkeeper, in Andalusia certain professional or wealthy men, dwelling in the village but living their mental lives in the city, "who represent the government to the pueblo, and who represent the pueblo to the government." In a suggestive phrase, Redfield wrote, "a peasant society is two connecting halves. We may be able to see a sort of link or hinge between the local life of a peasant community and the state or feudal system of which it is a

77. *Peasant Society and Culture*, pp. 26–33.
78. *Journal of Asian Studies* 16 (1956): 5–10.

part." [79] Redfield does not tell us how to determine which fields are hinged. We can get help at this point from anthropologist Frederick G. Bailey, who has been concerned for a decade with the relations between various culture elements and social relations in relatively isolated Orissa villages, with the larger contexts of Hindu and Indian culture, and the economic and political life of Orissa. Bailey gives great prominence to the political broker who facilitates transactions "between two sets of relationships and two sets of values, fundamentally different from one another." Bailey's type case of political broker had moved to town at the age of nineteen and established most of his relationships there. Through these relationships he could manipulate the state political system as it threatened the villagers. They did not trust him because, living outside, "he is not one of us." They nevertheless needed his mediation with administrators and ministers. They thought he made money on the transactions, and they regarded his interest as venal.[80]

Bailey gives us the suggestions we need to propose specific tests for the hinge or broker function. Are values shared among parties to transactions? Are those who act in the field a single reference group (do they think of each other as "we," not "they")? Is there a continuum of cognitive meanings, expressing and maintaining communication upon the subject matter of the transactions? By these three criteria we can operationalize Redfield's concept. If answers are "no," we should expect the need for a broker, or a series of brokers, in the field. We might then use his term, "hinged field," and conceive it as opposed to a field of shared values, identities, and communications which we might call a "linear field."

Already it is apparent that some fields are more likely to be hinged than others. Redfield invented the term to refer to situations characteristic of the governmental field; he found no use for it when describing fields of friendships or kinship. Bailey discovered the broker role operating between the village and the party-

---

79. *Peasant Society and Culture*, p. 27.
80. *Politics and Social Change, Orissa in 1959* (Berkeley: University of California Press, 1963), pp. 58–63.

legislator-minister power system, between the village and the district government. We might conceive of the governmental fields as most often hinged, caste and kinship least, market and worship somewhere in between.[81]

We have equipped ourselves to think precisely about the linkage sought to be developed and actually developed between the village and development administration. Administration does not enter the village de novo nor replace the established governmental field, or fields. The old line of revenue administration is a hinged, indeed multihinged field. The village headman, the *tehsildar*, the subdivision and district officers, all are brokers in our sense: each is perceived as doing, not merely a different job, but a job whose goals are not the village's; each translates communications, not into another vocabulary, but characteristically another language; [82] each is an outsider. No longer, however, is this field the exclusive channel to and from state power. The district Congress party chairman, the member of the legislative assembly, the minister or deputy minister, or as Bailey found, the unofficial broker, any or all may hold the new hinges of the political field in the Indian countryside.

Community development in India, sometimes in Pakistan, introduced a new field. The village-level worker, faithful to his training and to his Hindi name "servant of the village," was identified with the village; he was not a hinge. The broker was the block administrator, or the block extension technician. Of him the villagers characteristically thought, as we have seen, "he works for his raises in salary" or "to please his superior."

In the pilot projects no such officer appears, goals reach the villager intact, communications flow. We are in a position to suggest our third proposition:

Proposition III: *Community development reaches intended re-*

81. As an exercise during the Pittsburgh seminar, eleven monographic studies of Indian villages were coded for hinged or linear fields of government administration, elective politics, courts, marketing, employment, kinship and marriage, and worship. Methodology was too crude to warrant presentation here, yet the work encouraged the claim that the concept of fields could be operationalized.

82. This is a useful indicator of the difference between this brokerage and that mild mediation performed by each field echelon in any administrative system. Hinged–linear is a continuum.

*sults by developing linear fields connecting development admin-
istration with villages.*

Our own observations would suggest two corollaries: III.A:
*Linear fields reaching the villages cannot be developed by the
work of fields of higher administration.* Since both the internal
structure of the village and the culturally layered careers of the
administrative system are ordered by prestige, the ideas of participation which are intended to be planted in the new village
field can only penetrate by an effective command structure, or by
direct involvement of villagers with those committed to the ideas.

Some fields are characteristically hinged, some linear. Our second corollary is: III.B: *Development will be facilitated,* other
things being equal, *by channeling a transaction through a linear
rather than a hinged field.* We might see Comilla as testing this
proposition in two of its current experiments: distribution of con-
traceptives through existing retail merchants in the villages, and
use of the *imams* who officiate at prayers in the mosque to teach
both preprimary children and illiterate adults. Or we might compare fertilizer distribution through the market in Pakistan with
distribution through government and government-sponsored cooperative channels in India.

Redfield conceived his social fields as radiating outward from
a single village entity. To him in 1955, his peasant society was an
intermediate type in his folk-urban continuum. More recently,
Frank Young and his collaborators have subjected a more precise
concept to empirical validation.[83] Young, much more than Redfield, is interested in change. He finds a single sequence of small
community development starting with local autonomy and identity, moving through capacity to deal with community problems,
emerging in close and varied interdependence with the city or
the national social processes. "There is a single sequence and direction of community articulation in which 'inner' or institutional

---

83. Frank and Ruth Young, "The Sequence and Direction of Community
Growth: A Cross-Cultural Generalization," *Rural Sociology,* vol. 27, pp. 374–86
(1962). This uses international cases from the literature, plus the Youngs' field
data from 24 Mexican villages. Recently, Young and Isao Fujimoto confirmed a
slightly more modest version of the concept by coding all available (54) field reports of Latin American communities: "Social Differentiation in Latin American
Communities," *Economic Development and Cultural Change,* vol. 13, pp. 344–352.

growth is one side of the coin and 'outer' communications is another."

We do not have many detailed studies of Indian rural communities over a long enough time perspective to indicate whether the Redfield-Young concept holds in a caste-structured civilization. There are counterindications enough to warrant our considering modifications.

Revisiting a rapidly changing, irrigated area near Poona, Henry Orenstein found the inhabitants more generally and more intensively involved with town, district, or larger functional transactions than they had been in the early 1950's. Landowners are involved heavily in large-scale sugar mill cooperatives. Artisans are marketing their products in town, where their former village patrons now go to buy. Intercaste conflict is less in the village, but castes are organizing districtwide, even statewide. A faction within a landowning caste has hived off in a separate hamlet; in 1961 it observed Independence Day separately. "The failure of village-wide organizations contrasts with the relative success of more broadly based ones." Interpenetration with the town costs articulation of village groups and interests.[84]

Let us try, for the sake of analysis, to conceive a modification of the Young thesis which would deal with the phenomena of Gaon on the assumption that caste-structured civilization presents a special case. We have a clue from Redfield, who, though he offered no appropriate modification of his field theory, was quite clear about the significance of caste. "It is as if the characteristic social structure of the primitive self-contained community had been dissected out and its components spread about a wide area." [85] Orenstein takes us to the point. As we have already noted above, each caste may generate its own caste-field of extra-village relations: marketing, employment, politics, or administration. But the distinctive features of caste civilization go deeper, for they affect the basic territorial political field even in traditional society.

84. Henry Orenstein, *Gaon: Conflict and Cohesion in an Indian Village* (Princeton: Princeton University Press, 1965), chap. 13, and p. 298.
85. *Peasant Society and Culture*, p. 34.

One of the most decisive factors that prevented caste and class from destroying village unity was the existence of cross-cutting lines of cooperation and conflict. Neighborhood created dependence among people who might otherwise have conflicted. . . . The conflicts among brothers were often inherited by other close patrilineal kinsmen. . . . The opposed interests of classes were divided both by caste and by faction.

The basis of unity, to Orenstein, was that "conflict, which divided the whole village, also divided its parts." [86] In this broad context, not only would we expect subvillage fields, but we would not expect a single "nesting" set of territorial fields to have the strong traditional meaning that Redfield suggested was universal to peasant society.

Young saw the practical application of his theory as indicating which stage of differentiation/articulation might "take" in a developing community, and which would be too advanced. The implication of caste-structured civilization suggests additional risks for the developer. *Inappropriate demands upon village solidarity in caste society may not simply be frustrated, they may induce divisions in it.* This we can consider Proposition IV. Theoretically, it holds because demands for solidarity propose to remove cross-cutting cleavages, and therefore to present an unlimited threat to excluded groups. In fact, what we observe in Gaon is that the cooperatives, which the government had sought to organize on the basis of villagewide solidarity, had in fact grown only under the dominance of particular castes, or lineage-based divisions within castes—the village had four societies. Factions threatened further divisions. The *panchayat*, which the government had instituted for Gaon and a neighbor village, lapsed into inaction lest it be riven by factions. In a few other villages nearby, *panchayats* "had destroyed themselves in their efforts to take positive action." [87] Orenstein gives us two more specific indications where we may look for "inappropriate demands." "Government activi-

86. *Gaon*, pp. 305–308.
87. Ibid., p. 291.

ties impinged on the village to a much greater extent . . ." he found in 1961. "One of the effects of the innovations was a fragmentation of village society. . . . [Fragmentation] clearly had taken place at least partly due to the self-help movement." [88] There seems to be a suggestion here we can consider Proposition IV.A: *In caste society, programs requiring governmental action on the part of the village are most apt to induce factional division.* [89]

This proposition may turn out, if validated, to have explanatory value to the social scientist. It seems, at first glance, to be a discouraging proposition to the developer, for some development requires concerted action by villagers. We can distinguish two classes of required concert. Development technology may carry an area imperative: irrigation may require every landowner to join in routing field channels from the canal or tubewell, flood control may require joint action along the embankment, areal saturation may be required to upgrade seed or to suppress insects or weeds. Consolidation of many scattered plots into larger holdings practically requires government coercion. In these cases concert must be areal, though the area is not necessarily the village.

There are reasons for concert not inherently areal. Sociologists quite properly count on one success in self-help to build the confidence necessary to tackle the next. Economists see enhanced income from one improvement usable as investment for the next.

Capturing either benefit would seem to call for something like the Frank Young model of development: articulation of community interests and powers as part of intensified external involvement. But if we review our comparative analysis we realize that there are crucial alternatives of phasing and of the geographic or social range in which it is hoped concerted action can be induced. India's nationwide program, seeking a *panchayat* and a cooperative in each village (even though the village might be arbitrarily delimited), generated a maximum of factionalism. Etawah led

88. Ibid., p. 312.
89. In "Factions: A Comparative Analysis," in Michael Banton, ed. *Political Systems and the Distribution of Power* (London: Travistock Publications, 1965), Ralph Nicholas conceives factions as being essentially political, and to be found often in rapidly changing societies, pp. 23, 57.

off with increased farm productivity, then encouraged *panchayats,* and cooperatives only to meet a specific need. Comilla led off with cooperatives, but based each society on cohesion-in-being, not on the government-recognized village, and subjected each to supervision from a *thana*-level federation not initially responsible to the member societies.

Pakistan has, like India, shifted from the village council to the larger representative council (union and *thana* in Pakistan, block in India) as the key self-governing unit for rural development. Comilla experience agrees. This suggests Proposition IV.B: *In caste-structured society, the divisive potential or self-government decisions may be less at a level representing several or many villages than in the individual village.*

This proposition, per se, would argue for the location of the villagers' closest elective council in a market town or minor administrative headquarters, not necessarily so far away as the *thana* or block. If one thinks of the desirability of matching elective to administrative jurisdictions, we find ourselves strongly reinforced by two separate lines of policy recommendation. After a very realistic analysis, the M.I.T. conference concluded that while each agricultural development activity needs to be organized "in locality units appropriate to its own functions rather than forcing each of them into the strait jacket of a 'block' of predetermined size, . . . all activities can be coordinated by a single minor administrative unit of the government." [90] John P. Lewis argued that, from the point of view of developing economic enterprise, Indian rural development should radiate from small market towns.[91] Converting Proposition IV.B into our concepts of social fields, we have: In caste society, it may be easier to develop linear fields connecting village groups with the market town and converging in a self-government institution in the market town, than to convert the village into a self-governing community. But our work at this point is unfinished. Proposition IV is so vague as to risk circularity, while for IV.A and IV.B we have as yet no theoretical explanation.

90. Hapgood, *Policies for Promoting Agricultural Development,* p. 197.
91. *Quiet Crisis in India* (New York: Doubleday and Co., 1964), pp. 151–80.

Articulating the Culture of Development

Possible explanations emerge as soon as the cultural dimension of the development of peasant society is viewed in conjunction with the dimension of social structure. Here we will focus on the main distinctive features of caste society. Despite its reliance on cross-cutting cleavages for cohesion, the caste-structured village maintained strong legitimate leadership. This was because the caste village was a unit of exchange of services, tightly defined in the culture, and the exchange was not one of equality but in general of landowning, food-producing patrons, and traditional service castes. Furthermore, two mutually reinforcing prestige scales—landed wealth and ritual purity—supported a single structure of power. The legitimacy of traditional leadership was based on dependence and religiously sanctioned inequality.

Against this, the announced purpose of the national leaders is quite clear, and in India unqualified. The inequality of caste is attacked in principle; the dependence of traditional exchange of services is eroded by the market. A new basis of legitimate leadership is projected into the villages: the majority of equal votes. We are already in a position to understand that the actual choice presented to the villagers is modified to greater or less degree by the political brokers, not necessarily party workers, who hold the hinges connecting the state ministerial coalition or dissident group in the ruling party, or opposition party, with village groups. But this does not suffice to explain the virulence of factions, or their concentration in the village, rather than the representative levels of elective politics, e.g., in India the block or district.

So far the literature dealing with the heritage of Indian or Pakistani culture as it may affect rural development has focused on the high culture of Hinduism or Islam, under the impact of the high culture of Britain or the West. It is accepted on all sides that the culture of the peasants is different, but no one has conceived through what categories of life experiences high cultures could take on village reality. George Foster derived from much field work investigating changing folk and peasant cultures one such category. He calls it "the image of limited good." [92] Village wealth originates from the land. There is a fixed quantum of land in the village. What one family adds, another must lose. Yet, interrelations are close, inescapable. What is true of wealth is true of power, for it is power almost wholly over other villagers, or power to hold the single hinge connecting village power with the power of the outside government. More power for one leader means less for others.

Peasants do not seek more income or more power, therefore, save as they are ready to make enemies of other villagers, but they perceive the few who are born rich and powerful as born also immune from such restraints. It may seem proper to them, therefore, to give elective power to an ex-landlord whom they see as an exploiter rather than to a caste leader of their own status. Politics is a zero-sum game, except for the well-born and for those who have escaped "limited good" of the village by entering the new nonlanded economy and society of the town. Education is the most widely available lifeline out.

This explanation would permit us to understand why *panchayat* elections, or the question of who is to control one village cooperative society, would divide the village with such lasting bitterness, while similar decisions made by village representative meeting in the block or *thana* council might be accepted without lasting splits. It would also help us to understand why a decision taken by a village *panchayat* might be harder to enforce than one taken by a body slightly removed from the village. Orenstein tells why the Gaon *panchayat* had not been able to get house site owners to remove the rubble of abandoned houses. "They cited a Marathi proverb to the effect that when a kinsman pierces a baby's ears it hurts, but when the Goldsmith does so it does not. Action by a fellow villager would be taken as offensive, while that of an outsider would not." [93] Rooting democratic choice in the village may be seen by the outsider as substituting one value-basis of legiti-

92. "Peasant Society and the Image of Limited Good," *American Anthropologist* 67 (April 1965): 293–315.
93. *Gaon*, pp. 265–66.

macy, equality, for another, status. Villagers may see it as taking away from some of their close neighbors what is given to others, so that the stakes become too high to risk.

Does the perspective of limited good, which we have considered with reference to political choice, apply to economic motivation? "We assume, properly we believe, that every cultivator in every village desires to increase his agricultural production," write Carl Taylor, Douglas Ensminger, and their coauthors.[94] Kusum Nair's careful, though not scientific, observations indicated otherwise. Villagers of all castes in some areas and of some castes in many areas did not express economic ambition beyond mere subsistence.[95] There is absolute support for the idea of limited good in some of the most powerful and popular statements of Hindu ideals, for instance, Gandhi's: "If I take anything that I do not need for my own immediate use and keep it, I thieve it from somebody else." [96]

The point is not that an all-India cultural imperative translates all political choice or economic opportunity into a zero-sum game at the village level. The point is, on the contrary, that this may happen among particular villagers, if the development option is presented in a particular way, or if a series of options are presented in a particular sequence. Putting together our political and economic interpretations, we can state a series of propositions as to how "limited good" might explain the comparative results of community development we studied.

Proposition V: *Collective effort for self-help in peasant society is inhibited insofar as it is perceived in terms of limited good.*

Proposition V.A: *Villagers tend to perceive filling of village self-government offices, and making village government decisions, in terms of limited good.*

Proposition V.B: *Representative self-governing bodies at the*

94. *India's Roots of Democracy*, p. 562.
95. *Blossoms in the Dust.*
96. C. F. Andrews, *Mahatma Gandhi's Ideas* (London: George Allen and Unwin, 1929), p. 106. The virtually exclusive emphasis of Vinoba Bhave's moral crusade upon redistribution, not creation, of wealth is a contemporary application of this tenet.

union, block, thana, or district levels are less apt to be perceived through the image of limited good than village bodies.

Proposition V.C: *Decisions concerning a manifestly productive enterprise, particularly one of new technology, tend to escape the connotation of limited good.*

These propositions strengthen our previous explanations of the results at Etawah and Comilla as compared to nationwide community development. Etawah partly escaped perception as limited good by leading off with individual economic improvement. Comilla's cooperatives were vulnerable to this perception, except for their incorporation of two unconventional features: they set about at once introducing diesel pumps and tractors into the static economy, and they made lending decisions subject to firm external supervision. Even so, it is interesting to note that the sensitive observations of the academy detect a slackening of member deposits, once the economic position of the small peasants is back to where it is remembered to have been. On the other hand, we view with new skepticism the strategy of Indian community development to emphasize village elections regardless of the strength or weakness in the village of perceptions of the possibility of progress, and quite apart from decisions to introduce dramatic new productive technology.

We have been tracing the effect on development responses of a single cultural translation—we might, in analogy to our terminology regarding social relationships, call it a cultural hinge—the village perception of limited good. No doubt, we could find other such cultural translations. The point is certainly not that they are working in all the villages in the country; one of the unique values of Kusum Nair's books was that she presented the tremendous cultural contrast between a Guntur or Kaira district village and one in Gulbarga or eastern U.P. Village culture is part of a larger culture; it is also microculture. Here we come to Proposition VI: *Articulating the culture of village development requires learning the meaning of national purposes in terms of the perceptions of villagers.*

This is, of course, precisely what community development professes to be about. Prestige-ordered administration blocks this sort of learning, however. And it is very different from the characteristic cultural role of nation-building leaders, who project into the lives of villagers their own answers to the challenges posed by modernity to traditional high cultures. Finally, the "community development method" proves to carry with it blanket cultural assumptions (the village is the unit; all cultivators want to increase their incomes) which may not have the assumed meaning to villagers.

The organizational implication of Proposition VI is well put in a statement written, before Comilla was founded, by Arthur T. Mosher: "The task of finding and establishing an effective pattern of programs for rural development is itself a quest, and the pattern of administration appropriate to it is more . . . akin to that of a university, whose professors enjoy academic freedom, than it is to the straight line of authority commonly found in armies and colonial administration." [97]

We must be realistic about the kind of academic institution which can relate village microcultures to national development programs. It is work in an experimental rural area that gives the institution something to teach. It is evaluation and research upon village meanings of action programs that provide relevant understandings of village culture. In terms of our propositions II.A and III.A, the educational operation needs to extend as far up the administrative hierarchies and as far into village social structure as hinging of fields may occur. It is difficult to conceive of these educational functions being carried out save through the language which is current in the villages, though translation is bound to be required in the institution. Proposition VI.A: *Search for the microcultural significance of national purposes calls for an educational institution experimenting with action programs, feeding back into action its findings of village perceptions, and training participants so as to develop linear fields of program relationships.*

97. *Varities of Extension Education and Community Development,* Cornell State College of Agriculture, Comparative Extension Publication No. 2 (Ithaca, N.Y., 1958), p. 108.

Conclusions

We have been discussing the search for the meanings of national purposes to existing and immediately changing village cultures. Changing such cognitive maps as limited good is more apt to be a long-term transition, mainly intergenerational. Neither in India nor in Pakistan do we find a general, thoroughgoing harnessing of rural schools to this mission. Schools are, instead, the ladder from the village into the cultural elites. The strand of high cultures which reaches the village strongest and most intact is the religious strand. It is unlikely that a long-term reinterpretation and elaboration of peasant culture can be achieved without reweaving this strand in the whole fabric. But here also, it is the encounter of the villagers with an integration of their own high religious tradition with science and national purposes that gives meaning to rural development. One of the most profoundly significant of the Comilla demonstrations involves the training at the academy of the existing *imams,* who conduct prayers in the village mosques, so that they may teach preschool classes and conduct literacy training for adults. *Imams* have entered weekly training for the new tasks from 160 villages. Here again, we note how difficult it would be for one outside the culture to undertake so delicate a task of cultural reintegration. In a different context (meeting alleged Muslim objections to contraception) Akhter Hameed said: "I was not afraid . . . I was trained in theology, so I knew about the Muslim stand."[98]

We have returned to the ground on which we began. Community development defines itself as a method of uniting government programs to local community participation. Accepting this definition of our subject of inquiry, we observed our cases from a new perspective. We did not take village participation to be simply the resultant (dependent variables) of government programs (independent variables). We saw both interacting, but interact-

98. Akhter Hameed Khan, *Speeches of Akhter Hameed Khan,* pp. 2–6, 52.

ing as segments of a particular type of society and culture. Peasant society, seen from the village, is marked by weakly integrated relationships with the larger society, and by weak integration of the local nonliterate cultures with the great religious-literate-urban heritage. Seen as nations, Pakistan and India are bundles of extensive but partially integrated social systems, each partly sharing in its culture with the others, partly differing. We could list many such disjunctions between cultures or subcultures: Muslim–Hindu, Muslim or Hindu–secular, national–regional (linguistic), university–nongraduate, party–career administration, generalist–technician. National community development, decided upon and administered across these and other such gaps, fails to take root in the villages. Its champions hold that the very disjunctions that frustrate it provide the need for it; we cannot expect more. But pilot projects do take root. This is partly because, localized, they do not try to span all the gaps (e.g., their area is unilingual, and they need select from modern scientific and traditional cultures only elements they can integrate). Mainly, it is because they are learning projects. Save as they are learned, the bonds across the gaps of peasant society cannot be planned. It may be that through such working and learning the various elites and the various peasants in this kind of society discover the specific plans that will be developmental, and thus, in some part, the kind of nation they compose.

Chapter 3

Centralized and Decentralized Political Impacts on a Developing Economy: Interpretations of American Experience

Emmette Redford

The United States has been called the "first new nation." [1] Its statesmen at the beginning, like those of later new nations, wanted realization both of national identity and economic growth. The achievement of each in the course of history is strikingly apparent. The experience merits analysis from a variety of perspectives, not for specific guidelines for other nations seeking the same goals in different circumstances, but for glimpses of relevance.

Space is perhaps the most obvious feature in this "first new nation." The geographical dimensions are large, eventually comprising over three and two-thirds million square miles. It is, except for China and Russia, the largest common market and area of resource mobility in the world. Regional diversities in land, forests, minerals, and water resources (for use and for transport) allow development of regional economic specializations, symbolized in the period of agricultural dominance by such terms as "cotton kingdom" and "corn belt," but present also in the regional industrial developments around mineral resources and in commercial developments at harbor and river sites. Over such a vast space, numerous local markets would exist. Until transportation was developed, these would be semiautonomous. The village blacksmith, general store, and mill symbolize the localization of

1. Seymour Martin Lipset, *The First New Nation: The United States in Historical and Comparative Perspective* (New York: Basic Books, 1963); William Nisbet Chambers, *Political Parties in a New Nation* (New York: Oxford University Press, 1963).

economic activity in the agricultural period, as do the metropolitan concentrations in the industrial.

Space, though essential for the economic development which occurred, was only a setting on which cultural influences could be imposed. Technology, institutional structure, and human motivations, coincidental within a time span, would determine utilization of resources in the space dimension. It was not natural nor inevitable that the great possibilities for economic development in one vast midcontinent bowl would be realized. The resources in their natural state were not inherently conducive to efficient use for economic growth. They were spread over, or separated within, a vast area. A viable economy, aggregating use of these resources, would exist only if, along with other things, appropriate political actions were taken.

The unity, regionalism, and localism which developed in the economy has been paralleled by three-level political structuralization. The political structure has not neatly conformed to the allocation of resources—for the states, which form the middle tier in the political structure, developed without relation to regional resource locations, and the local units forming the bottom tier were created to meet needs that often differed from those which existed later. Nevertheless, in spite of the absence of close correlation between political organization and resource allocation and use, the three-tier structure has supplied the channels for political action in a large and diversified nation.

This three-level structure, particularly the federalistic nature of the relations between the top two levels, and the modifications of its operations through regional (cross-state) and metropolitan (cross-local) activities, has been a favorite theme of analysis for students of the American scene. On the other hand, the relation of this political structure to economic development has not attracted attention. It is my purpose to outline, first historically and then contemporaneously, the respective roles of centralized and decentralized political activity with respect to the economic development of the nation. Primary but not exclusive attention will be given to the role of centralized political action. Attention will be directed also to the interactions among centralizations as these have evolved in the economic and political sectors, but only for the purpose of showing how the role of centralized political authority came to be expanded. In the discussion the term "economic development" is not used in any technical sense but only as an alternative to "a developing economy" and is used comprehensively to include institutional development as well as quantitative expansion.

Initially, four descriptive propositions, to be substantiated in the discussion that follows, are stated.

First, centralized political decisions made possible a viable economy extending over a vast area and aggregating use of the resources therein.

Second, spatial allocation of the power to govern made possible centralized and decentralized initiatives for the promotion of economic development.

Third, economic development was facilitated by a variety of uncoordinated but pragmatic political responses by both centralized and decentralized governments.

Fourth, in the developed and mature industrial economy which has emerged, political decision-making has been greatly centralized to match the economic centralization that occurred earlier, but the decisions reflect functional and areal pluralisms that exist in the society.

The Preindustrial Phase

Many factors contributed to the unification of the North American midcontinent. Diplomacy, infiltration, and war built its territorial dimension. Political creativeness was necessary to construct a political unity. Less recognized is the effect of political creativeness in constructing the economic component of unity. The framers of the Constitution established more than a political structure; they created also a constitution for an economic system.

The American Common Market

The framers of the Constitution assembled because of obstacles in the political system to financial, industrial, and commercial activity, and they laid the political foundations for economic development over a large area. Madison said in 1786 that "most of our political evils may be traced to our commercial ones." [2] The Annapolis Convention of 1786, representing five states, was called to consider "how far an uniform system in their commercial regulations . . . might be necessary to the common interest and permanent harmony. . . ." It concluded vaguely that "other objects, than those of commerce" needed discussion and asked Congress to call a convention representing all the states. That Convention, responding to economic needs, prepared a Constitution which made these contributions to economic development:

1. It retained the interstate citizenship clause of the Articles of Confederation, which means that a citizen of one state in the Union can do business in all states on the same conditions as residents of the respective states.[3]

2. It retained the "full, faith, and credit" principle of the Articles, which meant that the courts of every state could enforce the commercial decisions of those in each state.

3. It insured the integrity of the commercial contract by prohibiting any state from "impairing the obligation of contracts."

4. It centralized the power "to coin money" and "regulate the value thereof" in the Congress and forbade the states to coin money, issue paper money, or make anything except gold or silver legal tender in payment of debts.

5. It likewise centralized the power to regulate foreign and interstate commerce (and trade with the Indians) in the Congress and the power to make treaties in the President and Senate.

6. It centralized in Congress the power to supply certain facilities of commerce: postal communications, post roads, common weights and measures, patents and copyrights.

7. It provided the elements of a strong government which could

2. Letter to Jefferson, March 18, 1786, in Gaillard Hunt, ed., *Writings of James Madison* (New York and London: G. P. Putnam's Sons, 1900–1910), 2: 228.

3. The exceptions evolved in Supreme Court decisions have had relatively little importance. The exception of corporations would have had great importance if substantial extension of the privilege to them by the states had not been general.

protect commerce on the frontiers and the seas and enforce national laws and the national constitution.

8. It created viable institutions for adjustments of conflicts of economic interests.

Although judicial interpretations and some legislation would be necessary to support the particulars,[4] the framers had constructed a "Grand Pattern" for economic development. The pattern was free commerce and free access to resources over a national domain, supported by integrity of contracts, a national monetary system, a central legislative power on matters affecting interstate and foreign trade, and a power balance in the Constitution acceptable to the many and diverse interests. Centralized political decision, to be legitimized in state ratifying conventions, had breached the disunities in the spatial spread and laid the basis for the development of a national economic system.

This, in modern terms, was institutional planning. In response to conditions, and with far-reaching perspectives on some of the essentials for economic development, the framers had provided a framework for such development. The tremendous significance of this institutional planning for economic growth can be understood by contrast with the restrictions on trade and use of resources which existed among small nations in Europe and which European statesmen still struggle to correct. Or by contemplating the opportunities for productivity in central North America created by free access to resources and to a market over an area theretofore not matched except in empires. Never perhaps had political decision contributed more for the development of an economy.

Political decision was, of course, only one of the factors facilitating a national economy in spite of space and diversity. There was for the entire area a common language, a common national experience in the Revolution, common secular traditions, use of the common law (except in Louisiana), and by decision from 1776 to 1791 submergence of religious conflict below the level of politics. There was common acceptance of the Calvinistic creed

4. For these details, as well as the full elaboration of the idea set forth here, see my *American Government and The Economy* (New York: Macmillan Co., 1965), chap. 7. On money, especially, legislation was required to supplement the Constitution, and it was long delayed.

of industry and thrift, secularized and popularized through *Poor Richard's Almanac,* and making every respectable citizen a creator of capital—whether in the form of barns and farm equipment, shops and inventories, factories, clipper ships, or other facilities of production and commerce. Also, the basic values of equality and individual achievement prevailed increasingly throughout the nation,[5] broadening initiatives in every section and keeping the society open and fluid.

In sum, there was much national unity in traditions and ideology. Also, the Convention decisions were followed by other national actions which facilitated economic development over a large area. Marshall's interpretations of the Constitution strengthened and stretched the protection of contracts, gave ample scope to the legislative power of the Union, and ruled out state exercises of power that conflicted with legitimate national uses of power. *Gibbons* v. *Ogden*[6] particularly had economic significance; it proscribed state laws on a matter of interstate commerce where national laws on the matter had been passed and thus impeded the resurrection of the local restrictions on commerce which had existed before 1787. Hamilton, first American to consciously propose a plan of economic development,[7] supplied leadership for restoration of the nation's credit, establishment of confidence in its finances, and protection for American manufacturing. These steps won for the new government the confidence and support of rising financial, manufacturing, and commercial interests. Jefferson, in turn, widened the support in the great agricultural interest. Jefferson and Jackson added to the formal political structure the informal instrument of the national party, through which the geographical and functional diversities of economic interest could be represented or submerged.

Meanwhile, the first decisions with respect to Western terri-

5. For discussion of American values see Lipset, *The First New Nation,* pp. 213ff.

6. 9 Wheat. 1 (1824).

7. Hamilton's plan included national assumption and funding of the public debt, establishment of a national bank, excise taxes, and sweeping measures to encourage manufacturing (encouragement of immigration, restrictions on export of raw materials, bounties for manufacturers and inventors, public construction of roads and canals, etc.).

tory were made. The great achievement of the Articles of Conferation was the pact for the cession by the states of their Western lands to the Union. This meant removal of a source of conflict among the states and allowed the development of uniform policy for sale of Western lands. The Convention, in one of its momentous decisions, accepted entry of new states on equal status with the original ones, thereby safeguarding the nation against artificial power balances between the East and West which could have impaired the development of the West and the unity of the economy. Jefferson in overcoming constitutional scruples about acquisition of territory, not only added to the Union the rich Mississippi Valley, but set the precedent for the aggressive land absorption which extended the one-market, free-access area to the Gulf and the Rio Grande on the south, 54° 40' on the north, the Pacific on the west, and ultimately to Alaska and Hawaii. By these decisions the lands were national, there would be no political discrimination against the new areas, and the economic area was enlarged.

From the foregoing discussion we can restate our first proposition: centralized political leadership created and extended a large common market and prevented political obstacles to free access and equal treatment within the vast resource area. It can be added that the unity existing within the nation was achieved not through mass political organization nor a centralized police, but primarily through the breakdown of economic barriers and economic growth within the one great market. And, also, that the unity was a loose one; it lay essentially in institutional framework within which individual and group, and public—national, state, and local—initiatives could be exerted.

Nevertheless, the system was threatened by the internal division between two regionally dominant economic systems—one based on free labor, the other on slave labor. The struggle of these two worlds within one for position in the underdeveloped West could not be submerged, absorbed, or resolved within the formal structure for compromise and adjustment established by the framers, or within the parties created by their heirs; politics again was the means of unification, but its instrument was "blood

and iron." The Civil War, although evidence of the failure of
political statesmanship, confirmed finally the unity of the nation
and the one great market and created also unity of the economic
system itself. Although regional differences would remain, the
whole economy would be based on free, mobile, wage-paid labor.

Political Aid for Economic Development

Historical research has now substantiated the proposition that
early Americans saw no inconsistency between the social contract and personal liberty; [8] on the contrary, they accepted government as regulator of diverse and conflicting interests,[9] as promoter of particular interests,[10] as broker of regional interests,[11]
and as promoter of economic development.[12]

The economic policies of the nation were developed at all three
levels of government. The framers had left intact the political
structures of the states, thereby preserving decentralized political
power. State powers of local legislation were extensive and, except for taxation of interstate and foreign commerce, their powers
of taxation were undiminished by the Constitution. Indeed, the
Supreme Court in the Taney period (1836 to 1864) liberally construed their powers: allowing creation of money through state-
chartered and state-supported banks; [13] establishing a more fa-

8. See Louis Hartz, *Economic Policy and Democratic Thought: Pennsylvania,
1776–1860* (Cambridge: Harvard University Press, 1948); Oscar and Mary
Flug Handlin, *Commonwealth: A Study of the Role of Government in the
Economy: Massachusetts, 1774–1861* (New York: New York University Press,
1947); James Neal Primm, *Economic Policy in the Development of a Western
State: Missouri, 1820–1860* (Cambridge: Harvard University Press, 1954); and
Milton Sydney Heath, *Constructive Liberalism: The Role of the State in Economic
Development in Georgia to 1860* (Cambridge: Harvard University Press, 1954).

9. See particularly, *The Federalist,* ed. Wright (Cambridge: Harvard University Press, 1961), No. 10.

10. While Madison conceived of government's role as compromise and balance
among interests, both Hamilton and Jefferson proposed to sponsor selected interests deemed important for the national welfare.

11. Jefferson and Jackson both made the national party the representative, and
therefore inherently the broker, of varied geographical interests. Clay, also, in his
American System sought to unify the interests of the West and the seaboard.

12. Note, for example, the following statement: "To aid, encourage, and stimu-
late commerce, domestic and foreign, is a duty of the sovereign, as plain and as
universally recognized as any other." Quoted by Hartz, *Economic Policy and
Democratic Thought,* p. 122, from the majority opinion in Sharpless et al. v.
Mayor of Philadelphia, 21 Pa. St. Rep. 147, 182 (1853).

13. Briscoe v. Bank of Kentucky, 11 Pet. 257 (1837).

vorable balance toward public power with respect to contracts; [14] and creating in the Cooley doctrine perhaps the most useful of all pragmatic rules of federalism, namely that states and their subdivisions could regulate interstate commerce, provided the purpose was local benefit, commerce was not obstructed or otherwise adversely affected, and Congress had not acted on the subject matter of legislation.[15]

For a long period of time—in fact, for roughly a century and a half—the states and their subdivisions, the local governments, would be the most active centers of economic legislation. Together they would maintain law and order and apply through their courts the rules on property, contract, and torts. Also, they enacted regulatory legislation. Hartz has shown that in Pennsylvania state and local authorities in the early nineteenth century passed a multitude of laws requiring licenses, regulating prices and standards, protecting labor, and doing other things. Moreover, before the Civil War they were initiating the modern systems of corporate, bank, and insurance regulation.

Nevertheless, the evidence is ample that Madison was wrong in his prediction that "the chief task of modern legislation would be the regulation of these conflicting and interfering interests." [16] The chief end of economic legislation in national, state, and local governments was the promotion of the economies in their respective areas. This is not inconsistent with the fact that they often interpreted the needs for economic development in terms of the promotion of particular kinds of enterprise, whether, for example, of manufacturing or of agriculture.

At the national level, statesmen like Hamilton, Albert Gallatin, Jefferson, Calhoun, John Quincy Adams, and Clay had plans for developing the nation's economy. Nevertheless, a positive national program for economic development did not come into being. The actions of the national government with respect to the economy were quite limited, though strategic in terms of the

14. Charles River Bridge v. Warren Bridge Co., 11 Pet. 420 (1837); West River Bridge v. Dix, 6 How. 507 (1848).
15. Cooley v. Board of Wardens of the Port of Pennsylvania, 12 How. 299 (1851).
16. *The Federalist,* No. 10

needs of the period. The nationally operated Post Office provided the communication facilities of the nation until the use of the Morse telegraph began in the 1840's. But in spite of Morse's proposal for government ownership and of active consideration of the proposal, Congress constructed only an experimental line from Baltimore to Washington, and then allowed it to pass into private ownership.[17] Protection was given to American settlers on the Western frontier and to American commerce on the high seas. Tariffs were enacted to protect American manufacturing, but they became the subject of sectional controversy and the rates went down in the decades preceding the Civil War. Explorations into the Western frontier were sponsored and financed. Land policy was progressively more favorable to Western settlers—tending to sale in small portions, at low prices, and on credit, and granting preemption rights to squatters.[18] The Army Engineers was created and the nation's first engineering school was established at West Point in 1802. Forest Hill has told the interesting story of how the national government's engineer corps trained at West Point, in addition to planning and constructing fortifications and coastal defenses, made surveys for canal routes, river navigation, roads and railroads, supplying this service both for the nation and for the states and chartered companies, and in the process developing additional engineering talent in the states.[19] But the thirty-year period prior to the Civil War was one of marked withdrawal of the national government from domestic activities.

The lack of sustained, positive national policy is most clearly revealed in the history of internal improvements. Internal improvements is the name used to describe the efforts to develop a transportation system for the spatially spread nation, and the importance attached to them in the early history of the United States is similar to that given to infrastructure in present-day planning

17. Leonard D. White, *The Jacksonians: A Study in Administrative History, 1829–1861* (New York: Macmillan Co., 1954), p. 457.

18. See Roy M. Robbins, *Our Landed Heritage: The Public Domain, 1776–1936* (Princeton: Princeton University Press, 1942).

19. Forest G. Hill, *Roads, Rails, and Waterways: The Army Engineers and Early Transportation* (Norman: University of Oklahoma Press, 1957). West Point and the Rensselaer Polytechnic Institute (with a one-year program) were the only engineering schools in the country prior to the creation of several in 1845 and the decade following that date. *Ibid.*, pp. 208–209.

in underdeveloped countries. The arguments made for public expenditure also are those applicable to other underdeveloped countries: the lack of private capital, and the deferred benefits which would be advantageous to the economy but would not provide incentives to private investors. (In the United States the sparse settlement on the frontier meant development for a population to be attracted to it.) National statesmen, notably Gallatin in a ten-year plan for development of canals in 1808 and Calhoun in a less extensive proposal of 1819, favored national expenditures for development of transportation to meet both military and commercial needs. The national government did make notable contributions through surveys, river and harbor projects, construction of the Cumberland Road and of military and territorial roads generally, purchase of stock in some canal companies, and by land and monetary grants to the states. But scruples concerning constitutional power of the national government hindered the development in the first quarter of the century;[20] and states' rights arguments and conflicts among the sections, fearful of their competitive position, brought a virtual end to national expenditures for the purpose after 1830.

The gap in national action was filled by the state and local governments. The story of the public contribution to the development of canals and railroads has been told exhaustively by Carter Goodrich. He found that in the period before the Civil War the state governments committed some $300 million in cash or credit to internal improvements and the local governments more than $125 million, whereas the national government's direct contribution was only about $7 million.[21] The sums spent by the state and local governments were tremendous for the economy of that day and constituted the largest item in state-local expenditure. Goodrich has concluded that the public expenditures made "major contributions to American development."[22] "It is difficult to im-

20. Jefferson suggested authorization of internal improvements by constitutional amendment, Madison in 1817 vetoed on constitutional grounds a bill which would have made funds available for construction of roads and canals, and Monroe, also on constitutional grounds, vetoed a Cumberland Road bill in 1822.
21. *Government Promotion of American Canals and Railroads: 1800–1890* (New York: Columbia University Press, 1960), p. 268.
22. Ibid., p. 281.

agine," he says, "what the nation's transportation system would
have been on the eve of the Civil War if there had been no public
subsidy." [23] He added that "the achievements of public investment might well have been still greater if federal resources had
been used in the early decades to carry out a national plan of internal improvements or if certain of the states had provided a
sounder basis for their more promising projects." [24]

While regional conflicts prevented planned and sustained national development, the existence of state and local interests stimulated a "booster spirit" in internal improvements. It seemed apparent to all that the route to state and local prosperity lay in
transportation links across the vast stretches of territory to resources and markets. Demonstration of this fact was provided by
the Erie Canal which, completed in 1825, gave a tremendous
thrust to economic development all the way from New York City
to the Great Lakes region. The great competition of the period
was among states and localities for the access to be created by
canals and railroads.

States and cities were pragmatic as to means to be employed.
Some states, and even cities, following the example of the state of
New York's construction of the Erie Canal, built canals themselves. In other cases funds were granted to private companies.
Yet the preference was for mixed enterprise, taking the form of
public subscription of part of the stock but leaving the management to private partners.[25]

The period of copartnership of the American state with private
enterprise came abruptly to an end in most of the states before
the Civil War. Poor planning and overextension of developments,
poor administration by amateur state administrations, and inadequate supervision of private partners were followed by fiscal difficulties. There was default or scaling of debt obligations in many
states and cities. As for the states, a period of withdrawal resulted
in new constitutional provisions inhibiting further contributions.
Many cities continued to make contributions to attract railroads,

23. Ibid., p. 280.
24. Ibid., p. 281.
25. Ibid., p. 289.

and the national government initiated a new period of assistance to railroad development in 1850. But grants to private railroad companies took the place of the mixed enterprise which had been preferred in the first flush of canal and railroad construction.

There were other ways in which economic development was fostered by state and local action. Aggregation of capital from groups of investors was facilitated by state grant of charters of incorporation to banking, insurance, canal, railroad, and manufacturing companies. After 1830 the states passed laws providing for limited liability of corporate investors, and beginning with Connecticut in 1837 general incorporation laws (allowing any group which met statutory requirements to obtain a charter) were passed in the chief manufacturing states.[26]

Banking authorizations by the states were especially significant for the nation's economic development. State-chartered banks supplied two needs for the economy: credit for land buyers, merchants, and others; and medium of exchange through deposit and checking accounts and, more especially, through state bank notes. Only three chartered banks existed in the United States at the time the Constitution was framed, and the framers of that document made no reference to the subject. They limited their decisions to authorization of national coinage and prohibitions on direct actions by the states to create money or to make anything except gold and silver legal tender in payment of debts. The issue of national authority to establish a bank was the first issue of federalism in the nation's history. Although the national government did establish a bank in 1791, and again in 1819, and although the constitutionality of such action was established,[27] the two national banks expired. The creation of banks was, however, a function exercised by the states from the 1780's on, and the vacuum in national action made this an essential state function. The regulation of these banks by the states was often weak, and loose banking practices caused economic crises on occasions. Moreover, delay

26. New York had passed such a law for small manufacturing concerns as early as 1811. See on the subject, Ross M. Robertson, *History of the American Economy* (New York: Harcourt, Brace and Co., 1955), pp. 213ff.
27. McCulloch v. Maryland, 4 Wheat. 316 (1819).

in the development of central clearance institutions, and the varieties of circulating bank notes, created serious inconveniences in commerce. Nevertheless, the state-chartered banks "brought about a steady and rapid development of the American economy which would have been utterly impossible without them." [28]

Finally, the state and local governments were laying the foundations for perhaps their greatest long-run contribution to American economic development. This was public education—the nation's greatest adventure in public enterprise. Although the national government, from as early as the Northwest Ordinance of 1785, set aside lands to provide for common schools, public education developed as a state-local function. By 1850 tax-supported, public schools for all children had become an actuality in most of the northern portion of the country. State universities had also been established. In time—that is, after the Civil War—the system of public education, supported and directed primarily by state and local governments, was to become universal in the United States.

General Features of Economic Development

The pre-Civil War period was one of tremendous growth. Population increased from about 4 million in 1790 to 31½ million in 1860. Agriculture, manufacturing, and commerce expanded tremendously. Great technological advances—the steamboat, the cotton gin, the reaper, substitution of coal for charcoal, and others —were made. Capital funds and capital assets accumulated in response to need.

The achievement was facilitated by unusually favorable circumstances. Undeveloped resources, expanding home and foreign markets, absence of large military undertakings or military structure were especially favorable to economic growth. Nevertheless, the result was a human achievement. Private individuals and companies pioneered, industry and thrift prevailed, there was willingness to take new risks and move to new areas, and there was the beginning of the aggregation of men and capital in larger un-

28. Robertson, *History of the American Economy*, p. 157.

dertakings. Even the great advances in technology were associated with the names of individual pioneers—Fulton, Whitney, McCormick, and Morse among others. On its face, the achievement shows the great potentialities of private initiative under propitious circumstances.

Yet government also made contributions of great consequence to the development. The greatest political achievement was national union—its creation, extension of its boundaries, and its final confirmation, although at great cost, in the Civil War. The economic consequence was the large common market with free access of people and capital to its resources. Additionally, there were the national protections for contract. And there was vigorous national protection for territory and commerce. Of great significance also was the contribution of state and local government. Government went westward with the settler, offering order and the protections of the American legal system for property and contract. State and local governments aggregated capital—through taxation and borrowing—to promote the transportation links needed for access to resources and to markets. State governments authorized, and to some extent regulated, the financial institutions necessary for the creation and supply of capital funds. Truly, the achievement was the result of the combined initiatives of the nation—private and public, and on the public side, national, state, and local.

At the end of the period the population was widely dispersed, the economy was still dominated by small-scale enterprise but included some large and successful corporations for railroads and other enterprises, and government was decentralized and bureaucracies relatively undeveloped. The national government with its 50,000 employees was larger than any state government. Its influence on technology through several of its agencies was important. Yet its contacts with the economy were minimal. The post office was its only daily reminder to most of the population. On the other hand, the state administrations included units related to corporate authorization, railroads, banking and insurance; and local governments licensed trades, supplied water, gave police, fire, and health protection, and educated children.

The Industrial Period: Transitional Phase

Beginnings and endings in social movements are rarely neatly marked. In the politico-economic development of the United States, the quite arbitrary separations of periods can be more easily made for the political than for the economic sector. In the political sector the Civil War is breaking point from the past and the Great Depression of the 1930's was watershed into the future. In the economic sector, industrialization began and was well on its way before the Civil War and the breaking point into present-day maturity is somewhere in the twentieth century. For convenience in analysis, the Civil War and the Depression are chosen as divisional events—marking the beginning and the end of a transition period.

On the political side, the great development of this period was the emergence of the United States as a major world power. The dates 1898 and 1914 are landmarks in the transition. But the consequences were evaded, and likewise the consequences of the revolution which had occurred in the economy. The nation had not matured to its modern responsibilities.

On the economic side, the great development was the corporate revolution, characterized by the growth of large private organizations to take advantage of technological advances, of the economies of scale, and of the vast American market. Although the large railroad corporation had won the field of transportation prior to the Civil War, its growth after the Civil War epitomized the corporate growth of the postwar period. Railroad capitalization grew from an estimated \$1.145 billion in 1860 to over \$10 billion in 1890.[29] Spectacular growth of corporations to huge proportions occurred before 1910 in such other major industries as oil, steel, durable goods manufacturing, food processing, and telephone and telegraph communications. Following these came the great mail-order houses to threaten the local wholesalers and retailers, and in the 1920's the emergence of the multibillion-dollar

29. Goodrich, *Government Promotion*, pp. 270–71.

electric and gas utility holding companies. By 1930 Berle and Means could record that 200 nonbanking corporations with assets of $90 million controlled 49.2 percent of all nonbanking corporate wealth.[30]

The growth of the giant industrial corporation was paralleled by a similar development in American banking. Huge banking institutions in the East financed industrial undertakings and placed representatives on corporate boards. They both facilitated the corporate revolution and participated in the controls over it.

In great measure the opportunities for growth of enterprise on this magnitude were the result of the existence of the one great market and resource area created by the political genius of 1787. On the other hand, the corporate revolution brought new regional and local concentrations in economic growth. Thus, railroad locations fostered the development of some regions and cities and hindered development of others, steel production developed in response to location of iron and coal, and banking concentration magnified the importance of New York and other financial centers. The differentiation of economic regions, which had been a feature of economic development prior to the Civil War, was continued under the impact of new factors. Nevertheless, the benefits would be nationalized as a result of the one market created in the preindustrial period, the corporate revolution of the transitional period, and national welfare legislation in a still later period.

The corporate revolution brought the large-scale mobilization of resources and men necessary for the modern phase of economic development. With it there came, dating from the last decade of the nineteenth century, industrial management, Taylorism, and the cult of efficiency. With it came also the transfer of Darwinian ideology from the plant and animal world to American capitalism, ruthlessness in treatment of rivals and of buyers and sellers, speculative profits from financial manipulation and price-rigging, inordinate "waste" of natural resources, and harsh conditions for American labor.

30. Adolf A. Berle, Jr., and Gardiner C. Means, *The Modern Corporation and Private Property* (New York: Macmillan Co., 1932), p. 29.

Although there were many large farms and large ranches, neither the corporate system nor large-scale enterprise was characteristic of agriculture. The corporate system and large-scale enterprise came slowly, or not at all, in some other segments of the economy. The farmer and many others who stood outside the corporate system viewed it with antagonism. The results were the rise of the politics of protest in the Granger, Populist, and Progressive movements, and of demands for public action. A further result was a kind of schizophrenia in the response of the diverse organs of government to the new corporate power.

Trends in Public Policy

Two kinds of influence operated to restrict the development of public policy in the transition period. Both were crystallized in what now became the chief organ of centralized political decision—the Supreme Court of the United States. The first was the notion of limited intervention of government in the economy. In the hands of the Court it became a general rule of "laissez-faire with exceptions." It incorporated the ideas of laissez faire economics and vested property rights. The notion did not prevent the expansion of government regulation, but it restricted the expansion and gave special protection to the corporate interests, particularly from stringent utility rate-making and undesired labor legislation. The second influence was the notion of states' rights. In the hands of the Court it created a mismatch between the geographical allocation of the power to govern and the economic centralization produced by the corporate revolution within the one national market. This notion too did not prevent national regulation, but it delayed enforcement of the antitrust statute of 1890 and led to Supreme Court invalidation of the first efforts of the national government to exercise positive control over industrial corporations. It is possible that the notions may have facilitated economic development; certainly, however, they produced delays in the development of public policy, and in the reallocation of political power, to meet the new situation created by corporate growth.

This does not mean that government did not have significant

effects upon economic development. Through two broad categories of policy government had an impact. Government policy was promotive and facilitative, even sometimes permissive. It was also regulative.

The most significant contribution of the national government to economic development was in the new policy, in part regulatory but primarily promotive, on banking and currency. Under pressures of wartime necessity Congress passed the banking acts of 1863 and 1864. In these acts it finally took the steps necessary to create a uniform national currency. It put a prohibitory tax on state bank notes, thereby terminating their issuance. It provided for the chartering of national banks, which would be instruments for issuance of bank notes to serve the commerce of the nation. Nevertheless, the "sound" money policies of the government in the decades following the Civil War may have created some lag in economic growth, and the banking system was not flexible enough. In 1913, fifty years after the initial banking act, Congress sought to correct its deficiencies. In the Federal Reserve Act it created the rudiments of a centralized banking system. A major objective of the system was to overcome local and regional shortages of credit by making the facilities of regional (Federal Reserve) banks available to the scattered commercial banks of the nation.

Promotional policy is patently evident in the grants for railroad construction. The national government, which had belatedly entered the field of internal improvements in 1850 with the initiation of large grants of land to railroads, now donated in the years 1861–1872 over 100 million acres to railroad companies to encourage extensive construction, particularly of transcontinental routes. Some of the states, mostly in the South, made monetary contributions, local governments gave large sums, and Texas added 27 million to the 5 million acres already granted by it.[31] By the end of the century the national government had substantially exhausted its ability to promote enterprise through land grants—a historic rather than contemporary form of aid—characteristic, as Walter Prescott Webb pointed out, of the day when sovereigns

31. Goodrich, *Government Promotion*, p. 269.

could give away resources without making any direct levy on their subjects.[32]

But the adoption of the income tax amendment in 1913 gave it a new source of revenue, and it promptly made use of it. With the advent of the automobile age the national government, in contrast to the hesitancy and meagerness of its actions a hundred years earlier, gave the impetus—through monetary grants to states initiated in 1916—to the construction of the highway system of the nation. The new transportation system would be entirely public, almost completely free (until the 1950's, when toll roads began to be mixed with the free), and built with the cooperative participation of all three levels of government. At the same time the national government initiated its grants for aid to American flagships on the seas. Meanwhile, also, it had begun the enormous expansion of its river and harbor expenditures.[33] Finally, the government had initiated programs for conservation and effective use of natural resources. Particularly noteworthy was the initiation of national leadership for preservation and rebuilding of forests through the national Forest Service,[34] the building of irrigation projects through the national Bureau of Reclamation,[35] and the assistance to farmers in land conservation through the nationally supported agricultural extension services.

From the beginning to the end of this middle period the national government promoted agricultural interests. The dominance of agricultural producers in most electoral districts gave

32. *The Great Frontier* (Boston: Houghton Mifflin Co., 1952).

33. The expenditures of the Army Engineers for this purpose expanded gradually from less than $250,000 in 1860 to over $54 million in 1920. W. Stull Holt, *The Office of the Chief of Engineers of the Army: Its Non-Military History, Activities and Organization* (Baltimore: The Johns Hopkins Press, 1923), p. 136.

34. A forestry agency was established under the commissioner of agriculture in 1876. In 1905 the forestry activities of the government were consolidated in a Forest Service in the Department of Agriculture, and in 1911 the Weeks Act provided for federal-state cooperation in forest protection. By 1911 the Forest Service had over 2,600 employees and a modest appropriation of about $6 million. Darrell Hevenor Smith, *The Forest Service: Its History, Activities and Organization* (Washington, D.C.: The Brookings Institution, 1930).

35. The Reclamation Act of 1902 laid down the national policies and authorized work by the Secretary of Interior in the Western states. Individuals, cooperatives, and states extended the acreage under irrigation, but after 1925 the national government was responsible for most of the expansion of irrigation acres. *Encyclopaedia Britannica* (Chicago, 1952), 13: 657.

them sufficient power in Congress to force positive promotion of their interests. By the Homestead Act of 1862 land was given to settlers who established residence on it. By the Morrill Land Grant Act of the same year the states were stimulated by federal land grants to establish agricultural colleges, and by subsequent monetary grants they were encouraged—through the extension services of the colleges—to provide for agricultural research and adult agricultural education. (Already, the federal government was stimulating the great increase in agricultural knowledge which ultimately contributed to the explosion of agricultural production.) In 1916 the government established a mixed public-private system of special credit institutions to supply long-term credit to farmers at lower interest rates than prevailed in the financial markets, and in the 1920's the system was expanded to include shorter-term loans. In the 1920's also the federal government took some steps to extend the prevailing prosperity of the nation to the farmers, whose production had expanded beyond peacetime markets during World War I. It regulated the processors of meat and sales of cattle in stockyards and encouraged agricultural cooperatives. Significant also for agricultural interests were two other developments: the federal aid to highway construction, and the rural free delivery system of the Post Office Department, which enabled the large mail-order corporations to create a national rural retail market for clothing, household goods, and all the other items which could be advertised in two-inch thick annual catalogues.

With respect to the new corporate structure, permissiveness and general lack of restraint of the corporations characterized public policy. Although attacks were to be made on the system and some regulations imposed, the promotive spirit of the states and the lag in exercise of national power allowed easy incorporation and subsequent regrouping of corporations into large combinations. One of the peculiar aspects of American corporate growth, explainable only as a mismatch between political power and economic developments, was the power of the states to grant charters that were good for interstate operations. There were some constitutional rights of control in the various states in which the corporations did business, but they were infrequently exercised and the constitutional power of the government of the United States to require charters for interstate operations appears not to have been seriously considered until the second decade of the twentieth century. Easy incorporation laws in certain states facilitated the use of the device and also the corporate combinations which began near the end of the nineteenth century. The Supreme Court of the United States extended some of the constitutional protections for individual rights to corporations in 1886 [36] and thus further facilitated their growth. The legislative power of the national government was not exercised over the finances of corporations, and hence their financial manipulations went unregulated. Not until the second decade of the twentieth century did security issues of corporations come under limited regulation, and then only from state governments. Finally, in spite of the passage of antitrust laws, there was a lack of effective national or state policy on corporate structure and behavior. It was an age of great corporate freedom, permitted and facilitated by government.

Viewing them in their entirety, the national promotional activities appear to have been episodic and limited, although greatly expanded in the twentieth century. There was little that could appropriately merit the label of "economic planning," the positive actions being pragmatic responses to particular pressures and needs, and the permissiveness with respect to the corporations being merely a slide with the course of events. In general, the same was true of the regulatory activities. Their scope and effectiveness were limited. National bank regulation began with national bank chartering, but its effects were limited by the coexistence of state banks and the "competition in laxity" in supervision by state and national banking authorities, each conscious of the dangers of driving their banks into the other system. National railroad regulation was initiated in 1887, but the controls over rates were notoriously ineffective before 1906, and not until 1920 did regulation extend to such essentials of effective regulation as control over security issues, entry and abandonment, and con-

36. Santa-Clara County v. Southern Pacific Railroad Co., 118 U.S. 394.

solidations. The 1920 legislation did embody a plan for an industry, but—whether because of a lack of realism or ineffective administration—it was abortive. The reaction to the corporate movement was the Antitrust Act of 1890, but except for the sixteen years prior to American entrance into World War I it was weakly enforced and weakly construed by the courts. The follow-up legislation of 1914 was riddled with statutory compromises and was weakly enforced. Regulation to protect the consumer from sale of impure foods and drugs was passed, but it was only a beginning toward the present-day system of controls. Legislation for protection of labor in transportation was enacted and the foundations for the present-day system of labor relations laid in the Railway Labor Act of 1926, but the first bits of legislation on industrial labor were held unconstitutional in two decisions of the Supreme Court.[37] It is clear, nevertheless, that the movement toward regulation of the new corporate structure was well on the way.

It was still, however, the states that constituted the primary centers of regulation. And the states were laboratories in which the features of the modern regulatory system were being developed. Much of their regulation was in fields in which the national government was also embarking on regulation, their regulation usually antedating that of the national government and remaining in effect to parallel it. This was true for banking, railroads, antitrust, and foods and drugs. Much of it was in areas in which the states and their local subdivisions had a monopoly of political power at that time. This was true of the licensing of professions and trades, the regulation of insurance, and the multitude of health and safety regulations for factories. Some of it was experimental in areas in which the national government would later become dominant. Such was the outpouring of laws to regulate hours of labor, limit child labor, prescribe minimum wages for women, and declare and protect labor's right to organize and bargain collectively. The state remained, of course, the authority which, except for participation of federal courts in interstate

37. Hammer v. Dagenhart, 247 U.S. 251 (1918); Bailey v. Drexel Furniture Co., 259 U.S. 20 (1922).

citizenship cases, developed the commercial law. Also, they and their subdivisions were still the centers for enforcement of law and order.

The importance of the states is particularly revealed in the field of utility service, where both promotional and regulatory objectives existed. Most utility enterprises were in this period, except for financing, intrastate in their operations. Excepting water supply, which in most cities was a public service, they were usually private enterprises. Initially, the localities gave permits to companies to offer service within their borders and sought to maintain controls to insure that the local monopolies offered adequate service and fair treatment to customers. Beginning in the first decade of this century the states generally assumed these functions. Still later, markedly in the 1920's, the typical utility company operated in many states, sold its service in interstate commerce, and was part of a huge and complicated corporate combine financially controlled from a national office. What was once local and locally promoted and regulated, then was extended beyond city borders and authorized and regulated by the state, was now by consummation of the corporate revolution national in scope and would shortly come under national regulation.

Features of the Period

One conclusion seems inescapable: the greatest impetus for economic development from the Civil War to the Depression came through private rather than public initiative. The Civil War itself, and World War I likewise, had stimulating effects; and the Civil War's confirmation of unity kept the one large market in existence. The legislation during the Civil War initiating a national banking system and providing a uniform national currency was constructive supplement to the institutional framework established in 1787. But from the Civil War to the Wilson administration (1913–1921) it may be doubted whether there were any political stimuli comparable in importance to Hamilton's measures for sound finance and the national, state, and local support for internal improvements in the first half of the nineteenth century. In a brief span of four years in Wilson's administration so many pieces of promotive and regulatory legislation were enacted that we could mark 1913 as the beginning of a new period but for the interruption of national initiatives for nearly two decades thereafter. It should not be overlooked, of course, that during the transition period the political foundations for economic development were still present: the one wide market with free access to resources and a common citizenship, and the freedoms and securities provided by the American legal system. Given these, and the additional favorable factors of abundance of resources and plentiful capital, private enterprise carried forward the American economic development.

Yet important areas had been staked out for public action: education, public promotion of transportation, public responsibility for an adequate banking and monetary system, conservation and development of resources, and the rules of the economic game. Also, pragmatic interventionalism overrode notions of laissez faire in a multitude of miscellaneous actions at all three levels of government.

By the end of the transition period the potential benefits of free access to resources over one large area and of sale within one wide market were being realized. Regional specializations had continued, and goods produced in advantageous locations and by organizations of great size were being sold increasingly in the interstate market. Henry Ford had even set the goal for the nation of a national mass market for the produce of industry. Nevertheless, regional diversities in resources, rates of development, and living standards were great. The South had not participated equally in industrialization or rise in living standards. Rural living standards were often lower than those in urban centers. Agricultural areas generally felt that they were not sharing equally the national gains. Mobility of population was not serving as an adequate corrective for these differences.

The power to govern was still highly decentralized. The state was the chief center of legislation, but the state was not an adequate center of economic legislation for an economy which now transcended state lines in its organization, financing, and operations. Regional diversities were reflected in the politics of the nation, which was still dominantly sectional politics.[38] But the regional demands and popular outcries for legislation could not be satisfied in the absence of allocation of national political power comparable to the allocation of national economic power.

By the end of the period the political action of governments was reflected in stable administrative structures. In the national government Departments of Agriculture, Commerce, and Labor had been added to the Treasury Department established in Hamilton's day. Regulatory commissions had been established. The bureau structure included organs important to economic development, such as the Bureau of Reclamation and the Bureau of Public Roads, as well as the older Corps of Engineers. In the states also there were stable departments, commissions, or bureaus to promote and regulate agriculture, banking, insurance, and other economic pursuits. The cities had water departments, port authorities, inspection bureaus, and many other administrative units servicing or regulating portions of the economy.

The Industrial Period: Maturity in Private and Public Sectors

The revolution in methods of economic enterprise initiated by corporate growth is in the process of completion. It can now more appropriately be called an organization revolution because size and organization have been extended to noncorporate areas, both private and public. Seventeen million laborers are organized in unions, the largest having over one million members and most of them federated in one organization. Agriculture, although not usually conducted under the corporate form, is increasingly large-scale enterprise. The corporate structure itself has been extended, notably in the giant mass-distribution enterprises for foods, drugs, textiles and other consumer products. Noteworthy also is the extension of the organizational structure in trade and professional associations. There is hardly any private functional area of en-

38. See Arthur N. Holcombe, *The Political Parties of To-day* (New York: Harper and Row, 1924).

deavor which is not represented by one or more associations, usually organized in territorial hierarchies and almost always peaked in a national organization.

Certain other developments in the private sector deserve mention in this discussion. It is now a job-dependent society, with most people's livelihood being determined by ability to find employment in the organized structure of society—public or private. Local or community dispersion has been decreased by metropolitan aggregations of industry, trade, and people. Regional diversities have been reduced by the spread of industry to the South and West, the diversification of agriculture within areas previously relying on one specialty, the reduction of disparity between rural and urban living standards, centralized public action to create a uniform social infrastructure, and other factors. Mobility of persons, although not sufficient to prevent pockets of regional and local depression, has since World War II altered the geographical distribution of persons and reduced the significance of geographical boundaries and regional, state, and local attachments. The Depression brought recognition of the interdependency of all parts of the economy. In sum, the existence of one market and free-acess area, the organization revolution, and the facilities for transportation and communication have led toward unity in the economy, uniformity in patterns of life, and national socialization of the population.

The major political effect of these changes has been the spatial reallocation of the authority to govern. A three-phase cycle in the evolution of the politico-economic system has been substantially completed. The momentary political centralization in the Convention of 1787 which created one wide market paralleled by dispersion of political power, and which was followed in the transition period by economic integration by way of the corporate revolution, has now been followed in the period of maturity by centralization of political power. The obstacles to national power in Supreme Court decisions of the transition period were overturned by the Court between 1937 and World War II. Since World War II the traditional preference of the people for state action, supported by the ideology of local self-government and the requirements arising from spatial dispersion of people, has given way to a habit of looking to the President and the Congress for solution of problems.

Developments in the Public Sector

Since the Depression six kinds of national governmental activity which have affected economic development may be distinguished. First, there has been a conspicuous expansion of corrective interventions in the corporate economy. In the Securities Act of 1933, the Securities Exchange Act of 1934, and the Utility Holding Company Act of 1935 the national government began its supervision over the financial affairs of corporations. In the legislation since 1935 it has established control over relations between organized labor and industrial corporations. It began by recognizing rights for labor in the corporate structure, resulting in a prewar quadrupling of the membership of unions. It followed this, in 1945, with a very comprehensive statute on labor relations and settlement of disputes. Moreover, through new legislation, vigorous enforcement, and sympathetic judicial construction the limitations on corporate action in the antitrust laws have gained new significance.

Second, in actions which are both promotive and regulative, it has developed the public organic law and public administrative structure for key industries. This is true for banking, agriculture, communications, power and gas utilities, atomic energy, housing, and new modes of transportation—namely, highway and airline. Sometimes the statutory-administrative system is rather tight, as in control over airline and television locations; in other instances the controls are loose, and in general the promotive purpose has been more dominant than the regulative. In transportation, for example, public highway construction promoted the road transportation industries, public subsidies promoted an airline industry, and public initiative is now supplying leadership for development of new means of mass transportation in metropolitan areas.

The legislation for particular industries has been adapted pragmatically to particular needs. This can be illustrated by reference to the power industry. The national government itself built and operated many public power projects, including some of the largest in the nation. It sells power to publicly owned local distributing companies, rural cooperatives, private distributing companies, and private users. It regulates wholesale interstate sales of power by private companies, and in so doing makes it easier for the states to regulate retail rates charged by private distribution companies. To bring electricity to rural users it sponsored and loaned money on very favorable terms to rural cooperatives. Through the Tennessee Valley Authority it merged power production with other purposes and developed a regional project for flood control, soil conservation, electric power production, and other purposes. In this program, too, it has collaborated with states and cities in a program of regional development. Diversity of method and cooperation with state and local governments are the characteristics of these approaches.

Third, the national government has been the leader in developing the social infrastructure consisting of social insurance, benefit payments to cover needs not met in the insurance system, hospitals, and medical research. It has recently extended the system through the antipoverty program, development aid for regions and localities which have become depressed areas, and medical insurance for the aged.

Fourth, it is the leader in the development of the "knowledge industry," which now absorbs about one-fourth of the gross national product. This includes research and development, on which the national government now spends substantially more each year than its total annual prewar budget, and education, on which the national government is developing new programs every year. An American college president has observed, "What the railroads did for the second half of the last century and the automobile for the first half of this century, may be done for the second half of this century by the knowledge industry." [39]

Fifth, the expenditures for national defense gave unprecedented stimulus to the economy from 1939 to 1945 and those for national defense and foreign aid have supported the economy since.

Finally, there has been an assumption of responsibility by the

39. Clark Kerr, president of the University of California, quoted in *The New York Times,* July 11, 1965, sec. 3, p. 1.

national government for promotion of economic growth, employment of men, and economic stability. This is sought primarily through indirect—that is, monetary and fiscal—controls. Also, presidents Kennedy and Johnson sought voluntary compliance with guidelines for wage and price increases suggested by them. Experience with compulsory controls over price and production during World War II confirmed the American antagonism against these forms of controls. Although such controls exist for certain industries, and although there is interspersed through the economy a considerable amount of publicly owned and operated enterprise, the interventions of the national government in the maturity period have, like the interventions of government in earlier periods, been characterized by retention of the dispersion of decisions on investment, production, and price through the private sector.

The exercise of national power has not resulted in the decline of state and local functions. It would be difficult to think of any function of magnitude of state or local government which has been lost completely to it by the assumption of power by the national government since the Depression. They have lost some of their independent position with respect to many functions. The scope of their activities has sometimes been restricted by the exercise of power nationally. On the other hand, national grants have stimulated the states and the local governments to embark on new functions or to expand old ones. The flow of money from the national treasury to states, and from states to localities, has been the chief cause of expansion of state and local functions. Approximately one-fourth of state revenue comes from national grants, and approximately one-third of local revenue from state grants. Also, national exercise of jurisdiction over interstate commerce has often increased the effectiveness of state and local control over local transactions. Finally, when the national government has built dams, developed power projects, or made rivers navigable, the prosperity of regions and localities has increased and correspondingly the ability of the state and local governments to obtain revenues.

The most significant aspect of state and local activities is that most of them are now performed by cooperation between two or more governments. Although partnership between the nation and the states in exercise of the same functions has always existed,[40] the partnership has become prevalent in so many areas that the concept of dual federalism, under which national and state governments have separate fields of power, has been largely replaced by that of cooperative federalism, under which there is national-state cooperation in performance of the same function. Moreover, there is cooperation by all three levels of government in health, welfare, road construction, and other functions. There is cooperation between states through the interstate compact and other means. The coexistence now of large metropolitan concentrations of population and the existence within these of a large number of local governments, and even sometimes several states, has necessitated arrangements for cooperation among local governments. The most recent development has been direct federal-municipal relations. These are rapidly being expanded in housing, slum clearance, transportation, and antipoverty programs.

Features of the Mature Period

In the mature period of American economic development the dominance of the national government has replaced that of the private corporation which characterized the transition period. If the corporations or any other fragments within the structure of the economy are to have a prevailing influence, it must be through the instrumentality of the central government. Its present power is a recent acquisition. It was defined constitutionally just before World War II and its dimensions have been influenced largely by events that began with the war. Its power is on the increase. It now determines the rules of the game through its regulatory activities, fosters new means of transportation and communication, promotes the knowledge revolution, determines the primary standards for the social infrastructure, fights poverty and area underdevelopment, and strives to maintain economic growth, employment opportunities, and price stability.

40. See Daniel J. Elazar, *Intergovernmental Relations in Nineteenth Century American Federalism* (Chicago: University of Chicago Press, 1959).

The significance of the new political centralization, and also the effects of areal (state and local) political units and organizations, are affected by four important factors in social structure. The first preserves, the other three diminish the impact of areal political structures.

The first is areal pluralism in the political structure. Pluralism is inherent in the multitude and variety of local, state, and interstate organizations. Each is a center of initiatives. The initiatives may be exercised independently through functions performed at three levels. They are frequently exerted competitively to attract industries directly or to develop the infrastructure which serves to attract industries. Even though the areal units of government often develop these attractions with the aid of the national government, their initiatives are still of vital importance in promoting economic development in the localities of the nation.

In addition, these units are centers of influence on higher levels of political organization. The decentralization within the American parties and within the system of geographical representation allows cities and counties, and their officials, to exert influence on state governments, and localities and states to exert influence on the national government.[41] The influences are exerted in combination with private individuals and organizations who share the interest in local development. The distribution of power within the national government itself affords multiple centers of access for such influence. The influences have effects in two ways. They force attention to regional and local diversities. And since they are exerted competitively for preferential favor, they force the brokerage (compromise and reconciliation) of sectional interests in the politics of the nation.

The second factor is functional structuralization and behavior. The private sector is now highly structured—in corporations, labor unions, professional organizations, trade associations, and federations of quasi-public agencies. On the one hand, the structure is sufficiently pluralistic to preserve the deconcentration of political power which has existed throughout our history. Within

41. See Martin Grodzins, "The Federal System," in *Goals for Americans: Programs for Action in the Sixties* (New York: Prentice-Hall, 1960), pp. 265–82.

the associations and federations the centrifugal pulls from areal or functional components, or from lack of loyalty of individual members, may be strong. In addition to this lack of cohesion within the organizations, they conflict with each other both in their economic activities (through competition and countervailing power) [42] and in their political influences. Moreover, they exert pressure at every level of government. On the other hand, they concentrate increasingly their attention on the national government. They often desire a uniform policy for the nation. Even when they seek to avoid this—as historically has been the case of oil and insurance interests, and of corporate interests seeking moderation of national labor policies by state legislation—they must defend their interests at the national capital.

The functional organizations in the private sector are correlated with similar structures in the public sector. Private associations maintain constant contact with governmental units which make or enforce policy related to the functions they perform. Leiper Freeman and others have shown how in each field of functional activity a triangular set of relationships develops among national administrative structures, parallel congressional committees, and private organizations.[43] Sometimes, indeed, state and localities become a fourth force, creating a quadrangular, rather than a triangular, set of influences. But the influence of areal governments may be small.

In addition to correlation of organizations sharing interest in the performance of a particular function, there is unification of functional occupational specialties. Liaisons develop among functional specialists serving in different governments, and even

42. The term "countervailing power" is used here to refer to all vertical checks and balances existing between buyers and sellers and between lenders and borrowers which supplement the horizontal checks and balances existing in competition. The concept of "countervailing power" comes from John Kenneth Galbraith, *American Capitalism: The Concept of Countervailing Power* (Boston: Houghton Mifflin Co., 1952). Galbraith's precise explanation of the term is on pp. 118–20.

43. See J. Leiper Freeman, *The Political Process: Executive Bureau-Legislative Relations* (Garden City, N.Y.: Doubleday & Co., 1955); Ernest S. Griffith, *The Impasse of Democracy* (New York: Harrison-Hilton Books, 1939), p. 182, and *The American System of Government* (New York: Frederick A. Praeger, 1954), p. 127; Arthur Maass, *Muddy Waters* (Cambridge: Harvard University Press, 1951); and Emmette S. Redford, "A Case Analysis of Congressional Activity: Civil Aviation, 1957–58," *The Journal of Politics* 22 (May 1960): 228–58.

among these specialists and those serving in private organizations. Areal influence may be enhanced through the activities of the specialists in state and local governments, or through organizations representing them, but these influences are shared with those of specialists outside government.

Functional correlation, both of organizations and of specialists, is accentuated by national policies which create mixed systems of public and private enterprise. For more and more types of functions public and private actions complement each other. Public and private coparticipation exists in the structure of the Federal Reserve (monetary control) System, the development of peaceful uses of atomic energy, the organization for development of a system of international communications (Comsat), the combination in housing of private building and private supply of credit with government insurance of loans and other promotional policies, the linking of industry to government through contracts for private construction of military hardware, the similar linking through contracts for research and development by private parties for the government, and, finally, in the partnership that frequently exists between regulatory agencies and regulated industries. There is often conflict between the public and private sectors operating in mixed systems, and also conflict among competing private interests; but there is a sufficient amount of complementary performance by public and private authorities in the fields referred to (named only as illustrations of a tendency) to justify the use of the term "cooperative functional federalism." [44]

The general effect of functional structuralization is to incorporate and submerge the areal influences. Three examples will illustrate this. State governments create and appropriate money to state universities. But the sovereignty of the state over a state university is limited. The development of the university and its policies is affected by a variety of influences bearing upon the performance of the "knowledge function." Among these are contracts with the national government for research, endowments from

44. Don K. Price describes "a new type of federalism" arising from government's contracting-out system in "The Scientific Establishment," *Proceedings of the American Philosophical Society* 106 (June 1962): 241.

private foundations, curriculum standards of professional associations, policy decentralization to faculties, professional standards of academicians, and the struggle of the university to attain or maintain national prestige. These and other factors limit the impact of the areal contribution.

The second example is banking. Although states create and regulate banks, nearly all of these voluntarily become members of the Federal Reserve System and insure their deposits in the Federal Deposit Insurance Corporation. In doing so they subject themselves to the regulations of the national agencies. State chartering of banks still has significance but it is limited by the subordinate position of the state banks in the total system of banking regulation.

The third example is public welfare. In this case the states still have significant power to vary standards of payment, and their officials and those of local governments can sometimes effectively resist national administrative pressures or force changes in national administrative plans and procedures. On the other hand, the effect of the areal influences is limited by the imposition of minimum national standards, and this is supported by groups interested in uniform standards and by the influence of professional workers at various levels in public and private organizations. Public administration experts have long been familiar with the conflicting imperatives of area and function in field administration.[45] The point here is that the functional organization in society encompasses the areal organization and limits its independent significance.

The third factor is rigidity in the areal structure. The sizes and boundaries of the states do not correspond with resource allocations or aggregations of economic activity. Yet the boundaries of the states are preserved by the Constitution and the sentiments of the people. Even if the will to change the structure existed, it would be difficult to devise a suitable plan for correlation of political boundaries with economic regions, and even if this could be done, the correspondence would perhaps be destroyed by later

45. See particularly James W. Fesler, *Area and Administration* (University Ala.: University of Alabama Press, 1949).

developments. The political effects of substitution of regional governments for state governments would be uncertain, but the effects would probably be dysfunctional for the economy if they prevented the matching of a mature national economy with adequate national powers of guidance and control. Nevertheless, in spite of the reservations that can be entertained about regional restructuring, it seems clear that states as small as Rhode Island and Delaware, or as lacking in resources as Mississippi or Idaho, are not as viable as some other units might be in promotion of economic development.

There are, however, means available for interstate cooperation on common problems. The states have used the interstate compact successfully in some instances. More significant, probably, for the economy is the adoption by the states of codes of uniform law. Also, through the Tennessee Valley Authority a program of regional development was effected through cooperation of national, state, and local governments.

More serious than state rigidities are those in local structures. The units of rural government developed for a rural society with slow transportation, and the multiple units of urban government developed in metropolitan areas are too limited in jurisdiction to serve as viable units for many local functions. Yet constitutions and charters, and interests served by each unit of government, prevent effective action to establish larger jurisdictions. The current reallocation of representation, forced by the Supreme Court of the United States and producing increased representation of the urban areas in the state legislatures, may force more attention to urban problems at state capitals. It can be expected, however, that the rigidities in local structure will lead to increased national jurisdiction. Already, cities are looking to the national government for aid on their functions, and already the national government has in a few instances required joint action among communities as a condition for obtaining aid.

The fourth factor is one already mentioned. Indeed, it is a major thesis of this paper. Political power must ultimately match the market. When within a common market economic development has reached the mature stage of national structural organization for exploitation of the possibilities within that market and of national mutual interdependence, then political centralization will be inevitable. The place of the areal subdivisions will be restricted by this overriding fact.

It is apparent that the factors noted above—functional cross-cuts absorbing areal influences, rigidities in state and local organization, correction of the mismatch between political and economic integration—alter substantially areal roles and relationships. Indeed, the quality of the areal allocation of function most evident in historical perspective is flexibility—showing that the reputed rigidities of federalism may not exist in an open and fluid society. And when the perspectives are shifted to the present it appears that, in spite of rigidities, the three-level structure may still meet tests required for viable institutions in a changing society. The existing structure has the advantage of legitimacy, thereby creating loyalties necessary for stability. The system as a whole is still being adapted to new needs, with preservation concurrently of initiatives at all three levels. The adaptations are not being made artificially through efforts to redraw lines of division of power, but through pragmatic arrangements for cooperation among all units of government able to contribute to the performance of particular functions.

Relevance of the American Experience for Other Nations

National experience will never be completely duplicated in another place or time. The relevance of any example to other situations is qualified by all the factors of difference which exist among societies.

There were many favorable factors in American experience which may not exist in other countries. A few can be quickly stated, with some repetition of the preceding story. The midcontinent was a vast resource space filled with "milk and honey." The institutional heritage held in common by settlers was extremely favorable. Land and other resources had not been engrossed by a

few, but were open to new generations of settlers and entre-
preneurs.[46] The values emphasized in the culture were industry,
thrift, equality, and individual achievement. The "symbiotic relationship between economic growth and the American value system" could hardly be overemphasized.[47] There were private
savings and high-level human resources. There was a kind of un-
planned foreign economic aid to the new nation—a foreign market for American wheat and other products, and an emigration of
investment capital and high-level human resources (mechanics,
engineers, and others). Much "waste" of resources could be tol-
erated. Peace prevailed over most of American history. Yet even
Americans would not accept the desirability of a full replica of
the experience, particularly with inclusion of the failure of statesmanship which produced the Civil War, and with the amount of
lag in national assistance and guidance to the economy.

There are, nevertheless, some factors out of this experience of
a new, underdeveloped nation which deserve consideration by
contemporary underdeveloped nations. First, the American experience illustrates the contribution to economic development
which may be made through organization of an economy over a
large geographical area, thus providing a large free market and
free access to the variety of resources which exist within such an
area. In doing so, it supports certain conclusions reached by Hanson. He says that no sane person would argue that every underdeveloped country "needs to build up its own autarchical industrial structure." "On the contrary, . . . what is needed is a series
of regional groupings of underdeveloped countries for industrialization purposes, so that wide markets may be created and the
fullest possible advantage taken of natural comparative assets." [48]
The difficulties in achieving these objectives when the impulses
in nation-building lead toward small states are certainly numerous, but national leaders could find a challenge to overcome these

46. For the effects of a lack of a feudal tradition see Louis Hartz, *The Liberal
Tradition in America: An Interpretation of American Political Thought Since the
Revolution* (New York: Harcourt, Brace and Co., 1955).

47. The quoted words are from Lipset, *The First New Nation*, p. 57. And see
generally for factors affecting American development Lipset's chaps. 1 and 2.

48. A. H. Hanson, the English scholar, *Public Enterprise and Economic Development* (London: Routledge & Kegan Paul, 1959), p. 13.

difficulties in the example of the framers of the American Constitution. The framers overrode existing geographical political disunity with a plan for removing geographical economic barriers. Even the details of their model offer guidance for any group of peoples seeking a similar result. Those details, in part fixed by the framers and in part elaborated or confirmed in subsequent action, included free mobility of persons, free access to resources, free trade, security against deterrents to confidence by action of local sovereignties, national ownership of unsettled lands, a supreme national court system, and central capabilities for defense and protection of foreign commerce. Whether all of these can be combined with separate national identities is doubtful, but the value of all of them in creating a favorable setting for economic development has been demonstrated in the American experience.

Second, the American experience shows advantages from the maintenance of numerous sources of initiative. It appears in retrospect that the three-level organization of political structure was well-adapted to the requirements of economic development over a large area. Both the state and the local governments have made, and continue to make, great and necessary contributions to economic development. Neither of these levels of government has ever operated as mere administrative districts for larger territorial organizations. Rather, they have been centers of initiative. Through most of their history they have been independent centers of initiative, and even now, in spite of the growth of cooperative government, they infuse local independence and conflict, as well as cooperation, into the political system. Interstate problems and metropolitan development bring still other initiatives into the system.

Private initiatives—of persons and of organizations—also were retained. It is undeniable that in the American development, private initiatives in accumulation of savings, choice of investments, aggregation of resources in giant undertakings, and expansion of markets have been lifeblood of economic growth. Private and public initiatives have been supplements to each other.

The existence of numerous sources of initiative has produced flexibility in the politico-economic system. Although many elements of rigidity exist now as a result of the organization revolution and the historical development of government structure, the pluralism in both the public and private sectors maintains numerous centers of initiative.

This model of a pluralistic structure may have value for underdeveloped countries. Shortcuts to centralization and monolithic structures may not produce equivalent stimuli to economic growth to those existing in a system where the initiatives of the people are encouraged and given opportunity to develop through numerous public and private organizations.

Third, the American experience illustrates the importance of facilitative public activities. Public support for development of transportation facilities has been a consistent policy of governments. Public action to facilitate development of credit institutions, through which capital funds could be aggregated and made available, is also a continuous thread of policy. The public education system, and now public support for research, has helped create the knowledge base for the economy. And, although American policy has seemed to be concerned only lately with redistribution of income, it has moved through all of the nation's history toward extension of opportunities to more people. Policies with respect to land, credit, and education have broadened opportunities and facilitated participation in economic development by millions of men.

Fourth, the American experience allows some observations which may be of value with respect to national economic planning. On the one hand, public policy has developed as empirical response to circumstances. Grand patterns of thought, whether of laissez faire or socialism, have not dominated the practice of American governments. Instead, governments have sought answers to particular problems as the felt needs of groups of people forced their consideration. In responding they have chosen those means which seemed most appropriate. They chose public construction and operation of schools but also accepted private schools; they chose private action in many other fields but also supplemented it with public promotion and regulation; recently, the empirical responses have yielded a variety of forms of mixed public and private action. On the other hand, planning has been characteristic of much of the activity of government. It has not usually manifested itself through specialized planning agencies nor has it taken the form of production schedules and market controls for the economy as a whole—except to deal with shortages in materials, supplies, and labor during World War II and the Korean military action. It has followed such patterns and dealt with such matters as seemed relevant at the time. The framers of the Constitution sat in one of the greatest planning sessions of all time. Their planning was institutional and yielded both a political constitution and a pattern for economic development. Planning was present in the promotion of canal and railroad construction by the states. Early national statesmen, like Hamilton and Gallatin, were economic planners. The comprehensive vision of early national statesmen was not fully carried into policy, for in the pre-Civil War period sectional disunities in the vast spatial spread were stronger than national purpose. From the Civil War to the twentieth century the tremendous burst of economic activity made public planning for economic development unnecessary. Some more public planning in particular areas might have avoided some later problems, but a planning mood would not have conformed with the spirit of the time. In the present epoch, however, planning is manifest in many activities of government. There is institutional planning, as when Congress established the Council of Economic Advisers, and there is policy planning for numerous functions of government. Planning is even motivated by large goals like economic growth and stability, maximum employment, and elimination of poverty. Nevertheless, planning reflects the traditional empirical mood, in that it consists of search for means for solving particular problems and realizing particular goals.

It is not likely that any other developing nation will make the same combinations as the United States between centralization and decentralization, public and private initiative, and planning and empirical response; but it is likely that all of them will find, as the United States has, that such combinations must be made if economic development is to accompany nation-building.

Chapter 4

The Prerequisites of Areal Deconcentration: The Soviet Experience

Jerry Hough

During the last ten to fifteen years the problem of areal deconcentration within large organizations has been relatively neglected in American political science.[1] In large part, this neglect has reflected a rather widespread feeling among political scientists that the problem is not a very lively one or perhaps not even a live one. In practice, American public organizations seem to be able to solve the problem of deconcentration on an *ad hoc* basis. The real authority to make decisions seems to flow informally to those levels at which various decisions should be made if the organization is to function effectively. Since political and administrative imperatives seem often to dictate the real division of responsibility with far more subtlety and flexibility than a written statement of principles would be able to do, it has seemed pointless to produce such a written statement.

When we examine administrative practices in the developing countries, however, we find that the centralization-decentralization problem is a much more serious one. It may be true that an organization cannot function effectively or, indeed cannot function at all, unless its field agents are permitted to make types of

The author would like to express his gratitude to Professors Carl Beck, Murray Edelman, Merle Fainsod, and Robert Scott for valuable comments on an earlier draft of this article. It goes without saying that these men are not responsible for errors that remain.

1. Dwight Waldo, after surveying recent scholarly discussions of centralization and decentralization, has concluded that the work done has been "rather thin." Dwight Waldo, "The Administrative State Revisited," *Public Administration Review* 25, no. 1 (March 1965): 13, n. 13.

decisions. Yet, as Faqir Muhammed forcefully emphasized in our discussions, it is also quite possible that the organization may, in fact, not function effectively or may not even function at all. Such a situation is frequently encountered in development administration.[2]

In Western literature on development administration, there is general agreement that "governments must decentralize authority to make decisions as rapidly as is practicable in order to accelerate economic and social development and to make the effects of their programmes lasting."[3] Yet, American consultants and students of public administration have "universally" spoken of the "terrific congestion of business and decision-making at the center, especially at the higher levels,"[4] and some of the examples of overcentralization which are cited are striking indeed.[5] Again and again, one finds references to an administrative atmosphere which Lucian Pye found existing in Burma:

> The urge to withhold confidence in subordinates permeates almost all hierarchical relationships within the present-day Burmese bureaucracy. . . . There is an increased need to emphasize status considerations in order to insure one's security in the hierarchy. The result is an enveloping sense of isolation and loneliness. . . . The feelings of isolation and insecurity of course breed further distrust and the belief that discipline should be more strongly enforced, which, when combined with the basic Burmese desire for status but fear of decision and choice, tend to choke off the flow of communication within the administrative

2. Of course, as Chester Bernard has reminded us, this phenomenon is far from unknown in the most industrialized countries. Indeed, Barnard asserted, "Successful cooperation in or by formal organizations is the abnormal, not the normal condition. What are observed from day to day are the successful survivors among the innumerable failures." *The Functions of the Executive* (Cambridge: Harvard University Press, 1960), p. 5.

3. United Nations Technical Assistance Program, *Decentralization for National and Local Development* (New York: United Nations, 1962), p. 6.

4. Fred W. Riggs, *Administration in Developing Countries* (Boston: Houghton Mifflin, 1964), pp. 391–92.

5. See, for example, the UN's *Decentralization for National and Local Development*, pp. 6–7; Henry Maddick, *Democracy, Decentralization, and Development* (London: Asia Publishing House, 1963), pp. 34–37; Henry Hart, *New India's Rivers* (Bombay: Orient Longmans, 1966), pp. 141–44.

service. Superiors cannot share their problems with subordinates, and subordinates find it necessary to adhere rigidly to correct form and procedure in all their dealings with their superiors. . . . Confronted with a pervasive sense of insecurity, everyone must fall back on the safest course of action; everyone must adhere strictly to form, procedure, to ritual.[6]

When a student of the Soviet administrative system reads about the obstacles to deconcentration in development administration, it is not surprising that he finds much that is familiar. While the Soviet Union is often included among the "advanced" industrial nations by students of development, its leaders have (particularly in the Stalin period) faced many of the problems of a developing nation: a population in which 76 percent of those nine years old and over were illiterate and which as late as 1928 was 80 percent rural; a peasantry which had been in serfdom until 1863, which at the time of the Bolshevik Revolution still primarily lived within the village commune (*mir*), and which had an inertia and resistance to change that were legendary; an unproductive agricultural sector which had been unable to avoid famine in the 1890's and which in the late 1920's was beginning to provide dangerously small amounts of grain to the cities; a population composed of a great variety of peoples with very diverse languages and cultures; a bureaucracy known neither for its progressive attitudes nor its efficiency.

One also finds many signs of the centralization which seems prevalent in the developing nations. Indeed, never has a more centralized economic and political system been established in a large country. Almost every aspect of economic life is administered by governmental agencies, and a great many decisions which would be made in the United States by a private citizen on the spot are made—or at least directly approved—by officials at rather high levels in the Soviet government. And, of course, any reader of the American press has been exposed to innumerable examples of irrationalities (in fact, absurdities) which have oc-

6. *Politics, Personality, and Nation Building* (New Haven: Yale University Press, 1962), p. 228.

curred in the Soviet Union because of central decisions which unduly restrict the freedom of action of local officials. For example, who has not heard of Khrushchev's corn program and the resulting planting of the crop in the most inappropriate places, even within the Arctic Circle?

Yet, for all its centralization, the Soviet administrative system has managed to function. And if we are to judge by such indicators as rate of industrial growth, reduction in the mortality rates and the levels of illiteracy, increase in the number of trained specialists, and development of space technology, the system has actually functioned fairly well. Few persons in history can have been more suspicious and distrustful than the man who led the Soviet system during the first quarter of a century of the industrialization drive, but he obviously was still somehow able to insure that many of those decisions which "must" be made by officials on the spot actually were made there.

In this paper, we will attempt to ascertain the reasons that the Soviet Union was not—particularly in the early period of rapid industrialization—plagued by the inability to delegate to the field to the same extent as other developing nations. How is it that, despite Stalin's inherent suspiciousness and the insecurity his lethal purges must have created in his subordinates, the Soviet administrative system was able to develop the subtle ability to distribute real decision-making power through the hierarchy in such a way that the system could function fairly effectively? Why, "confronted with a pervasive sense of insecurity," did not Soviet administrators, like their Burmese counterparts, "fall back on the safest course of action . . . [and] adhere strictly to form, procedure, to ritual?"

In this article we will first describe the ways in which authority has been informally deconcentrated in the Soviet administrative system, and we shall then ask how the feeling of confidence that permitted this informal deconcentration could develop both in the center and in the field. Since this article is based in large part upon a research project focussing on industrial decision-making in the post-Purge period, most of the examples will deal with industrial administration, and many will be drawn from the experience of the 1950's and 1960's. However, the discussion is meant to be generally applicable to the entire administrative system, and a point will not be illustrated with a quotation from the more recent past unless the author is confident that it relates to a situation which also existed in the 1930's.

In the concluding section, we shall attempt in a tentative manner to draw broader generalizations from the Soviet experience. We shall explore the possibility that each of our major explanations for areal deconcentration in the Soviet Union may be a general prerequisite for areal deconcentration, and we shall speculate briefly on ways in which the prerequisites might be met in non-Communist settings. While this discussion will take the form of a search for prescriptive lessons suggested for the developing nations by the Soviet experience, we do not mean to imply that the analysis is relevant only for countries in the relatively early or middle stages of industrial development. We believe that one can explain the ability of, for example, the United States to cope informally with the problem of areal deconcentration by referring to the same general factors that are present in the Soviet Union—factors, however, which naturally take quite different forms in a political and economic system that is quite dissimilar from that found in the Soviet Union.

I

To many readers it may seem strange to turn to the Soviet experience for enlightenment on techniques of decentralization. The Soviet Union is depicted by the American media as having a grossly overcentralized administrative system, and anyone can see that this image has at least some basis in fact. In industry, decisions concerning investment, product mix, change in product design, organization chart within the factory, and the basic wage scale have often been made by agencies located in the center, or at least they have required the approval by a central agency or, more usually, a number of central agencies. In agriculture, not only have the crop plans been distributed to the farms in a fairly arbitrary manner,[7] but the highest officials have also at times

---

7. The central authorities have not concerned themselves with the plans of individual farms. Rather, they have established quotas for the republics, and these

issued countrywide edicts about the precise timing of sowing or harvesting—edicts which fail to take weather differences into account. In trade, managers have, in the past at least, been unable to hire extra clerks or waitresses even if this would be profitable to them in monetary terms nor did they have the authority to lower prices in order to move excess inventory. Until recently, there has not been a purchasing system that would assure the store managers the possibility of acquiring the sizes and styles of goods their customers desire. And, of course, there has been similar centralization in those spheres of administrative activity we in the United States normally associate with governmental action.

Yet, this is scarcely the entire story about the Soviet administrative system. Most of the very striking examples of overcentralization within the administrative system reflect not so much an inability to deconcentrate authority as a fairly conscious attempt to achieve some particular result. For example, the restrictions on the freedom of the store manager to hire extra clerks or effectively to order the sizes and styles he desires may have caused inconvenience to the consumer and may have been irrational from some points of view. However, this policy did keep distribution costs extremely low in comparison with the United States and did relieve manufacturers of the burden of adapting their production schedules to a wide variety of different-sized goods. And this is what the regime wanted. Its prime goal has been to divert as much material resources, labor force, and managerial talent into heavy industry as possible, and the cost to the population— whether in terms of low wages, poor housing, poor service at restaurants, or the need to cut clothes down to the proper size— has been a secondary consideration until recently. Analogous examples could be drawn from agriculture, where the prime goal (particularly under Stalin) was not the maximization of production but the securing of a certain minimum level of deliveries to the city and the driving of the talented and ambitious off the farm into industry. The problem faced now by the Soviet leaders is that

---

quotas are then broken down successively by the officials at the republican, regional, and county level. In the process, however, the counties generally have received quotas which give their officials little leeway in determining the plans of the farms. In fact, the quotas have often been so high as to preclude the possibility of proper programs of crop rotation,

better food and service for the consumer are becoming more important concerns. The fact that these may require more deconcentration of authority to the enterprise level does not necessarily mean that the older system was overcentralized in terms of the tasks that it was originally given to accomplish.[8]

If we look at aspects of the Soviet development program where deconcentration of authority is required for the realization of important goals and where this deconcentration will not have a negative impact on other, more important programmatic goals, we find that even Stalin was able to permit the field officials to make many decisions more or less independently. To be sure administrators have been given a very detailed plan which establishes not only gross output figures and the expected rate of profit, but also the size of the labor force, the number of employees that can be hired in various categories, the wage bill, the organization chart, the cost figures, the prices of goods, the assortment of goods, the supply plan (including the name of the supplier for each item), etc. Repeatedly Soviet authorities have declared that "the plan is law," and that every indicator must be fulfilled unconditionally.

Despite the specificity of the plan and the multiplicity of formal limitations on the authority of the manager (phenomena which continue to exist after the 1965 industrial reorganization), the plan has not restricted the manager nearly as much as would appear from the legal documents. As David Granick and Joseph Berliner have graphically demonstrated in their studies of industrial management in the 1930's,[9] the director has had considerable

8. We do not mean to imply that changes in the priorities of the Soviet leadership are the only cause of the increasing concern with more managerial autonomy. Another factor is the increasing size and complexity of the economy. Detailed planning of supplies in the center becomes increasingly difficult as the number of supply relationships mushrooms and as the supplies become technically more differentiated. Still another factor is the increasing need to give the manager the ability and—most important—the incentive to improve his product or make it more acceptable to the customer. Such an incentive was not provided by the older reliance upon gross product as the prime criterion for judging managers. In the earlier stages of development when it is more rational simply to copy the more advanced technology of the West, product innovation is relatively unimportant and in many cases wasteful; in later stages it becomes much more crucial. For our purposes, however, it is important to note that in all these cases the problem of overcentralization became severe for the Soviet Union not when it was "underdeveloped" but when it became more industrialized.

9. David Granick, *Management of the Industrial Firm in the USSR* (New York: Columbia University Press, 1954), and Joseph Berliner, *Factory and Manager in the USSR* (Cambridge: Harvard University Press, 1957).

freedom to maneuver within the framework of the law and the plan indicators—and, indeed, outside their framework as well. Granick actually argued—and solely on the basis of information from the press of the 1930's (including that of the Purge period) —that the manager had so much freedom of action that he could not be called a bureaucrat in the Weberian sense of the term. Granick devoted one whole chapter to "plant management's independence," and then on the last page of his book he summarized his findings: "Throughout this study we have seen the great powers granted to directors and the considerable autonomy left to them. From the point of practical independence in making concrete decisions, the Soviet director may be conceived of as an entrepreneur." [10]

Many American economists specializing in the Soviet Union have privately expressed unhappiness about Granick's use of the word "entrepreneur," feeling that the word should be reserved for the type of independence in the creation of organization and in the investment of funds that the Soviet manager clearly does not have. Yet, it is instructive that a recognized authority should feel compelled to use this particular word, and it is true that the use of the term "bureaucrat" (in the sense of an official who follows a precise set of rules established at higher levels) is probably more misleading in the other direction.

The reasonably successful deconcentration of decision-making power to the field in the Soviet Union is reflected in several types of administrative behavior that is formally illegitimate, but is implicitly permissible—and functionally quite vital for the operation of the administrative system. One type is found in the planning process. The phrase "democratic centralism," which was first used to describe the ideal way in which the Communist party should function, has also been applied in a general way to the administrative system, and it connotes considerable participation by the lower levels in the early stages of decision-making.

In making suggestions about the nature of next year's plan and in requesting the funds necessary for realizing it, lower administrators are supposed to take a national perspective. Their duty as a party member is, it is constantly repeated, to propose a plan that

10. Granick, *Management of the Industrial Firm*, pp. 107–33 and 285.

is as ambitious as possible and to request the lowest possible level of appropriations. In practice, the process follows quite different rules. Even during the 1930's, the managers did not hesitate to fight for as easy a plan as they thought possible and for more investment funds and supplies than they really needed.[11] Such behavior has continued to exist, and in 1960, it was described in very picturesque terms by a Soviet correspondent:

> The basic principle of the economic administrators, regardless of the post they hold, remains the principle: "Give [me]!" On the lips of a baby this word sounds . . . touching and nice, but even then the parents try with all their strength to suggest to the little one that giving to others is not a bit worse. Our economic administrators have long ago left the diaper stage, but you can bet your life that no one has yet chanced to see a supply agent who would offer anything without asking something in return.
>
> And they do not say simply, "Give," but rather "Give as much as possible!" How many statements for equipment are compiled each year with excessive requests? If, for example, a plant needs 100 tons of castings to fulfill its production plan, the supply officials defend a request for 150 tons, having called on the help of the plant designers, technologists, and their own quick wit.[12]

This type of managerial behavior has been criticized in the Soviet Union, and the desire to create an incentive system which would not encourage it has been one of the prime factors behind the recent emphasis upon the profit indicator. Nevertheless, there has long been a general recognition among high Soviet officials that such behavior is natural and inevitable under existing conditions. In the words of the director of the giant Kuznetsk Metallurgy Combine,

> Who would believe that a leader of the enterprise would himself fight for an increase in the plan? It can't be. . . .

11. Berliner, *Factory and Manager*, particularly chaps. 6 and 7.
12. *Ekonomicheskaia gazeta*, June 10, 1960, p. 3.

However, it is necessary to understand the director. He seeks a desirable plan not because he wants to live peacefully or because he does not intend to seek reserves for increased production. The system of planning itself in large part compels him [to act in this way].[13]

Recognizing this to be the case, the higher officials do not treat the unrealistic requests of the lower administrators as unpardonable activity, but instead they simply deal with the problem in the manner familiar in the West: they refuse to allocate as much as requested while continuing to push for higher production. They essentially follow what Joseph Berliner has called "the ratchet principle in planning: they take the level of production achieved by the enterprise in the current year and then demand that the planned output next year be higher by a certain arbitrary percentage."[14] They may also require the plant to introduce specific new products or to make innovations in existing ones.

Thus, instead of an inflexible response, the higher officials handle the problem as a game-situation. Granick reports one case from the mid-1930's which illustrates well the atmosphere which has existed in this process:

At the VIIth All-Union Congress of the Soviets, the Commissar of Heavy Industry reported on progress in 1934. He gave the coefficients of blast-furnace use for several firms, cleverly mentioned that of the Petrovski Firm in an order of firms where it would appear at its worst. When the Commissar gave the coefficient of 1.24 for his firm, Director Birman interrupted from the floor of the Soviet to say that the coefficient was down to 1.15 in December. With this interruption, the Commissar snapped the trap, demanding of Birman that he promise to achieve a coefficient of 1.15 throughout 1935. Politburo member Voroshilov laughingly shouted out, "You're trapped, Birman!" and the hall filled with laughter

13. *Sovetskaia Rossiia*, January 5, 1965, p. 1.
14. Berliner, *Factory and Manager*, pp. 78–79. In the words of a contemporary enterprise director, "the plans everywhere are composed on a simple principle: base your calculations on the achieved indicators plus an obligatory supplement for the next year." *Sovetskaia Rossiia*, January 5, 1965, p. 1.

and applause. Birman had to give his word to achieve this coefficient throughout 1935. In many later speeches, Birman denied that he had been tricked by the Commissar and claimed that he would have promised this coefficient in any case, but his frequent repetition only emphasized that nobody believed him.[15]

Soviet public meetings have seldom been so lively in recent years, but the attitude revealed in the exchange with Birman has continued to prevail through the years. We can recall one case in which a Soviet correspondent asked a number of directors how they could justify their general practice of inflating their requests for funds and supplies. He was told that this had to be done "because Gosplan will cut them." The correspondent then went to Gosplan and asked why they habitually cut the directors' requests. The answer was simple: "Because the directors inflate them."

Of course, an industrialization drive with a tempo which presses resources to the limit compels the planners to cut more deeply than the managers would actually prefer. However, even after the plan has been approved and the plan year has begun, the managers have still had the opportunity to continue to appeal for items which they have not been allocated but which they still consider absolutely essential. The higher officials do not allocate all funds and supplies at the time that the plan is drawn up, but instead, they keep for themselves a small reserve so that they can make adjustments where the allocations actually prove insufficient to secure plan fulfillment in key enterprises.

A second way in which decision-making power has been deconcentrated to the field has been by permitting the manager to violate or at least to bend his regulations and plan indicators if he thinks this is necessary to realize the overall production goals. As both Berliner and Granick amply document, the manager did not hesitate to take such actions in the 1930's nor has he since then. He may fail to fulfill his assortment plan, tending to neglect those items which are the most difficult to produce in terms of their contribution to the gross output plan; he may violate (to a cer-

15. *Management of the Industrial Firm*, p. 122.

tain extent) the technological norms and the labor regulations if this is needed to increase production to the required level; he may send out illegal expediters (*tolkachi*) to speed up crucial deliveries by methods which do not always conform to the legal norms; he may illegally trade supplies which have been rationed to his plant for some other material which it needs more; he may turn to the black market to buy (at very expensive prices) some spare part which his plant badly needs; he may circumvent the organization chart and the basic wage scales by appointing men to positions which have little to do with the job they are really performing. And so forth. In nonindustrial spheres, the details of the administrators' irregularities have been somewhat different, but their general pattern has been much the same.

For our purposes, there are two interesting aspects to these activities. The first is simply the willingness of the lower officials to treat formal regulations in the way they have. We should emphasize once more that Berliner and Granick drew their material almost exclusively from the 1930's and that they found managers taking such actions even during the period of the blood purge—a period difficult to match in administrative history for its atmosphere of mutual suspicion and general insecurity.

Even more interesting from our point of view has been the response of the Soviet leadership to this behavior. While it has dealt very harshly with certain law violations by administrators (for example, bribery and embezzlement), the violations discussed in the last paragraph have been handled in quite a different manner. They are repeatedly and vigorously denounced in the Soviet press both in general terms and in reference to individual administrators, but concrete action is not taken against the violator unless the violation becomes particularly flagrant. Again and again, we read of cases in which a director issued an illegal order and in which his superiors knew of the transgression and ignored it. In one instance, the director of a large plant issued a formal (and illegal) order which permitted his shop heads to authorize overtime pay and even to require workers to work on their off-day. The ministry was informed but took no action for six weeks. Even then, it simply annulled the director's order. In the words of the Soviet article reporting the incident, *"It is characteristic* that [the director] himself was not punished." [16] Indeed, managers themselves are often willing to state in a matter-of-fact manner in the press that circumstances have forced them to violate some rule or some plan indicator, and they obviously do not fear punishment for their revelation. [17]

In practice, then, many of the rules and plan indicators are recognized by the higher officials as ideals to be approached rather than precise prescriptions, and the manager is recognized as having the job in large part of determining, in an endless series of concrete cases, the extent to which he should conform or deviate from the various rules established for him. Soviet leaders seem to believe that tactically it is not wise to acknowledge this recognition formally, and thus the speeches and newspaper editorials continue to demand absolute adherence to the letter of the law and the plan. [18] However, the official attitude appeared quite clearly in one exchange between two party secretaries and a newspaper correspondent who had come to inquire as to why a particular manager had not been punished for a series of irregular actions. The secretaries refused to apologize for their inaction. The regional party second secretary explained that the violations had been required "for the sake of production." The secretary of the city party committee was even more curt: "You try to lead such an enterprise! How can you possibly get along without law violations?" [19]

Of course, if the violations are not committed "for the sake of production," if they become so severe as to raise questions about the general ability of the manager, or if they do not secure fulfillment of the gross output target, then the attitude of the higher

16. *Trud*, September 3, 1955, p. 2; my italics. The director of this plant, I. V. Okunev of the Ural Railroad Car Construction Works, continued in his job at least until 1965.

17. Granick, *Management of the Industrial Firm*, p. 121.

18. There seems to be a feeling that the pressures of the administrative situation (particularly the incentive system) will be sufficient to compel violations and that prescriptive articles should be used to try to keep deviations within bounds. Moreover, so long as all violations are formally prohibited, the leadership always has ample legal justification to intervene anytime that it believes that the situation has gotten out of hand.

19. *Sovetskaia Rossiia*, April 8, 1960, p. 2.

officials can be quite different. The policy of the leadership is sometimes summarized in the press by the use of the Russian proverb: "The victors are not judged" (*Pobeditelei ne sudiat*), and the Soviet administrator has had to meet achievement standards before he is considered a victor.

A third way in which decision-making power has been deconcentrated to the field has been through the empowering of the provincial party organs to authorize still further rule deviations by local governmental and economic officials. This policy, like that of permitting deviations by local administrators themselves, is not formally recognized by the Soviet leaders. The provincial party organs, who (in the words of one of the last *Pravda* editorials of the Stalin era) have had the duty "to unite, to direct, and to lead the Soviet and economic agencies," [20] have constantly been bombarded with demands that they enforce the "strictest" party and state discipline. Yet, while the local party officials often have functioned as a control agent enforcing central priorities, the fact that their work has been judged primarily on the basis of their area's economic performance has given the local secretaries a very strong incentive to overlook those violations which aid overall economic performance.

In a certain sense, of course, any control agency which operates in a situation of permissible rule violations (and at least to some extent, all control agencies must operate in such a situation) actually has the responsibility of insuring that the rules are violated in such a manner as to further the interests of the regime. Or, to phrase it differently, it has the authority to "authorize" deviations by failing to intervene in cases when it thinks they are justified. Through the pattern of its interventions it should help to convey to lower officials a clear sense of the limits of deviation and should provide the leadership with an instrument through which it can conduct a widespread campaign against deviations that seem to have gotten out of hand.

In the Soviet Union, however, the provincial party officials can

20. *Pravda*, February 26, 1953, p. 1. The rest of Section 1 is based on chapter 11 of Jerry F. Hough, *The Soviet Prefects: The Local Party Organs in Industrial Decision-Making* (Cambridge: Harvard University Press, 1969).

and do authorize violations of the law and the plan in a more direct and positive manner. We do not mean to suggest that an administrator who wants to deviate from the plan or his regulations has gone to the party organs for permission. On the contrary, such an appeal would only put the party officials in the position virtually of being compelled to enforce the law, and hence the administrator must be willing to act on his own, counting on the party officials to look the other way. The provincial party organs intervene to authorize deviations only when the party officials are convinced that the deviation is required for the fulfillment of more important rules or plans of other administrators in the area.

The most frequent such intervention of the local party organs occurs when there is a conflict between the regulations and/or plans of two local offices or enterprises subordinated to different functional hierarchies. Since all local officials are ultimately subordinated to the same party leadership, such conflict would not occur if every official were carrying out his duties in accordance with precise rules which are clearly defined by the center. In the real world, however, such precision is neither possible nor usually desirable. Although the policy directives of all Soviet officials may ultimately derive from the central party leadership, it is inevitable that they will not always be completely consistent by the time they reach operating levels. The failure to define the policies of the different functional hierarchies in a noncontradictory manner,[21] differences in emphasis in the decrees of these different hierarchies, the existence of departmental self-interests, simple misunderstandings of central wishes—all of these can and do result in conflicts among lower administrators. These conflicts are not merely due to differences in individuals, but rather are the

21. This is a point much emphasized by James Fesler. For example, he has warned that "those who clamor for areal coordination of an agency's functions . . . should first wrestle with the problem of the agency integration at the center. For unless the agency head at the center can truly unify his confederation of bureaus and so underpin the role of generalists throughout the agency, it is futile to expect his counterpart in the field, the area generalist, to exhibit signs of strength." *Area and Administration* (University, Alabama: University of Alabama Press, 1949), p. 76. Of course, to paraphrase a comment by Reinhold Niebuhr about democracy and irrationality, if it is integration at the center which makes areal coordination possible, it is the impossibility of complete integration which helps make it necessary.

inevitable consequences of (to quote Henry Landsberger) "different organizational subgoals [and] interdependent activities that need to intermesh." [22]

Let us consider, for example, a dispute which arose between an energy shop and a construction trust in an outlying district:

> They had finished building the boarding school. There was already frost in the air, but there was no heat in the building. The line [to the central heating system] had a section of several yards which was not insulated, and an argument raged: should the line be hooked on or not? The builders were in favor, but the "bosses" of the heating system—the officials of the energy shop of the Aznakaev Oil Administration were against. The specialists argued for five hours until they were hoarse. While they talked on, the heating system of the boarding school began to freeze. [23]

But how was the impasse to be overcome? It was not a dispute that could be solved by referring to a book of regulations, for both sets of officials were "right" within their own frame of reference. The officials of the energy shop knew that sending heat through an uninsulated section was not proper procedure, and undoubtedly there was a strict regulation against it. If the pipe burst, their initiative in breaking a rule was not likely to be rewarded. The construction officials, on the other hand, knew that the freezing of the school's heating system would lead to unfortunate and wasteful consequences. In many of these "horizontal" problems the officials involved can, as Henry Landsberger emphasizes, resolve the matter informally, [24] but in this case the cost of a mistake was so high for both sides that the chance for an informal agreement was not great.

In many hierarchical situations a normal answer to this type of problem would be to refer it to a common supervisor. However, in this case, the common superior was a regional economic council official over a hundred miles away in the regional capital—too far

22. Henry A. Landsberger, "The Horizontal Dimension in Bureaucracy," *Administrative Science Quarterly* 6, no. 3 (December 1961): 300.
23. *Sovetskaia Rossiia*, March 13, 1960, p. 2.
24. "The Horizontal Dimension in Bureaucracy," pp. 303ff.

away in terms of distance, his knowledge of the local scene, and the scale of questions with which he deals. Under the ministerial system (either before 1957 or after 1965) there would have been no common superior short of the republican or (more often) the USSR Council of Ministers. If the conflict in regulations involved an industrial manager and a governmental official outside of industry, the disputants had no common governmental superior short of the republican or national capital, even during the *sovnarkhoz* period.

In the Soviet Union, the leadership has taken advantage of the fact that all important administrators are members of the Communist party and that the principle of democratic centralism subordinates each party member to the party hierarchy. It has empowered the provincial party organs to serve as a local common superior who can authorize one or both sides in a conflict to deviate from their regulations or plans. Thus, in the dispute over the boarding school construction, the question was taken to the head of the industrial-transportation department of the local district party committee. He decided that the heat could be attached despite any regulations to the contrary, and "nothing terrible happened." If something terrible had occurred, then it would have been the responsibility of the party official, not the heating shop.

At times, the provincial party organ itself may choose to intervene in a dispute which it sees developing, but it is more normal for the lower governmental officials to initiate the action. Or, more usually, the official who is not in a position to compel another to take some desired action appeals to a provincial party organ for support. In the words of the journal of the Party Central Committee, "It is not the regional Party committee (*obkom*) which makes demands on the regional (*oblast*) organizations, but, on the contrary, the leaders of these organizations which present their endless demands to the regional committee: do this, interfere in this, give such an instruction." [25]

Almost any type of conflict can be taken to the party organs, and their quantity seems limitless. It has been reported, for example, that in the city of Orsk (population 176,000) "not one

25. *Partiinaia Zhizn'*, no. 4, February 1958, p. 5.

significant question which falls outside the framework of an [individual] enterprise is decided without the advice of the city Party committee and without receiving its support." [26] The most frequent of these questions involves not the priority to be given to conflicting regulations of different officials, but rather the priority to be given their conflicting plans. The educational officials may have a plan for in-factory training which local plant directors say will interfere with the fulfillment of the industrial plan. Both a factory and the trade administration have a planned construction project which is to be done by the same construction trust; both declare that they will not be able to fulfill their annual plan unless their project is completed first. A half dozen local agencies assert that their plan fulfillment depends on being given the highest priority in the delivery of their order of lumber. During a period in which use of electricity begins to exceed the power limit (and this frequently occurs), the regional agricultural officials, the plant managers, the educational officials, all demand that *their* electricity allotment not be reduced. And so forth.

The process by which the relative priority of these different plans is determined can be a complex one, but it has been the provincial party organ, responding to a desperate appeal from the official receiving relatively low priority, which has very frequently made the real decision as to which of the plans should be given priority in the short run. Here the party officials are not so much authorizing deviations from the plan as they are determining which plan must, in fact, be sacrificed or threatened so that others may be fulfilled.

In addition to resolving conflicts that are brought to them by officials of the different functional hierarchies, the party organs may themselves initiate action compelling one official to violate his regulations or plan in order to aid another administrative agency or the community as a whole. The Soviet leadership has long emphasized the need for the more fortunate enterprises and institutions to render "brotherly help" to those in a less fortunate position. In ideological terms, this is often depicted as "patronage" (*shefstvo*) by the proletariat in the enterprises over the peasants,

26. *Sovetskaia Rossiia*, April 29, 1960, p. 2.

the children, the community. Ideally, the workers may provide labor and advice in their off-hours, but it is recognized that the equipment and materials will be provided from enterprise funds.

The help given by the Makarov Cellulose-Paper Combine to a state farm illustrates the type and amount of assistance which the leadership expects to be involved in *shefstvo*. In 1961 the "collective" of the combine provided the equipment for the mechanical delivery of water and repaired the automatic drinking trough in the cow shed and the pigsty. It set up a suspension way for transporting feed, made capital repairs on two DT-54 tractors, and built a new pigsty. During 1962 it pledged to equip all the cattle yards of a division of the state farm with intrafarm transport, to place a heating and ventilating network in the building for mother pigs, to set up automatic water basins in all the cattle yards, and to build a feed preparation area, a fertilizer storehouse, and a water-tower.[27]

While the assistance in the Makarov case was almost exclusively of a material nature, official Soviet spokesmen also indicate great happiness when the plants help the farms by temporarily sending them specialists who can teach better bookkeeping methods, better methods of organizing agitation-propaganda, better methods of machine repair, and the like.[28] However, during the Stalin years in particular the aid seems to a very large extent to have been of a material nature—often involving the most basic necessities. In 1951 the institutions and enterprises of just one borough of the city of Ulianov sent the farms seven tons of steel and 12,000 instruments, while a factory there gave a farm such things as 3,000 rubles in cash and 20 pairs of leather boots.[29]

Assistance to the schools is another type of *shefstvo* which receives very favorable mention in the Soviet press:

> Recently the question of polytechnical education has twice been discussed at sessions of the bureau of the [Elgav] city Party committee. One of the preconditions for successful polytechnical education is assistance to the schools from the

27. *Lesnaia promyshlennost'*, March 15, 1962, p. 1.
28. *Trud*, March 30, 1965, p. 2.
29. *Pravda*, June 20, 1951, p. 2.

factories, works, state and collective farms. Taking this into account, the bureau of the city Party committee studied all sides of the question of aid to the schools from the enterprises of the city, and it confirmed a list of patrons (*shefy*) who should help the individual schools. Now each school has its own patron which renders great help. It supplies instructors, machines, and raw materials to the school workshop, and if necessary, it assigns some of its engineers to the school as instructors.[30]

The city institutions may also receive help from the factories—as evidenced in this complaint which the industrial officials of the city of Sterlitamak made in the newspaper *Trud:*

[From a letter of the head of personnel of the Sterlitamak Synthetic Rubber Works] Why does the city soviet write to the enterprise directors, "Assign eight men to the meat combine for a month." "Direct eight qualified men for fourteen days to the city statistics inspectorate." "Send twenty specialists for a month to the Construction Administration No. 1 and 2 of the Ishimbai Housing Construction Trust.". . . ? Moreover, each time it is suggested that the assigned workers be freed from their basic work but that they be paid by their original place of work. . . .

"Correctly written!" confirmed an official of the personnel department of the Soda-Cement Combine, Comrade Mudryi. "Sometimes over 100 men are occupied for weeks on the site, fulfilling different tasks."

The deputy director of the chemical works said, "There are months when fifty or more men are not at the works for several days. They are occupied at the construction sites and institutions of the city."[31]

Although Soviet images of *shefstvo* emphasize its voluntary, brotherly nature, it is quite clear that the provincial party officials

30. K. Tolmadzhev, ed., *Na novom puti* (Riga: Latviiskoe gosudarstvennoe izdatel'stvo, 1957), pp. 80–81.

31. *Trud*, April 8, 1965, p. 2. The complaint was directed against the city soviet. However, since the soviets do not have the authority to demand this kind of aid from the plants, the complaints were really directed against the city party officials who stood behind the soviet's requests.

can be insistent that the voluntary aid be given. Even, for example, when the managers of the important Kalinino Railroad Car Construction Works were bitter about being asked for 12 skilled workers and engineers to help in the hay harvest and 400–500 of them for the potato harvest—all at the plant's expense—they still had to send them. In the words of the plant's party secretary, "That is the decision of the Party district committee, and we are obligated to fulfill it." [32] In 1962 Khrushchev complained that the provincial party organs exempted no enterprise from the responsibilities of *shefstvo*, even though in many cases the aid given was very costly to the economy.[33] The Central Aviation Research Institute (TsAGI) built a cattle yard for a collective farm out of dura-aluminum, while a regional party committee "forced" a factory producing apparatus for space flights to work out apparatus for the automation of cow-milking.[34]

It should not be thought that the local party organs limit themselves to making demands upon the industrial sector. The party officials are judged primarily on the basis of the degree of fulfillment of the economic plan, and at times they may be able to call upon nonindustrial sectors for aid in promoting the smooth functioning of industry. An additional or perhaps simply a prompt delivery of food for the plant dining hall, a somewhat larger housing allotment, an increase in some municipal service—any of these may help a key plant acquire and retain the kind of working force that it needs. If the completion of the construction of a shop at a plant requires 200 skilled workers, then party organs can recruit them temporarily from other institutions in the city.[35] If keeping an important industrial administrator in the region can be accomplished only by the admission of his son to the local polytechnical institute, then the party organs may be able to intervene with the proper authorities.

32. *Sel'skaia zhizn'*, July 21, 1962, p. 2.
33. N. S. Khrushchev, *Stroitel'stvo kommunizma v SSSR i razvitie sel'skogo khoziaistva* (Moscow: Gospolizdat, 1962), 7: 133 and 151.
34. Ibid., p. 151. See also Granick, *Management of the Industrial Firm*, pp. 122–23, for a 1935 case in which a recalcitrant director was expelled from the party for refusing local party demands. Granick concludes that the director had been correct in standing up to local authorities, but we believe that this conclusion is true only on a formalistic basis.
35. For such an example, see *Partiinaia zhizn'*, no. 22, November 1964, p. 23.

In effect, then, the provincial party organs have, in practice, been delegated the authority not only to resolve conflicts between the regulations, plans, or self-interests of different departments, but also to shift resources within the area in such a way that the different programs and policies are fulfilled in accordance with the relative priority which the leadership gives them. At times the party officials are simply shifting resources in order to promote their most efficient utilization. One would strongly suspect, for example, that the enterprises are usually called upon to provide manpower to other institutions during the first ten days of the month when their own production load is at a low level awaiting the arrival of supplies. Only if there were an impending disaster in the harvest would the party officials be likely to require an important plant to send out production personnel during the last ten days of the month—its own "storming" period. On the contrary, it is then that the party officials will be quite likely to overlook violations of labor regulations by the plant management—including the law that Sunday is not a workday—and then that they will demand that the important plants are well supplied with different municipal and communal services. At other times the party organs must make the judgment that other goals are more important than the industrial plant at the particular moment. The harvest must be brought in, or the population must be given some concession to avoid a dangerous political explosion.

In carrying out this work, the party officials have essentially been agents of the center in the sense that they have been attempting to insure that the relative priorities of the central leadership are fulfilled. It is the center which appoints and removes the provincial party officials, and it is the center which must be pleased. In essence, the provincial party officials have served as the prefects and subprefects of the Soviet system, and their role has had much in common with that of Napoleon's original prefects: "govern in Napoleon's name . . . interpret by his own sense of the nation's interest, what Napoleon would wish in the circumstances." [36] The local party officials realize that the ac-

36. Brian Chapman, *The Prefects and Provincial France* (London: G. Allen & Unwin, 1955), p. 17.

counts of their area's institutions will be audited and that the governmental superiors of local administrators will be asking questions about deviations. They know that they may be required to defend their actions if these superiors of local administrators complain to higher party organs. They are also certain that the higher party officials will be examining the performance reports of the different institutions of the area. They need not be told that if they make demands in such a way that the housing construction and municipal services plans are fulfilled 100 percent and the heavy industry plan is fulfilled 90 percent the consequences for their career will not be pleasant.

Yet, if the provincial party organs serve as an instrument to enforce central priorities, this does not change the fact that areal deconcentration is entailed in the work of the party secretaries— deconcentration that involves frequent violation of regulations and plan discipline. While the factors discussed in the last paragraph impose real limitations on the provincial party organs, the important point for our purposes is that the limitations are almost exclusively of an indirect, ex post facto nature. If a provincial party organ gives an administrative official a categorical instruction—or at least one which demands immediate execution and which is within his physical power to fulfill—there are few circumstances in which the instruction would be disobeyed. This is even true of demands that the administrators carry out such formally illegal actions as diverting materials and production to nonplanned recipients, sending workers to other institutions while continuing to pay them, accepting "above-plan" orders at a time when there are still planned orders which are not filled. The fact that the party officials can make such demands requires a very considerable independence of judgment on their part, for the line between a demand for illegal action which is praised by higher officials and one which is condemned can be fuzzy indeed.

II

In this paper we have spent a great deal of time in describing the informal deconcentration of power within the Soviet administrative system. We have suggested that the most obvious examples of real (as contrasted with paper) administrative overcentralization have usually been explicable in terms of the latent functions they serve for the Soviet leadership. We have suggested that—despite the suspicions and insecurities engendered by a cataclysmic economic-social revolution and by the existence of terror and secret police—the Soviet administrative system has not been excessively bothered by the psychological problems described by Lucian Pye (and others). There has been sufficient mutual confidence for the Soviets to develop the one indispensable feature of a properly deconcentrated system—the willingness and ability of lower officials to violate regulations and rules to some extent when performance considerations seem to dictate such violation.

We still, however, are faced with the problem: how can we explain the presence of this feature in the Soviet system?

Clearly, one of the reasons that the psychological barriers to effective areal deconcentration have been less severe in the Soviet Union than in other developing nations has been the psychological functions served by Marxism-Leninism and by the requirement of party membership for a great many "purely administrative" posts. To be sure, the Marxist-Leninist value system is very authoritarian, and it certainly has not produced any tendency toward the type of devolution of authority to the localities which is implied in the theories of local self-government. However, in both direct and indirect ways it has made much easier the deconcentration of power within the administrative system itself.

On the simplest level, of course, the ability of the party leadership to destroy all other parties and to insure that only its own members hold significant administrative posts has worked to weaken any fears of the leadership that there might be grave political dangers in areal deconcentration. Even in such a technical realm as industry, the leadership had by the beginning of the industrialization drive insured that nearly all managers of important plants were members of the party. In the 1920's and to a considerable extent in the early and middle 1930's these were often men without higher education who had been appointed for their political reliability and organizational ability. While originally these men rarely had higher education, increasingly they were chosen from among party members who had been taken from political, administrative, or factory work in their mid-twenties and sent to industrial institutes.[37] The Great Purge catapulted these men up the administrative hierarchy in a short period —indeed, some of them even above the top provincial posts. For example, Aleksei Kosygin—now Chairman of the USSR Council of Ministers—graduated from a textile institute in 1935 at the age of thirty. He served as a foreman and then shop head in a textile factory, and in 1937 he became the director of the factory. In 1939 he was named People's Commissar (Minister) of the Textile Industry of the USSR.[38] The presence of such men throughout the administrative hierarchy meant that Stalin would have an administrative elite who not only were party members but who also were politically too inexperienced to offer an intraparty threat to the Soviet leader.

Communist party membership for administrators has not only increased the leadership's sense of political security, but has also tended to insure that both central and field officials have had a more or less common value system which has been conducive to areal deconcentration. We are not suggesting that all party members are "think-alikes" (*edinomyshlenniki*) in the sense that the leadership can count upon Communists in the field seeing all matters from the national, "party" perspective.[39] Far from it. In a great number of concrete administrative situations the decisions of the Communist administrators have proven to be strongly influenced by considerations of self-interest and localistic perspective. Indeed, the whole Soviet discussion of the Liberman proposals takes this fact for granted; the debate has centered on the type of incentive system which will insure that self-interest will lead the administrators to take decisions more in accordance with central priorities.

37. By 1928, 89 percent of a sample of 770 directors of large plants were party members. Three-quarters of these "Red Directors" had only elementary education, while 3 percent had higher education. *Bolshevik*, no. 8, April 30, 1928, p. 64. By 1936 (when almost all significant directors were party members), the percentage with elementary education had dropped to 40 percent, while 46 percent had higher education. Granick, *Management of the Industrial Firm*, p. 43.

38. *Who's Who in the USSR* (New York: Scarecrow Press, 1962), p. 390.

39. The word *edinomyshlenniki* is found in the opening lines of the party rules.

In a broader sense, however, Communist party membership is associated with a set of values which contributes very significantly (if indirectly) to the willingness of the leadership to permit lower administrators some leeway in decision-making and the willingness of the lower administrators to exercise some initiative. As a number of observers have noted, there is in Marxism-Leninism something of the nature of a dogmatic religion. There is in it the sense of absolute certainty that it and only it has the key to understanding the course of human history and the nature of the economic, social, and political system at any time or place. The man who can accept Marxism-Leninism is likely to avoid some of the problems connected with the identity crisis, and an administrative system with such men both at the top and in lower administrative positions is likely to be less plagued by the problems of the transitional period Pye discussed.

Even more important than the sense of self-assurance that Marxism-Leninism may develop is the fact that it could hardly be better constructed to promote the values of industrialization. Communist ideology represents a frontal attack upon the traditional past: the old political institutions, the economic arrangements, the church or tribal gods, and many traditional customs and beliefs are described as overwhelmingly decadent and oppressive. In addition, it provides a "faith—faith in the words of Saint Simon, that the golden age lies not behind but ahead of mankind." [40] It preaches that both change and progress are an inherent part of life, and it depicts industrialization as absolutely required by the laws of history. Like early Calvinism, it creates in the man who accepts it strong psychological pressures to be in tune with the inevitable, and it also places strong emphasis upon many of the same values of the early Calvinists: hard work, sacrifice, saving. Moreover, because of its tenet that the workers are too instilled with trade-union consciousness and the peasants with private-property mentality (for both of which, read in part "traditional values") to understand their own long-term interests, Marxism-Leninism has also cloaked in self-righteousness any

40. Alexander Gerschenkron, *Economic Backwardness in Historical Perspective* (Cambridge: Harvard University Press, 1962), p. 24.

rather ruthless policy the party leadership decides is good and necessary.

Of course, if many administrators have entered the party without really accepting Marxism-Leninism, the general correspondence between the values of leaders and the lower administrators would not occur nor would there necessarily develop the necessary self-confidence at all administrative levels. And, naturally, any person seeking a career has faced a great temptation to join the party whatever his beliefs. However, the leadership retained Lenin's original concept of an elite party, and it went to considerable lengths to try to insure that party members had made a clean break with the traditional past. Long before the late 1930's there were repeated party purges (in Russian, the word literally means "cleansing"), and particularly in the 1920's and the early 1930's these often centered on members who found it difficult to break their ties with the past—who still retained an interest in family land, who visited their villages in a suspiciously frequent way, who tried to maintain some contact with religion, and the like.[41]

While the requirement of Communist party membership for lower administrators helps to meet the psychological prerequisites for areal deconcentration in the Soviet Union, this policy alone does not provide a complete explanation of the Soviet ability to deconcentrate authority to the field. A second explanation has been the educational policy of the party. If personnel are scarce, it is highly likely that they will be concentrated in the center. Even if relatively unqualified persons are found to staff lower positions, the central leaders are likely to find it impossible to trust them sufficiently to grant any real authority to them. Conversely, if a government does send out a flood of qualified field officers, this by itself will almost inevitably compel some deconcentration. There comes a point when the business at the center really becomes too great to be handled there and when the field literally must be permitted some leeway, if not through more

41. Merle Fainsod, *How Russia Is Ruled* (rev. edition; Cambridge: Harvard University Press, 1963), pp. 260–61.

formal delegation of authority then through the center's inability to exercise persistent, detailed control.

As Merle Fainsod has emphasized,[42] one of the really crucial aspects of the Soviet development program has been its large investments in the educational field, and much of this has been directly related to the preparation of men for administrative posts. Investment statistics are open to some question, but one can gain some sense of the magnitude of the effort by examining statistics about growth in number of students and trained personnel. Thus, in 1914–1915 there were 9.7 million children in the elementary and secondary schools; in 1940–1941 there were 35.6 million in these schools.[43] Those enrolled in the institutions of higher education increased from 127,000 to 1,247,000 persons during this period.[44] The expansion in the training of those with secondary specialized education was particularly great. In the period 1920–1928 the number of graduates in this category averaged 18,000 a year; in 1929–1932 (the first years of the five-year plans) they averaged 73,000 a year, in 1933–1937, 125,000 a year, and in 1938–1940, 226,000 a year.[45] The result of these education policies was a most rapid expansion in the number of persons with higher and specialized secondary education employed in the economy: 190,-000 in 1913, 521,000 in 1928, 2,401,000 in 1941.[46]

Such an increase in the number of those with specialized education was not accomplished by the expenditure of money alone. The Soviet leadership was not content to wait until an expansion in the elementary and secondary school system provided the base for a large increase in the number of college students, but instead it took special steps to accelerate this process. During the 1920's the Soviet leadership embarked upon a substantial adult education program with "workers' faculties" (*rabfaki*) being established

42. Merle Fainsod, "Bureaucracy and Modernization: The Russian and Soviet Case," Joseph LaPalombara, ed., *Bureaucracy and Political Development* (Princeton: Princeton University Press, 1963), pp. 265–66.
43. *Narodnoe khoziaistvo SSSR v 1963 gody* (Moscow: Gosstatizdat, 1965), p. 555.
44. Ibid.
45. Ibid., p. 574.
46. Ibid., p. 486.

in an attempt to raise the knowledge of the poorly educated rapidly to the level where they might benefit from specialized education. In the late 1920's a crash training program was launched, as the regime directed into the institutes thousands of men and women in their middle or late twenties who had demonstrated political loyalty and who had shown some ability in minor administrative jobs, in low-level political and trade-union work, and even at the factory bench. These were the men who, we have noted earlier, were the major beneficiaries of the Great Purge— and who, incidentally, provided the reservoir from which most of the Soviet leaders of 1970 have been drawn.

It is interesting to note that most of the training provided these future administrators was of a technical nature. The training varied, of course, depending upon the type of development work into which the man was entering, but an attempt was made to insure that the lower specialized administrator had the appropriate specialized training for his post—that the head of the district health office was a physician, that the head of the district agricultural office was an agronomist, that the factory director was an engineer. To permit the student, who often was not very well prepared, to master his subject, the leadership followed the policy of providing rather narrow specialties, e.g., "engineer of food industry technology" rather than "electrical engineer" or "mechanical engineer."

The more general administrators—including party officials— were also increasingly chosen from among the administrators with specialized training and work experience who proved successful. In those cases in which the general administrator has not had this background (and they were quite numerous in the Stalin era), he has been almost invariably chosen from among those without higher education who began their career directly in post-revolutionary political or—more rarely—lower administrative work. In contrast to many other countries, the man with a legal education has almost never been found in general or specialized administrative or political posts at any level (except for administrative posts within the legal or judicial fields themselves).

It may well be that the nature of the training of the lower ad-

ministrators helped to create the material basis for areal deconcentration as much as did the sheer expansion in numbers of
trained personnel. If legal training—particularly of a rote nature
—may imbue many of its graduates with an excessive sense of
legalism (which is absolutely fatal to areal deconcentration in
nonroutinized administrative situations), then technical training
may give a man more of a sense of the importance of the overall
task and a sense of impatience with rules that interfere with its
realization. Moreover, the specialized nature of the training,
although conceivably not being the best background for the
whole career of the graduate, provided the kind of training that
would help him cope rather well with his first, more specialized
jobs in the field and which would increase the confidence of the
leadership of his performance.

A third explanation for the ability of the Soviet leadership to
achieve effective areal deconcentration can be found in the nature
of the control machinery established. While a leadership may
permit—or be forced to permit—devolution of authority to occur
on certain questions without taking steps to insure that the authority is exercised wisely, it will scarcely do so willingly on matters it considers of central concern. As the authors of a United
Nations study on decentralization stated after listing a large
number of positive and negative controls imposed over devolved
functions, "Where these controls do not exist, local authorities
have very restricted functions. The availability of control facilitates devolution particularly of responsibility for technical services." [47] The same is, of course, true for deconcentration of
authority, for here we are concerned with matters which the
leadership feels compelled to have administered under central
direction.

In the Soviet Union, as everyone knows, the leadership has
been extremely thorough in meeting this condition for deconcentration. Elaborate statistical and accounting systems have
been established, and the accountants in lower enterprises have
been made responsible not only to the manager but also to higher

47. United Nations Technical Assistance Program, *Decentralization for National
and Local Development*, pp. 26–27.

financial organs. There are the Ministry of Finance and the State Bank to exercise financial control from above, the Ministry of State Control (later called the Committee or Commission for Soviet Control and now the Committee of People's Control) to investigate criminal wrongdoing or mismanagement. There are the courts, the prosecutor's office, and the secret police. And, finally, the Party organs both within the enterprise and above it have been made fully accountable for anything which happens within it, and they have been given the mandate to supervise its work closely.[48]

More than anything else, it has been this vast system of over-lapping controls that has given the Soviet administrative system the appearance of irrationality and overcentralization—the appearance of being, in the words of Joseph LaPalombara, "a chaotic and archaic public administration."[49] Yet, while the number of control agents may be excessive, it would be wrong to think that the deconcentration of authority would have been increased if none of them were to have existed. No large institution undertaking nonroutinized tasks can function effectively without the existence of formal or informal control instruments which destroy the neatness of the real organization chart. (One may ask, for example, whether the real organization chart in American industry is any less chaotic than in the Soviet Union if we take into account governmental and trade union controls.)

Although a control system is required if the leadership is to have the confidence to engage in effective areal deconcentration, it is also vital that the control instruments—particularly those of a more negative nature—not be in a position to enforce all rules and regulations literally. In the Soviet Union, as we implied in the last section, the negative control instruments are not in such a position but actually have had a very prescribed role with respect to the development administrator. Berliner and Granick

48. For a fuller discussion of this point see my article, "The Soviet Concept of the Relationship between the Lower Party Organs and the State Administration," *Slavic Review*, 24, no. 2 (June 1965): 215–40.

49. Joseph LaPalombara, "Bureaucracy and Political Development: Notes, Queries, and Dilemmas," LaPalombara, ed., *Bureaucracy and Political Development*, p. 54.

make it absolutely clear that during the heart of the industrialization drive in the 1930's the financial institutions were the least of
an honest manager's worries while the Ministry of State Control
was not much more of a threat.[50] The negative control instruments
might provide a check against the administrator's enriching himself through illegal actions, they might provide a generalized
restraint on his administrative actions in the sense of keeping
him within certain general limits, but they have not had the authority to pre-audit his operating expenses nor to take significant
independent action against those illegal activities which are in
the interests of production. Although their formal powers sometimes seem impressive when examined in a legal code, their real
powers have largely been limited to taking relatively formalistic
or meaningless action or to appealing to the line officials (the
ministry or the provincial party organs) for real corrective action.
When the financial controls have threatened to restrain a manager
seriously (as when funds begin to run out), the ministries have
always shown a willingness to appropriate the extra funds which
are needed.

It is most symptomatic that the Ministry of Finance—the institution which in many developing countries is among the most
powerful—has always occupied a somewhat secondary position
among the central administrative bodies in the Soviet Union.
Soviet administrative structure has varied considerably over
time, but the four or five top industrial administrators have normally been given the additional authority of being deputy chairmen of the Council of Ministers. Except perhaps for a brief period
in 1948, the minister of finance has not held this post.[51] Similarly,
although the minister of finance has been a member of the Party
Central Committee—a sign that the ministry is not unimportant—
he has never been a member of the ruling Party Presidium (now
called the Politburo). Only for a few months in late 1952 when

50. Thus, for example, see Granick, *Management of the Industrial Firm*, pp.
162–88.
51. Aleksei Kosygin was named minister of finance for a short period at this
time, and he would be an exception to all our generalizations about financial
officials. However, this was a very short interlude in his career and it represents a
most atypical deviation from the normal Soviet patterns.

the Presidium was enlarged to include twenty-five full members and eleven candidates did the minister of finance become a candidate member of the Presidium. Even then his status was inferior to the six deputy chairmen of the Council of Ministers who were full Presidium members.[52]

It is also symptomatic that the men who work in the negative control instruments are seldom moved on to general administrative posts. After studying a decade of the Soviet republican press, we can recall only a single case in which a republican minister of finance later became the chairman of the republican council of ministers. Likewise, one finds many factory directors, institute directors, and other specialized administrators among the provincial party secretaries, but it is extremely rare for a man to be transferred to party work after a career in the financial organs. There has also been a strong tendency for the Ministry of State Control and its successors to be primarily a dead-end post for older party officials.[53]

With the negative control instruments occupying a less than dominant role, the really significant limitations on the freedom of decision-making by a development administrator have been those exercised by his own ministry (or *sovnarkhoz*) and the party organs. While these agencies are responsible for maintaining observance of codes, regulations, and details of the plans, they are judged primarily by their ability to reach overall production goals. They are men who themselves "must meet a payroll" and who must develop a sensitivity to the imperatives of production.

Indeed, to a considerable extent the lower development administrators have been controlled not so much through detailed directives as (since 1931 at least) an incentive system and the ratchet system of planning. Or, perhaps it is more accurate to say that the administrator has received so many directives—according to the Soviet press, far more than he can ever read—that the incentive and ratchet systems almost inevitably become the

52. Fainsod, *How Russia Is Ruled*, p. 278.
53. This tendency became temporarily less strong with the changing of this institution into the Party-State Control Committee in 1962. The USSR chairman of this committee was a man in his mid-forties, Aleksander Shelepin. However, this experiment was very short-lived.

major instruments of control. A large portion of the administrator's pay and (more important) the fate of his career have depended upon his ability to guarantee the fulfillment of the main development program—in industry expressed as the gross output target. An official who consistently fails to meet his output goals knows that he faces demotion.

This use of an incentive system—and particularly one based on the achievement of an overall production target—has been a fourth important factor in the achievement of areal deconcentration in the Soviet Union. In many situations the field officer's psychological insecurity is not the only explanation for his failure to take initiative. If a man can lose his job only through committing a mistake or violating a rule, it should not be surprising if he acts quite cautiously—especially if he does not have a strong achievement ethic or sense of calling. In a society in which this ethic is weak, the use of an achievement-oriented incentive system and of a threat to demote those who fail to meet positive achievement standards can help to overcome this caution. If, as in the Soviet Union, the administrator knows that the failure to fulfill the overall target will have more serious consequences for himself than minor violations of regulations and other plan indicators, his insecurity can be at least partially harnessed and be made to serve the development program.

A final administrative technique that has greatly facilitated Soviet areal deconcentration has been the existence of a coordinating prefect in the provincial party organs. Earlier, we discussed the powers of the party organs simply to demonstrate the degree of areal deconcentration in the Soviet Union, but it also should be understood that this is not a chance type of deconcentration within the functional hierarchies themselves.

The importance of a coordinating agency to regulate the "horizontal" relationships among field agents of different functional hierarchies was emphasized in a most striking if indirect manner by several American administrative theorists just prior to World War II. Thus, David Truman, following the lead of Luther Gulick and May Dhonau, raised directly the question: What fairly concrete indicators can be found to judge the degree of decentralization which exists within an organization? One key indicator, he concluded, is the existence of areal coordination:

> It can be assumed . . . that where provision is deliberately made for the coordination of an organization at the field level those in charge of the establishment have desired to secure the advantages of decentralization. Moreover, since the exercise of coordinating authority at any level requires discretionary action, coordination in the field assumes considerable decentralization. It might be reasonable to conclude, therefore, that an organization is decentralized if it concludes coordinating points at the field stage of the "scalar process." [54]

The point can, of course, be expressed in the reverse manner. If one wants areal deconcentration in a complex organization or set of organizations, one must have effective mechanisms to insure that the activities of the field agents intermesh in a meaningful manner. As James Fesler has pointed out, these mechanisms may be pluralistic as in a complex Western society, but in an authoritarian country it would seem imperative that the areal coordination be entrusted to a representative of the center—to a man or institution more-or-less similar to a prefect. Moreover, as Henry Maddick has emphasized, the fact that lower administrators may not be as well trained as might be wished makes the general area administrator particularly important in a developing nation:

> [During the transitional period] the well-trained general administrator can be of the greatest assistance for he can take general responsibility for overseeing a variety of services. Thus it becomes possible to use personnel of a low caliber when compared with the top ranks at headquarters. . . . Visits by traveling inspectors from the departments concerned will provide technical guidance and periodic supervision. But on day-to-day problems and emergencies or

54. *Administrative Decentralization* (Chicago: Chicago University Press, 1940), pp. 56–57.

immediate difficulties arising from the areal implementation or national policies, there will be the generalist officer to act as adviser, referee, and general supervisor on the spot. In this way much can be done to provide services in situations where otherwise the "technical" departments would be unwilling to leave a relatively low grade officer in charge.[55]

Of course, in the Soviet Union it has not been imperative that the prefectoral role be filled by the provincial party organs, and governmental institutions (for example, the executive committees of the soviets) could have been used to perform the prefectoral functions. Yet, in many ways the choice of the party organs was very natural. After all, the prefect in France and Italy has had the responsibility of maintaining political stability and even at times of mobilizing electoral support for the government, and it is the party organs who must almost inevitably assume at least part of these functions in a Soviet-type system.

The selection of the provincial party organs for the prefectoral role also strengthens the psychological preconditions for areal deconcentration we discussed earlier. If Napoleon looked upon his prefects as "little Napoleon's," the party leadership may find it reassuring that its prefects—those men who sanction and require violations of the letter of the law—are the official representatives of the party in the countryside. It must be comforting that a provincial party secretary may look upon himself in the way in which Anastas Mikoyan (then secretary of the Nizhnii gubernia Party Committee) did in 1922. Speaking of the gubernia party committees in a debate on the role of these committees, he stated, "We, as the Party of the working class . . . cannot not lead economic work. Of course, we should not interfere in administrative details, in trifles, but we should predetermine the policy of economic work."[56] Stalin must have liked that "we."

Finally, the use of the provincial party organs as the Soviet prefects may also help to insure that the prefect has the authority needed for his difficult task. As James Fesler has pointed out,[57]

55. *Democracy, Decentralization, and Development,* p. 51.
56. *Protokoly odinnadtsogo s'ezda RKP (b)* (Moscow: Partizdat, 1936), p. 455.
57. *Area and Administration,* pp. 82–83.

the areal coordinator in a system of dual supervision normally has difficulty in maintaining his position vis-à-vis the different specialists under him, and this problem can become especially severe in development administration where the diversity among the various technical services can be quite great. The fact that the Soviet areal coordinator can bang the table and say "the party demands" greatly enhances his ability to overcome this problem.

Even more important than the name of the institution assigned the prefectoral role, however, has been the willingness of the leadership to give that institution the capabilities it has needed to perform its functions. Rather than creating a one-man prefect the leadership came to accept the necessity of a differentiated institution. Besides a first secretary, the regional party committee, for example, has had a secretary for industry, one for agriculture, and one for ideological-cultural-educational affairs, and these secretaries have had a staff (organized in departments—*otdely*) to assist them.[58] Throughout the post-Purge period there has been a very strong (and growing) tendency for these specialized officials to be selected from among those with specialized education and with substantial administrative experience in the appropriate technical service. Indeed, increasingly the first secretary himself has been chosen either from the state apparatus or from the lower secretaries with their earlier specialized experience.

This differentiation within the party committee has been a crucial element in its ability to serve the functions we have described. It provides a number of officials other than the first secretary who can authorize or require rule deviations and thereby helps to alleviate somewhat the terrible work burden of a prefectoral official in a system in which the complex developmental work is undertaken. Moreover, it gives the first secretary the possibility of obtaining independent advice and information when a question arises on which he has no specialized knowledge.

58. Between 1940 and 1948 the regional committees had not a single secretary for industry but rather a number of deputy secretaries for different branches of industry. The secretariats of the city and district committees are smaller, but the city committees invariably have a specialized secretary for industry while the rural committees have one for agriculture. Both have a secretary for ideological-educational work.

III

In explaining the steps taken by the Soviet leadership which have facilitated areal deconcentration, we have often referred to the broader problems the Soviet policy has helped to overcome. In this concluding section we would like to explore whether the Soviet solutions to these problems may be generally relevant to the developing nations.

Social scientists have learned from painful experience, of course, that the transfer of institutions and practices from one culture to another is a most difficult and doubtful process, and it is certain that the Soviet experience cannot be indiscriminately utilized in the non-Communist world. In 1917 the Bolsheviks inherited an economic and administrative system that was much more developed than those often found in Asia, Africa, and Latin America, and they were able to follow policies that would have been quite impossible in, for example, Western Africa. Moreover, the willingness of the Soviet leaders to exercise political power ruthlessly and their decision to administer all aspects of the economy directly created a framework for areal deconcentration quite unlike that in more pluralistic societies.

Yet, if we are correct in suggesting that the Soviet experience illuminates the general psychological, educational, and administrative prerequisites for effective areal deconcentration, then at a minimum the Soviet experience does point to a series of problems that must be confronted in any country. Moreover, because the Soviet Union has been at a sufficiently early stage of development to be required to seek solutions to these problems, its experience may be somewhat more suggestive than that of the more industrialized nations, which came to their solutions more unconsciously.

If there are lessons for the developing nations in the Soviet experience, many of them are of a general and indirect nature. Clearly, for example, the psychological preconditions for areal deconcentration can be met in other ways than through Communist party membership for the leadership and the lower administrators, for there are non-Communist nations in which areal deconcentration is handled as well or better than in the Soviet Union. In the United States the Protestant Ethic and the general commitment to "Americanism" and "the American Way of Life" serve the same functions that we have ascribed to Marxism-Leninism in the Soviet Union.

But to say this is to make a point which is not always emphasized by developmental theorists. There has been a tendency to treat values as a dependent variable (or "superstructure" to use Marxist language) which reflects the basic economic stage of development. Peasant or tribal society is said to produce a "traditional" value system, whereas industrialization is said to result in more rational-legal, achievement-oriented values. We would not want to deny that industrialization tends to have such an impact, but Soviet experience tends to substantiate the contention of Max Weber himself that the causal relationship between industrialization and "modern" values is not unidirectional.

As Weber argued in *The Protestant Ethic and the Spirit of Capitalism*—a book that should never be forgotten when reading his later discussion of rational-legal authority—the creation of rational-legal attitudes and particularly the creation of a drive toward rationalization are not inevitable in human society.[59] On the contrary, the development of such a set of values has been very rare and might even be considered unnatural. There has, of course, been vigorous scholarly debate about Weber's theory about the role of Calvinism in Western industrialization, but even those who deny Calvinism and the Protestant Ethic as an important causative factor seem to agree on its importance as a reinforcing element. The fact that both Marxism-Leninism and the value system in Japan—the one Asian country to accept industrialization readily and fully—have had many of the same psychological consequences as Calvinism is very suggestive.

If effective areal deconcentration (and economic development

---

59. (New York: Charles Scribner's Sons, 1958). We have cited the paperback edition in order to refer the reader to Talcott Parsons' discussion of this point in his introduction to that edition, pp. xiii–xvii.

in general) requires a fairly common value system throughout the developmental administration—a value system centered on a rationalizing, achievement-oriented ethic—the question still remains: how can these values and attitudes be built into a developing nation and particularly into its development administrators? [60] Unfortunately, if there were an easy answer to this question, industrialization itself would not have proven so difficult to launch in the non-Western world. The changing of values is at best a very slow undertaking, and there are no panaceas.

Nevertheless, this is perhaps one of those problems whose solution is made at least a bit easier simply by an awareness of it. The value systems of any culture have many ambiguities in them, and any value system almost surely has elements within it which can serve as the functional equivalent of the Protestant Ethic or Marxism-Leninism. For example, the sense of the importance of national dignity and of equality with the West—a value quite widespread among the newly educated elite in the developing nations—lends itself readily to the development of a sense of importance of economic development and of the need to serve the nation. The problem is to emphasize and reinforce such values and, in particular, to be sensitive to the dangers of reinforcing contrary values. Thus, to romanticize the village past and the folk wisdom of the peasant may serve certain useful purposes, but it may also strengthen an administrator's ambivalence toward the development program, especially if he is aware of its eventual impact upon the values of the countryside.

The Soviet experience in developing the psychological preconditions for areal deconcentration can do little more than suggest a general problem which needs attention, but some of the concrete Soviet educational and administrative measures may be of more immediate relevance to many of the developing nations. Here too it is impossible to present some universally applicable program, for the great variation among the developing nations demands similar variation in the specific recommendations one

60. This is, of course, the major focus of concern of David C. McClelland. For a very brief reference to the relationship of Communism and *n* Achievement, see *The Achieving Society* (Princeton: D. Van Nostrand Company, Inc., 1961), pp. 412–413.

would make. A man concerned with a specific developing country will have a far clearer idea as to which Soviet measures might be relevant to his country's particular situation and as to how these measures might be modified to meet the different conditions found in it.

We would suggest, however, that the Soviet educational programs, particularly those geared to the training of lower administrators and specialists, deserves very careful study by those interested in development administration. The sending of young adults with political ability to college for specialized training, the concentration upon technical education rather than legal training, the emphasis upon very narrow specialties to facilitate the training of those relatively unprepared—any of these measures might be profitably utilized by almost any developing nation, but especially by those which are beyond the stage of being compelled to use almost every educated person as a responsible official.

The Soviet policies in the administrative sphere are, of course, much more difficult to transfer directly to countries with quite different political-economic systems, but the possibility of indirect use of certain of these practices should not be ignored. The use of incentive systems with pay, promotion, and even retention of job depending upon the fulfillment of some kind of output goal would seem to have widespread applicability. It should be remembered that economic development in the West was carried out in large part by organizations without civil service personnel policies, and one should be very cautious in transferring the civil service concepts of Western bureaucracy to development administration in any sweeping manner. The Soviet experience suggests that the differences in payment and tenure practices between American civil service and business have reflected not the "proper" difference between public and private administration, but in a deeper sense the "proper" difference between the more routinized activities traditionally conducted by government and the more nonroutinized activities associated with development. If areal deconcentration in the development field may, in some part, depend on the willingness of the lower administrator to cut corners when the interests of the project demand, then it is vital that cutting corners not be the only way that an administrator can get into serious trouble.

Associated with such pay and promotion policies is, as Merle Fainsod has emphasized, the need to give the specialist "an honored place in administration, sharing the perquisites, the prestige, and the responsibilities which were formerly reserved exclusively for the elite administrative service." [61] Nothing seems more tragic than for a developing nation to have a great excess of college graduates in central offices and an insufficient number of such men in the field. The reasons for this phenomenon are understandable, but they do not appear to be insuperable. It is difficult to believe that the problem of inducing men to go into the field could not be greatly alleviated by judicious changes in the pay and promotion patterns. Persons interested in this question will find a vast and detailed Soviet literature on it—one that contains a multitude of concrete suggestions, many of which may be adaptable to non-Soviet conditions. Such persons should, however, be aware of the fact that incentive systems must vary with conditions and that many of the practices now being criticized in the Soviet Union were actually of great use in earlier stages of development.

Finally, the Soviet use of an areal coordinator also deserves careful consideration. In a country which relies on the private sector and the marketplace for many decisions about economic development, particularly in one which is politically well integrated and whose citizens agree on fundamental values, areal coordination can be handled fairly well by a variety of elective and appointed officials in conjunction with the developed network of private institutions. When, however, government assumes more direct developmental responsibilities in a country not so well developed politically, the use of a prefect or prefectoral institution seems quite advantageous for the reasons that David Truman and Henry Maddick present. Moreover, in a country with scarce resources, the availability of a local instrument for coordinating the delivery of resources can also be beneficial. An agricultural proj-

61. "The Structure of Development Administration," Irving Swerdlow, ed., *Development Administration* (Syracuse: University of Syracuse Press, 1963), pp. 11–12.

ect may need the simultaneous receipt of financing, machinery, spare parts, seed grain, and the like, and often intervention may be necessary if one of the technical agencies is lagging in providing one or the other. In the city too, construction is a very complicated process, and there may need to be a specific agency that can expedite the delivery of certain supplies, that can resolve conflicts with building codes and the inspectors who enforce them, that can see that service institutions are created.

The precise nature of the areal coordinator can vary, depending upon the local situation, but the Soviet practice of dramatizing this position by giving it to an extraordinary institution has much to recommend it. In a one-party system the party organization is a natural choice for the job. The Ghanian solution of giving the responsibility to a special political subminister might also be appropriate. A special Ministry of Development Coordination, headed by the national leader, might have the type of name which would attract the most qualified men. But in any case it would seem useful—and maybe imperative—to avoid such a drab title as "the District Collector."

It is also imperative that the coordinator should be responsible to higher levels and should be removable by the higher levels if the development programs are not properly fulfilled. (We are assuming, of course, that the development program for an area will have a fairly realistic possibility of being fulfilled.) If the area administrator is locally based, the prospects for areal deconcentration will be very seriously affected. It is probably wise, however, to follow the example of the French prefectoral system and to provide the prefect with an elected council with advisory functions.

Certain of the more detailed features of the Soviet prefectoral system may also have more general applicability for the developing nations. A clear recognition of the dual subordination of local technical services both to their functional hierarchy and the areal coordinator would certainly aid in avoiding situations in which one or the other of these supervising institutions does not even know of a key decision, yet alone participate in it.[62] The develop-

62. Arthur Macmahon makes the same point about dual supervision in his *Delegation and Autonomy* (Bombay: Asia Publishing House, 1962), p. 36.

ment of a differentiated prefectoral organization, staffed in part by technical personnel, would seem a natural answer to the problem of overwork for a single official. Finally, the Soviet practice of drawing party secretaries from a wide variety of developmental agencies and enterprises also deserves attention. Even in terms of job performance, the man who has proven his ability to "meet a payroll" in the development field and who has shown some general political ability (perhaps through holding a junior prefectal post or through participation in elected advisory councils) would seem a more likely success as an areal coordinator than a man with a legalistic training and with no developmental experience. Moreover, if these lower areal coordinators were regarded as one of the main sources of recruitment for higher administrative jobs, the practice of drawing the areal coordinators themselves from a wide variety of local administrators might be one of the ways of making technical field work more attractive to the ambitious young man.

In concluding this article, we should emphasize once more that the Soviet experience, like the American experience, cannot be universally transferred to the developing nation and that it certainly should not be utilized without careful thought as to the concrete conditions in a particular country. We recognize that in the cultures of a given country there may be many obstacles to the introduction of this or that concrete policy. Indeed, often no obstacle is greater than the ambivalence of the political leadership itself about industrialization and about achievement norms. Yet, if there is a serious desire to achieve effective areal deconcentration and an effective development program, the prerequisites for this deconcentration must be met and functional equivalents for the Soviet (and American) measures to meet these prerequisites must be found. To the extent that there is considerable fascination with the Soviet model in the developing countries, it may be useful for those in charge of development programs to study in detail how the Soviet administrative system really works and to consider how some of the lessons of the Soviet experience may be utilized without paying the penalty of the Soviet political system.

Chapter 5

Intra- and International Movements of High-Level Human Resources

John C. Shearer

Introduction

There are certain major intranational and international movements of human resources to which neither development theorists nor practitioners have given the systematic attention that such movements warrant. Insofar as movements of human resources affect the rapidity and nature of the development of underdeveloped areas, such spatial considerations should be included in the array of variables of explicit concern to development administrators. Lack of concern can be very costly in its consequences. This chapter concentrates on movements of "high-level" human resources. It is not concerned with more traditional areas of interest, such as the movement of supposedly homogeneous "labor" from rural to urban occupations.

I do not use the term "human resources" as a synonym for the term "human beings," but rather to focus attention on those characteristics of human beings which have major economic significance, are identifiable and, to some extent, measurable. Perhaps the characteristics that best fit these criteria are a population's educational attainment and the nature of its economic activity as expressed in its occupational structure. This is no way implies that investments to increase human knowledge and skill (that is, "education," in its broadest sense) are made solely to develop the capacities of human beings as producers of goods and services. Educational investments in human beings have many noneconomic goals, but educational investments are also the means for increasing the potential of humans as producers. Education is, therefore, among many other things, the developer of human resources.

Education consists of both formal and informal means to develop human knowledge and skills. Formal education is, perhaps, the most significant of these means and that most susceptible to measurement. Measures of formal educational attainment may often constitute good approximations of the human resources potential of a given population. Occupational data provide other useful measures of human resources—in this case human resources in certain discernible economic roles as producers.

Human resources often constitute the key to development. They are the only active factor of production. Other factors of production produce value only as human resources activate them. Natural resources and capital become meaningful as factors of production only as human resources organize, combine, and control their uses.

The term "high-level human resources" represents those human resources which by virtue of their relatively high educational attainment or the nature of their occupations embody significantly greater than average knowledge or skill. These are the persons at the apex of the educational or occupational pyramid. They include the leading thinkers, innovators, planners, administrators, adapters, and appliers of modern techniques and technology, in short, the organizers and combiners of all other factors of production.

The crucial importance of high-level human resources for development is emphasized in the worldwide studies of the Inter-University Study of Labor Problems in Economic Development.[1] It has been stated:

I would like to acknowledge the many helpful suggestions made by the organizers and members of the research seminar and, especially, the substantial contributions of the seminar leader, James Heaphey, and of the special consultant for this paper, Frederick Harbison.
  1. Summary volumes include: Clark Kerr, John T. Dunlop, Frederick Harbison, and Charles A. Myers, *Industrialism and Industrial Man* (Cambridge: Harvard University Press, 1960), and Frederick Harbison and Charles A. Myers, *Education, Manpower and Economic Growth* (New York: McGraw Hill, 1964).

The goals of modern societies . . . are political, cultural, and social as well as economic. Human resource development is a necessary condition for achieving all of them. A country needs educated political leaders, lawyers and judges, trained engineers, doctors, managers, artists, writers, craftsmen, and journalists to spur its development. In an advanced economy the capacities of man are extensively developed; in a primitive country they are for the most part undeveloped. If a country is unable to develop its human resources, it cannot develop much else, whether it be a modern political and social structure, a sense of national unity, or higher standards of material welfare.[2]

Useful definitions of what constitutes high-level human resources will vary roughly with levels of development. Nevertheless as a rule of thumb for many underdeveloped areas, high-level human resources may be characterized as those persons who have attained at least secondary education or whose occupations require an equivalent level of knowledge or skill. Unfortunately, there are few data concerning the quality of human resources. Quality may vary greatly among persons, areas, and nations despite similar educational and occupational labels. This fact argues strongly for the qualitative tempering of quantitative measures in this field.

Data concerning intra- and international movements of high-level human resources are scarce. Fortunately, however, some relevant data has recently become available for several Latin American countries. This chapter concentrates on these data. They suggest certain conclusions which may have general relevance. The dangers of generalizing from limited arrays of data are well known; for most underdeveloped areas these dangers are multiplied. If any relevant data exist, they are often of questionable precision. Nevertheless, the new data I use represent gains in knowledge that may have important implications for the spatial aspects of development administration.

In Section II of this chapter I consider certain intranational

2. Harbison and Myers, *Education, Manpower and Economic Growth*, p. 13.

movements of high-level human resources based mainly on the recent work of others. In Section III I draw mainly from my own work on certain international movements of high-level human resources. In Section IV I discuss some of the implications for development administration of such spatial movements and suggest some means whereby public officials might influence these movements and thereby the course of development. I do not attempt to cover all movements of human resources that might significantly influence development. My purpose is limited to the consideration of some recent findings that may have important consequences for development administration.

Intranational Movements

The following information will help orient our discussion of intranational movements of high-level human resources in Latin America:

1. Studies by the United Nations substantiate that "the intensive urbanization process witnessed by Latin America during the last twenty years is one of the most noteworthy characteristics of the pattern followed by the region's population trends." [3]

2. They further suggest that "the urbanization process was concentrated mainly in the principal cities of Latin America." [4]

3. In most Latin American countries the largest metropolitan area is also the wealthiest area. The United Nations estimates that throughout Latin America per capita incomes in the richest (largest), urban areas are usually on the order of ten times those in the rural areas. Similar ratios for the United States, Spain, and Italy are, respectively, 2.5, 4, and 5. [5]

4. In all of the twenty Latin American republics, except Brazil

---

3. United Nations, Economic and Social Council, Economic Commission for Latin America, *The Economic Development of Latin America in the Post-War Period* (E/CN. 12/659), 7 April 1963, 1: 142.

4. Ibid.   5. Ibid., pp. 124–25.

and Ecuador, the capital city is also the largest city. It tends, therefore, to have not only the greatest concentration of economic wealth and opportunity but also the greatest concentrations of political, administrative, social, and cultural activities and opportunities.

Two recent field studies, one of Mexico [6] and the other of Chile,[7] contain the most relevant data known to me on the internal movement of high-level human resources in Latin America. Much of the information was obtained from government, academic, and other sources available only in the two coutries. These data reveal large movements of population from the poor to the richest areas of Mexico and Chile. They further reveal heavy concentrations of high-level human resources in the composition of these movements. Because these migrations were not influenced by civil disorders, such as *la violencia* in Colombia, they may be considered as representative of "natural" intranational movements of high-level human resources.

Table 1, from Herrick, presents some internal comparisons of the concentrations of population in the largest (usually capital), cities of twelve Latin American nations. The table shows significant concentrations of population in the capital cities and significant increases in these concentrations for almost all countries when compared to earlier years.

For the two countries that concern us most, we find that between 1940 and 1960 the concentration of population in Santiago, Chile, increased from about 18.8 percent to 25.9 percent of national population and that of Mexico City from 8.3 percent to 13.9 percent. Within the twelve Latin American countries listed, Santiago ranks second in concentration behind Montevideo, Uruguay, with 32.9 percent (1955), and Mexico City ranks seventh. Other

6. Charles Nash Myers, *Education and National Development in Mexico* (Princeton, N.J.: Industrial Relations Section, Princeton University, 1965), 148 pp.

7. Bruce Hale Herrick, "Internal Migration, Unemployment, and Economic Growth in Post-War Chile" (Ph.D. diss., M.I.T., 1964), 177 pp. The published version is: *Urban Migration and Economic Development in Chile* (Cambridge: M.I.T. Press, 1965). Except for footnote 8 and for the source of Table 1, all other citations of Herrick are from the published version. The two citations of the dissertation draw on data not incorporated in the published version.

Table 1. *Centralization of Population: International Comparisons*

Country	Capital [a]	Date	Percentage of population in capital [a] city	Date	Percentage of population in capital [a] city
Argentina	Buenos Aires [b]	1958	18.6 [b]	1947	18.7 [b]
Bolivia	La Paz	1957	10.2	1942	11.0
Brazil	São Paulo [a]	1960	5.6 [b]	1940	3.1 [b]
Chile	Santiago	1960	25.9	1940	18.8
Colombia	Bogota	1959	8.1	1951	5.6
Ecuador	Guayaquil [a]	1960	10.5	1950	8.1
Paraguay	Asuncion	1960	17.6	1950	15.7
Peru	Lima	1960	11.6	1940	7.4
Uruguay	Montevideo	1955	32.9	—	—
Venezuela	Caracas	1959	20.8	1941	9.4
Cuba	Havana	1953	20.9	1943	16.4
Mexico	Mexico City	1960	13.9	1940	8.3
Canada	Montreal [a]	1956	10.1	1941	9.7
U.S.	New York [a]	1960	6.0	1940	6.6

Source: Bruce Hale Herrick, *Internal Migration, Unemployment, and Economic Growth in Post-War Chile* (Ph.D. diss., M.I.T., 1964), Table 3.1(a), p. 37.
a Or largest city. Population of the metropolitan area.
b Population of the city proper instead of the metropolitan area. In 1955, Greater Buenos Aires contained about 60 percent more people than the city proper; São Paulo about 25 percent more.

data from Herrick show that in the same countries the capital cities are from five to ten times the size of the second largest city.[8]

For eleven Latin American countries Herrick relates the recent growth rates of the capital cities to the national growth rates. These data are presented as Table 2. For the ten comparable metropolitan areas all except La Paz, Bolivia grew at much faster rates than did their countries. This is particularly impressive in view of the fact that to Latin America belongs the dubious distinction of having the highest rate of population growth of any large area in the world—approaching 3 percent per year.[9]

For the ten comparable Latin American countries in Table 2 the arithmetic average of the growth rates of the largest cities is more than twice as large as that for their respective nations. For

8. Herrick, *Internal Migration, Unemployment, and Economic Growth in Post-War Chile*, Table 3.2, p. 39.
9. U. N., *Economic Development of Latin America*, p. 140.

the period 1940–1960 the ratio of capital city to national growth rates for Mexico is 2.07 and for Chile is 1.85. A wider and, perhaps, more meaningful differential is that between the capital city's rate of growth and that of the rest of the country. Herrick cites such data for Chile (1952–1960): Whereas Greater Santiago grew at a rate 1.78 times that of all Chile, it grew at 2.4 times the rate of Chile less Greater Santiago.[10]

Table 2. *Growth of Population in Nations and Their Capitals* [a]

Country	Period	Percentage growth rate of Capital	Nation	Capital city [a] growth rate divided by national growth rate
Argentina [b]	1947–60	2.1	1.8	1.17
Bolivia	1942–57	0.8	1.3	0.63
Brazil	1940–60	5.1	2.3	2.17
Chile	1940–60	3.5	1.9	1.85
Colombia	1951–59	6.9	2.2	3.12
Ecuador	1950–60	5.5	3.0	1.86
Paraguay	1950–60	3.5	2.3	1.49
Peru	1940–60	4.4	2.2	2.04
Uruguay	—	—	—	—
Venezuela	1941–59	7.4	3.0	2.46
Cuba	1943–53	4.4	2.0	2.21
Mexico	1940–60	5.4	2.8	2.07
Canada	1941–61	3.1	2.2	1.11
U.S.	1940–60	1.0	1.5	0.68

Source: Herrick, *Urban Migration and Economic Development in Chile* (Cambridge: M.I.T. Press 1965) Table 3.2, p. 29.
a Or largest city.
b Data for the growth of Buenos Aires are not comparable with those of the other cities, since only the city proper is considered.

It seems clear from these data, then, that Mexico and Chile are fairly representative of Latin America (1) in their concentration of population in the capital city, (2) in the increases in these concentrations, and (3) in the fact that their growth rates are more than double those of the high growth rates of the rest of their countries.

The main explanation of these significant differentials in popu-

10. Herrick, *Urban Migration and Economic Development in Chile*, p. 44.

lation growth rates lies in the considerable migration of people to the capitals. Myers presents data on the extent and nature of Mexican internal migration. He demonstrates that "the migration between 1940 and 1960 went primarily to the Federal District, Mexico City, and the northern states." [11] These are the richest areas of Mexico.[12] In 1950, 1,303,343 residents of the Federal District (46.4 percent of its population), were born elsewhere, compared to 12.9 percent of the national population who were born in states other than that in which they were then residing.[13]

For Chile, Herrick states that "because Santiago's rate of natural increase (birth rate less death rate) was almost exactly equal to that of the rest of the country, any difference in total population increase must have been due to migration." [14] He cites census information which shows that between 1940 and 1952, 45 percent of the population increase of Santiago Province (which includes the metropolitan area and many outlying towns and rural areas) was due to migrations from other provinces.[15] The 1952 census shows that of Santiago Province's 1,755,000 enumerated people, 32 percent had been born in other provinces.[16] A labor force survey by the Institute of Economics of the University of Chile (June 1963) estimated migrants as 37 percent of the population of Greater Santiago and as 53 percent of its labor force of 778,000.[17]

Profound economic, social, and political implications result from the increasing concentration of population caused by the heavy movements of people to the capitals of Mexico and Chile, and from similar heavy movements to other Latin American capitals. One of these major effects, largely ignored in the development literature, is that in countries where such movements are heavy they constitute a heavy subsidy of the richer by the poorer areas. The natal area usually bears the costs of the gestation, birth, rearing, and education of future migrants until they leave. It also bears many of the direct costs of migrating. Most migrations con-

11. Myers, *Education and National Development in Mexico*, p. 71.
12. Ibid., p. 12.
13. Ibid., Table 7, p. 69.
14. Herrick, *Urban Migration and Economic Development in Chile*, p. 44.
15. Ibid., p. 46.
16. Ibid., p. 46.
17. Ibid., p. 46.

tain high concentrations of younger people, especially those near
the beginning of their most productive years.[18] Herrick conducted
a survey in 1964 of economically active migrants who had arrived
in Santiago within the previous ten years.[19] It indicates that very
few of this group migrated during childhood when much of the
rearing and educational costs would be incurred after the move
to Santiago, whereas almost 50 percent were at or near the beginning of their working lives (ages sixteen to twenty-five). In
these cases most or all of the preemployment costs were incurred
in the poorer areas from which they migrated, whereas most or
all of their productive years would contribute to Santiago's income.

Thus, the migrations represent movements of heavy investments
in human resources made by the poorer areas. The migrants and
the capital city, already the richest area, harvest the fruits of these
investments.[20] These investments in human resources, large in absolute terms, represent relatively greater costs for the poorer areas
than similar investments would represent if incurred in the capital. The magnitude of the subsidy varies with the proportion of
migrants who are high-level human resources, for they bring with
them the highest levels of investment.

Among the concentrations of wealth in the advanced areas, and
especially in the capital cities, are heavy concentrations of high-
level human resources. Table 3, from Myers, shows how in Mexico such concentrations vary among advanced and less advanced
areas. In the Federal District the proportion of population with
secondary education or more is almost four times the national
proportion. The proportion of the capital's labor force in the cited
high-level occupational categories (professionals, technicians, and
managers), is almost two and a half times the national proportion. In contrast, all the less advanced areas listed have corresponding proportions significantly below the national proportions.
Four of the seven have less than one-fifth of the national proportion of persons with secondary education or more. The concentra-

18. Ibid., p. 71.
19. Ibid., Table 6.2, p. 76.
20. Of course, migrants may share their gains with the poor areas by sending
remittances to relatives there.

tion of high-level manpower is further pointed up by the fact that Mexico City, with 13.9 percent of the national population in 1960 had 53.0 percent of all Mexicans with secondary education and more than 56.2 percent of all those with sixteen years of education or more.[21] This is largely a consequence of the fact that educational opportunities, especially at the university level, tend to be

Table 3. *Mexico: Stock of High-Level Manpower, 1960, by Selected Areas*

Area	Percentage of area population with secondary education (12 yrs.) or more	Percentage of area labor force listed as professionals, technicians, and managers
The Republic	1.1	4.4
Advanced areas:		
Federal District	4.2	10.5
Baja California Norte	1.2	6.2
Sonora	0.9	4.6
Chihuahua	0.8	4.5
Coahuila	1.1	5.2
Nuevo Leon	2.1	6.3
Tamaulipas	1.1	4.3
Less advanced areas:		
Zacatecas	0.2	2.1
Hidalgo	0.4	2.4
Tlaxcala	0.3	3.1
Guerrero	0.2	2.2
Oaxaca	0.2	1.7
Chiapas	0.2	1.9

Source: Charles Nash Myers, *Education and National Development in Mexico* (Princeton, N.J.: Industrial Relations Section, Princeton University, 1965), Table 4, p. 27, and subject to notes thereto.

heavily concentrated in the capital city. Mexico City, with 10.4 percent of national university-age population in 1940 had 64.9 percent of national enrollment in higher education. The corresponding figures for 1960 are 15.1 percent and 73.2 percent.[22]

The great concentration of educational opportunities enables richer areas to generate high-level human resources at much

21. Myers, *Education and National Development in Mexico*, pp. 111–12.
22. Ibid., Table 13, p. 106.

faster rates than can poorer areas. There is available a means for comparing national outputs of high-level manpower: the Harbison-Myers (C. A. Myers) composite index of human resource development. One of Charles Nash Myers' most original contributions is his application of the Harbison-Myers index to areas within Mexico. The Harbison-Myers composite index was developed

> to distinguish among countries in terms of four "levels of human resource development" which we have labeled as follows: Level I, underdeveloped; Level II, partially developed; Level III, semiadvanced; and Level IV, advanced. The composite index which is the basis for slotting seventy-five countries into these four levels is simply the arithmetic total of (1) enrollment at second level of education as a percentage of the age group 15 to 19, adjusted for length of schooling, and (2) enrollment at the third level of education as a percentage of the age group, multiplied by a weight of 5. In our judgment, higher education should be weighted more heavily than second-level in such an index. A weight of 10 and a weight of 3 gave somewhat different results, but not significantly different.[23]

Harbison and Myers demonstrate statistically the generally very high correlations between their index and other major indicators of economic development [24] such as gross national product per capita, in United States dollars, for which the correlation is .888.[25] Table 4, from Harbison and Myers, groups seventy-five countries according to their composite index.

By applying the Harbison-Myers index to areas within Mexico, Charles Nash Myers demonstrates in Table 5 the great regional disparities in the production of high-level human resources and the increase in these disparities between 1940 and 1960. While the national index increased from 12.5 (Level II), to 26.2 (II), the index for the Federal District increased from 71.4 (III) to

---

23. Harbison and Myers, *Education, Manpower and Economic Growth,* pp. 31–32.
    24. Ibid., pp. 34–48.   25. Ibid., p. 40.

Table 4. Countries Grouped by Levels of Human Resource Development According to Composite Index

Level I, Underdeveloped		Level III, Semiadvanced	
0.3	Niger	33.0	Mexico
0.75	Ethiopia	35.1	Thailand
1.2	Nyasaland	35.2	India
1.55	Somalia	35.5	*Cuba*
1.9	Afghanistan	39.6	Spain
1.9	Saudi Arabia	40.0	South Africa
2.2	Tanganyika	40.1	Egypt
2.6	Ivory Coast	40.8	Portugal
2.95	Northern Rhodesia	47.3	*Costa Rica*
3.55	Congo	47.7	*Venezuela*
4.1	Liberia	48.5	Greece
4.75	Kenya	51.2	*Chile*
4.95	Nigeria	53.9	Hungary
5.3	*Haiti*	53.9	Taiwan
5.45	Senegal	55.0	South Korea
5.45	Uganda	56.8	Italy
7.55	Sudan	60.3	Yugoslavia
		66.5	Poland
		68.9	Czechoslovakia
Level II, Partially developed		69.8	*Uruguay*
		73.8	Norway
10.7	Guatemala		
10.7	Indonesia		
10.85	Libya	**Level IV, Advanced**	
14.2	Burma		
14.5	*Dominican Republic*	77.1	Denmark
14.8	*Bolivia*	79.2	Sweden
15.25	Tunisia	82.0	*Argentina*
17.3	Iran	84.9	Israel
19.5	China (Mainland)	85.8	West Germany
20.9	*Brazil*	88.7	Finland
22.6	*Colombia*	92.9	U.S.S.R.
22.7	*Paraguay*	101.6	Canada
23.15	Ghana	107.8	France
23.65	Malaya	111.4	Japan
24.3	Lebanon	121.6	United Kingdom
24.4	*Ecuador*	123.6	Belgium
25.2	Pakistan	133.7	Netherlands
26.8	Jamaica	137.7	Australia
27.2	Turkey	147.3	New Zealand
30.2	*Peru*	261.3	United States
31.2	Iraq		

Source: Frederick Harbison and Charles A. Myers, *Education, Manpower and Economic Growth* (New York: McGraw-Hill, 1964), Table 1, p. 33.
Note: Italicizing of Latin American countries is mine.

101.1 (IV), and the index for poor Oaxaca increased only 2 points, from 2.2 (I) to 4.2 (I).

The much higher capacity of the capital to train high-level manpower tends to perpetuate and increase the already wide educational and economic gaps between the rich and poor areas. An additional force tending to widen these gaps still further is the

Table 5. *Harbison-Myers Composite Index of Enrollments in Middle and Higher Education, Selected Areas, 1940 and 1960*

	1940		1960	
Entity	Index value	Level	Index value	Level
The Republic	12.5	II	26.2	II
Advanced areas:				
Federal District	71.4	III	101.1	IV
Nuevo Leon	17.4	II	61.9	III
Less advanced areas:				
Republic minus Federal District	6.0	I	13.0	II
Republic minus Federal District and Nuevo Leon	5.9	I	11.3	II
Oaxaca	2.2	I	4.2	I

Source: Myers, Education and National Development in Mexico, Table 15, p. 109.

proclivity of students drawn from elsewhere by the capital's education magnet to pursue their careers in the capital, rather than return home after completing their studies. Of course, those who *do* return home, and those few highly trained natives of the capital who work elsewhere, represent contributions of the capital's educational institutions to the development of high-level human resources for the poorer areas, thus tending to narrow the gaps.

Unfortunately, there is little data on the magnitudes of such movements. The Harbison-Myers enrollment ratios cover all, including migrant, students. Significant migrations of students might seriously reduce the usefulness of the Harbison-Myers index for areal comparisons. A region or country which is a net trainer of "foreign" students will have a correspondingly higher index number whether or not they return home. On the other hand, a low index number may omit substantial numbers of students who pursue (better) educational opportunities elsewhere and who may or may not return home. To the extent that students from poor areas study in rich areas and then return home, the Harbison-Myers index, useful as it is in many ways, is not an accurate measure of the net educational benefit accruing to the area being considered. Since student migrations are much heavier at the university than at the secondary level, the quintuple weight given by the index to the enrollment ratios in higher education will greatly magnify the effect of student migration on the index numbers.

In 1961 about 20 percent of those entering Mexico City's National University (by far the largest in Mexico) were from elsewhere.[26] Myers suggests that "a sizable number will remain in the Capital once their studies are completed." [27] He further states that

it is likely that many graduates with middle and higher education from the less advanced states are now living outside them. Upon completion of each phase of their education, ambitious students are often forced to migrate in order to pursue further study and later to find employment opportunities commensurate with their level of education, as well as living standards potentially equal to their expectations. . . . University education of high quality and diversity often necessitates travel to the Federal District, and once having left the poorer states, many students do not return.[28]

In summarizing his findings Myers states:

the advanced regions and particularly the Federal District have been favored by internal migration. The arrival of educated migrants from other areas has often increased the disparities that motivated their migration in the first place, and the increased disparities, in turn, caused increased migration. Equally important has been the arrival of students from other

26. Myers, *Education and National Development in Mexico*, p. 31.
27. Ibid., p. 32.   28. Ibid., p. 74.

regions of the republic. . . . The better students, if they can possibly arrange it, attend institutions in the Federal District or in the north, where many of them remain after graduation. . . . Early development of education and economic capacity allowed these regions to grow most rapidly since the Revolution. They have become the dynamic areas of the nation, drawing financial and human resources from other regions.[29]

For quantification of the high-level manpower component of migration to the capital city we turn again to Herrick's data for Chile. They indicate that in terms of education and occupation the high-level manpower component of migration to Santiago is

Table 6. *Chile: Greater Santiago: Occupational Distribution of the Male Labor Force, June 1963*

Occupation	Natives	Migrants
Professionals and technicians	8.0%	10.3%
Owners and managers	9.3	14.5
Office workers	11.4	11.6
Salesmen	12.1	9.7
Farmers and miners	1.3	2.1
Drivers and deliverymen	7.5	5.0
Artisans and operatives	35.1	29.5
Unskilled manual workers	4.6	4.8
Personal service workers	7.9	11.3
Unclassified	1.6	0.9
Seeking work for the first time	1.2	0.3
	100.0%	100.0%

Source: Herrick, *Urban Migration and Economic Development in Chile,* Table 6.9, p. 86, from unpublished data from the employment surveys of the Institute of Economics of the University of Chile.

significantly greater than the corresponding component of the population from which the migrants came and is generally even greater than the corresponding components of the native Santiago population. In other words, migrants from poorer areas, where high-level manpower is in relatively poor supply, bring to the capital, already comparatively rich in human resources, a higher com-

29. Ibid., pp. 141–42.

ponent of high-level human resources than that enjoyed by the capital's native population.

Table 6 presents occupational data which compare the group of male migrants to Santiago to Santiago natives. Most significant, perhaps, are the first two (high-level) occupational categories in which the migrant males were much more highly concentrated than were native males.

Table 7 shows that migrants (male and female together), to

Table 7. *Chile: Educational Attainments of the Population More than Fourteen Years Old*

| Highest level of education attained | Percentage distribution | | |
| | Outside Santiago 1960 | Greater Santiago 1958 | |
		Natives	Migrants
None	21.4	3.5	8.8
Primary	57.1	49.1	53.0
Technical & special	4.2	6.4	4.6
Secondary	16.2	36.4	27.8
University	1.1	4.6	5.8
	100.0%	100.0%	100.0%
	Cumulative percentage distribution		
More than secondary	1.1	4.6	5.8
With at least secondary or technical	21.5	47.4	38.2
With at least primary	78.6	96.5	91.2

Source: Herrick, *Urban Migration and Economic Development in Chile,* Table 6.4, p. 78.

Santiago were considerably better educated than the population from which they came. Although migrants were not so well educated as Santiago natives, at the highest educational level—the level with which we are most concerned—the situation is quite different. The migrant group had more than five times the proportion of university-educated than did the source group and a proportion more than 25 percent greater than that for Santiago natives. At all levels migrants' educational pattern is generally much closer to that of Santiago natives than to that of their source group.

Table 8 shows the striking similarity of educational attainments of economically active males in the migrant and native groups. The main exception is the considerable advantage in university education enjoyed by the migrant group, especially among the younger men.

In summary, a major phenomenon throughout Latin America is the pattern of heavy migrations which result in increasing con-

Table 8. *Chile: Greater Santiago: Educational Attainments of Economically Active Males over Fourteen Years Old, 1958*

Highest educational level attained	Age			
	15–24	25–44	54–64	Total [a]
None				
Native	2.0%	2.3%	5.3%	2.7%
Migrant	2.6	4.0	8.8	5.5
Primary				
Native	58.4	51.5	45.7	52.5
Migrant	58.6	53.5	44.1	51.6
Technical & special				
Native	8.7	4.9	8.2	6.5
Migrant	4.6	6.5	6.7	6.2
Secondary				
Native	29.5	34.2	32.2	32.4
Migrant	29.6	28.1	31.8	29.0
University				
Native	1.4	7.1	8.7	5.8
Migrant	4.6	8.0	8.6	7.7

Source: Herrick, *Urban Migration and Economic Development in Chile*, Table 6.5, p. 80, from unpublished labor force survey of the Institute of Economics, June 1958. a Total includes those people over sixty-five.

centrations of populations in the capital cities. The available evidence for Mexico and Chile, which can be considered representative, indicate that the migrations from the poorer areas to the capital (richest) area contain disproportionately heavy concentrations of high-level human resources. Furthermore, the evidence suggests that these movements are both caused by and contribute to the great and increasing disparities in wealth and opportunities between the capital and the poorer areas.

International Movements

In this section I discuss certain international movements of high-level human resources. These movements include emigration (particularly to the United States), immigration, and certain other more specialized outflows and inflows of high-level human resources. I do not attempt to assess the "balance of trade" in the "international commerce in human skills." My purpose is to examine certain significant flows in order to suggest their implications for development administration.

Outflows

Outflow to the United States—The United States, which has not until recently used quotas for immigration from Western Hemisphere countries, attracts great numbers of Latin American immigrants. Table 9 shows that this flow has been increasing rap-

Table 9. *Latin American Immigration to the United States* (approximate)

Origin	1940–49	1950–59	1960–69
Central America [a]	21,700	44,800	80,000 (estimated)
South America	21,800	91,600	200,000 (estimated)

Source: John C. Shearer, *La Importación y Exportación de Recursos Humanos* (Santiago, Chile: Instituto Latinoamericano de Planificación Económica y Social, April 1964), p. 6, based on annual reports of the U.S. Immigration and Naturalization Service.
a Does not include Mexico, which in 1962 alone sent approximately 55,300 immigrants to the U.S.

idly and that, based on the experience of the early 1960's, much greater immigration was expected in this decade. However, these estimates antedate the Immigration Act of 1965, which includes limitations on immigration from Western Hemisphere nations.

Included in this heavy and rapidly increasing flow are large numbers of high-level human resources. This is part of a larger phenomenon in which the United States attracts many high-level human resources from all over the world. For example, during the thirteen years from 1949 through 1961 about 33,000 engineers and 10,000 scientists, a combined average of more than 3,300 per year, immigrated to the United States from all countries. For the five years, 1957–1961, the South American countries lost 1,556 engineers to the United States, an average of over 300 per year.[30] Although the absolute numbers of migrant Latin American engineers and scientists, for example, are small compared to the widely publicized brain drain from countries such as the United Kingdom and West Germany to the United States, Kidd terms the loss for poor areas, and specifically for Latin America, a "catastrophe" because of the relatively small numbers of engineers and scientists in those countries. Large numbers of many other categories of Latin American high-level human resources, including many medical personnel,[31] also emigrate to the United States.

Using United States immigration data, Horowitz presents information on the numbers of Argentine immigrants admitted to the United States during the period 1951–1961.[32] Among almost 4,000 such immigrants in the professional and technical category, Horowitz calculates the numbers of immigrants in certain professions as percentages of all graduates of Argentine universities in those same professions during the same eleven-year period. A number equal to about 8 percent of all engineering graduates from 1951 to 1961 became United States immigrants during that period. The corresponding figure for all geologists, physicists, and biologists is more than 6 percent; for chemists, 6 percent; for doctors, 5 percent; and for architects, 3 percent.[33]

Table 10 presents selected occupational information on United States immigrants in 1962 for selected countries, including those Latin American countries sending most immigrants during that year. It shows the high proportions of Latin American immigrants in several categories which include most high-level occupations.

30. Based on data from Charles V. Kidd, "The Growth of Science and the Distribution of Scientists Among Nations," in *Impact of Science on Society* (Paris: UNESCO, 1964), 14, no. 1: 5–18.

31. See, for example, Doris W. Krebs, "Necesidades y Recursos de Enfermeria en Chile," mimeographed study for the Chilean National Health Service (1961).

32. Morris A. Horowitz, *La Emigración de Profesionales y Técnicos Argentinos* (Buenos Aires: Editorial del Instituto, September 1962).

33. Ibid., p. 3.

Table 10. Selected Occupational Pattern of Immigrants to the United States in 1962

Country or region of birth	Total number immigrants	Number immigrants with reported occupation	Professional, technical and kindred workers	Managers, officials and proprietors	Clerical and kindred workers	Craftsmen, foremen and kindred workers
			(Percentage of immigrants reporting occupation)			
All countries	283,763	134,824	17.6	4.1	15.6	12.7
(All countries, total, 1947–1961)	3,542,189	1,671,003	15.7	5.0	13.0	16.1
Western Hemisphere (except Canada)	108,441	53,368	10.6	3.7	10.9	8.3
South America, total	17,592	7,488	24.9	5.6	23.9	11.2
Argentina	2,985	1,328	34.3	5.9	14.8	16.7
Brazil	1,560	617	30.2	4.7	21.9	10.4
Chile	1,137	508	25.0	4.7	28.8	7.1
Colombia	4,391	2,051	22.2	7.2	30.0	9.2
Ecuador	2,562	1,205	17.2	5.5	20.4	12.7
Peru	2,667	985	18.6	2.5	23.0	8.9
Venezuela	1,037	245	23.2	6.9	35.1	12.6
Others	1,253	548	34.9	5.8	24.6	10.0
Rest of W. Hemisphere (except Canada)	90,849	45,880	8.3	3.4	8.8	7.8
Costa Rica	1,407	770	12.8	2.5	22.4	11.6
Mexico	55,291	28,113	2.5	0.8	2.7	6.1
Panama	2,098	942	11.6	1.2	19.8	10.6
United Kingdom	21,189	12,226	26.8	4.7	29.7	9.9
(% occupational distr. of U.S. labor force, ave. 1947–1961)			9.2	10.4	16.0	13.5

Source: Calculated from Annual Report of the U.S. Immigration and Naturalization Service (Washington, D.C., 1962), Tables 8 and 8A, pp. 31–32.

Almost one-fourth (24.9 percent) of the immigrants from South America [34] who reported an occupation were in the important category "professional, technical and kindred workers." This is more than two and a half times the proportion of the United States labor force (9.2 percent) in this category. It is also much larger than the corresponding proportions for immigrants from all countries in 1962 and for the 1947–1961 total for all countries.

Despite the fact that at about this time the government of the United Kingdom became openly concerned about its loss of high-level manpower to the United States,[35] Argentina, Brazil and the "other" South American countries (not reported separately) showed, proportionately, considerably higher losses in this category than did the United Kingdom. The overall proportion for South America (24.9 percent) is close to that for the United Kingdom (26.8 percent). The concentration, then, of this key category of high-level human resources was (1) much greater in South American than in all immigration, (2) comparable to that in immigration from the United Kingdom, and (3) very much greater than the concentration of this category in the United States labor force.

Table 10 also shows significantly higher percentages of South American immigrants in the categories "managers, officials and proprietors" (5.6 percent) and "clerical and kindred workers" (23.9 percent) than is true for all countries (4.1 percent and 15.6 percent). For "craftsmen, foremen and kindred workers" the South American proportion (11.2 percent) is only slightly lower than that for all countries (12.7 percent).

This heavy flow of high-level human resources constitutes a

34. In the following analysis I cite "South America" rather than "Western Hemisphere" because of the many non-Latin countries and colonies included in the latter designation, and because of the large and unusual immigration from Mexico—itself more than three times the South American total. Mexico's propinquity to and special relations with the U.S. result in extremely high proportions of Mexican immigrants in two unskilled categories not cited in Table 12: "unskilled agricultural workers" (28.1 percent) and "other unskilled workers" (38.4 percent).

35. The Minister of Science, Viscount Hailsham, "charged the U.S. with living 'parasitically on other people's brains.'" According to London University physicist G. O. Jones, the scientists lured to the U.S. are "'always the most adventurous, energetic and gifted. The loss to Britain is thus far more serious than mere numbers suggest.'" "The Brain Drain," *Time* 81, no. 11 (March 15, 1963): 56.

major "reverse flow of foreign aid" from these poor countries to the world's richest country. In relative terms, this "aid," in sharp contrast to planned foreign aid, costs the sending countries much more than it is worth to the receiving country. This is because the flow of high-level human resources goes from countries very poor in these resources to the country richest in them, in terms both of proportions of labor force and of the ability of their educational systems to develop these resources.

Outflow to international organizations—An outflow of high-level human resources, which assumes major proportions for some Latin American countries, results from what I term the "international organization syndrome." International organizations usually seek some national "balance" in their staffing. This is based on national populations rather than on the relative densities of high-level manpower. The practice creates, at the same time, relatively greater opportunities for nationals of the poorer countries and relatively greater losses for these countries when their nationals join international organizations.

Observations by myself and others who have taught multinational professional groups in international agency training programs suggest that student diligence is often not a reflection of strong desire to serve their homelands. Rather, it often reflects their admitted desire to "escape" from home by increasing their chances for employment abroad, often with an international organization.

The only relevant data known to me concerns Latin Americans who received some statistical training in the United States.[36] It may be representative of the general outflow to international organizations of Latin Americans, especially those with overseas training. My calculations, based on this information for approximately twenty years through 1962, reveal the following: Of 431 professionals who had at least six months of United States training, 61 (14.2 percent) were with international organizations. The majority of the 61 (34, or 56 percent) were employed in the

36. Inter American Statistical Institute, *Latin Americans Receiving Some Statistical Training in the United States (From about 1942 to December 31, 1962)* (Washington: Pan American Union, 1963).

United States, 18 (29 percent) were employed in other countries, and only 9 (15 percent) were employed in their own countries by the international organizations. Haiti, the poorest country, was the heaviest loser. Exactly half of the 32 Haitians trained were employed outside that country. Of these 16, 13 were with international organizations, of which 9 were employed in the United States and none were employed in Haiti.

Inflows of Human Skills

In this subsection I consider certain significant inflows of high-level human skills to Latin America. Although they tend, in a numerical sense, to offset the heavy outflows, there is considerable evidence that these inflows are often of much greater apparent than real benefit to Latin America. The following four parts deal, in turn, with immigration; the importation, under contract, of foreigners by private and by public organizations; and the inflow of high-level knowledge and skill through the training of Latin American students in the United States.

Immigration—As in the case of North America, European immigration has played an important role in providing high-level human resources for Latin America. Although a few countries, particularly Mexico, now strictly limit immigration, even of persons with important and scarce skills, most are anxious to receive such immigrants. Many of the relatively recent European immigrants were refugees. For example, Spain's Generalissimo Franco is widely credited with providing Latin America with considerable high-level manpower.[37]

The richest of the Latin American countries, Venezuela and Argentina,[38] have attracted by far the largest proportions of for-

37. *El Mercurio* (Santiago, Chile), May 3, 1963, p. 5, reports the following estimates (following my translation): More than 200 university, 400 secondary, and 600 primary teachers; almost 400 doctors; about 200 engineers, 400 lawyers, and 100 writers; almost 300 ex-military officers (now mainly in teaching or private business); and 150 economists, are among the Spanish intellectuals who now live in Latin America.

38. Recent estimates show a substantially higher per capita income for Venezuela ($648) than for any other Latin American country. Argentina is second with $490. Venezuela has a higher per capita income than such European countries as the USSR ($600), Italy ($516), Hungary ($490), Poland ($475), Greece ($340), Spain ($293), Yugoslavia ($265), and Portugal ($224). Harbison and Myers, *Education, Manpower and Economic Growth*, Table 7, pp. 47–48.

eigners.[39] Some recent data for Venezuela reveal especially high proportions of foreign-born among its high-level human resources. The following data are from a recent national survey of 5,709 establishments.[40] The workers covered were about 16 percent of total national employment, excluding agriculture and government service. Whereas 12.51 percent of the 183,800 adult workers enumerated were foreign-born, the proportions of foreign-born were much higher in the two broad occupational categories which include most high-level occupations: 21.3 percent for professional, technical, and kindred workers, and 31.7 percent for administrators, managers, and executives.[41]

For Caracas, with about one-third of the enumerated employment, the proportions of foreign-born are higher than for the entire nation for all workers and, especially, for the high-level categories. In some specific occupations a large majority of Caracas workers are foreign-born. For example, of 598 Caracas engineers, 60 percent were foreign-born and of 177 physical scientists (except chemists and physicists), 74 percent were foreign-born.[42]

The survey makes no distinction among the foreign-born between immigrants and others, most of whom are employed on a contract basis by foreign (mainly United States) companies, which are heavy importers both of capital and of high-level manpower into Venezuela, as into many other Latin American countries.

Importation of foreigners by United States firms in Latin America—In many countries, and especially in Venezuela, Brazil, Mexico, Colombia, Peru, Argentina, and Chile, foreign (especially United States) companies have significant investments which are usually accompanied by significant inflows of high-level human resources, generally from the United States. A survey of 646 United States companies shows that of their 24,659 American employees abroad, 10,493 were in Latin America where they repre-

39. Instituto Interamericano de Estadística, *América en Cifras, 1963* (Washington, D.C.: Pan American Union, 1964), 2: 44, Table 201–10.
40. República de Venezuela, Instituto Nacional de Cooperación Educativa, *Encuesta Nacional para Capacitación de Mano de Obra* (Caracas, May 1962).
41. Ibid., p. 3 Table I–1,
42. Ibid., pp. 55–56.

sented about 2 percent of total Latin American employment of these firms.[43] These flows appear to add substantially to the available high-level manpower in Latin America and thereby appear to constitute substantial offsets to the outflows. However, my study of the high-level manpower policies and practices in Latin America of 52 representative United States firms [44] casts considerable doubt upon the efficacy of this inflow, either for the United States firms or for the host countries.

My study focused on the development and utilization of high-level human resources, nationals and non-nationals (usually North Americans) by the Brazilian and Mexican subsidiaries of 23 of these firms, mainly in manufacturing. My main sources of information were interviews with about 300 executives, government officials, educators, and the like, in the United States, Brazil, and Mexico.

Almost all the home-office executives in the United States stated that their company policy was to employ the "maximum possible number of nationals" in order more easily to adapt their foreign operations to their overseas environments and to avoid the high costs of employing North Americans abroad. The direct costs of merely sending a United States family abroad usually exceed $15,-000 for Mexico and $30,000 for Brazil.[45] In addition, there are great costs related to learning language and methods of operation in a new environment. One executive estimated that it took at least one and one-half years before the average North American executive began to earn his salary in Latin America.

The salaries paid to North Americans are very high. Base salaries are usually 20 to 25 percent higher than for comparable posts in the United States. To this are added the myriad special overseas allowances for such things as children's education, housing and home leaves. I estimate, conservatively, that on the average, the direct, recurrent costs of employing North Americans in high-

43. Syracuse University, Maxwell Graduate School of Citizenship and Public Affairs, *American Business and Overseas Employment* (Syracuse, N.Y., June 15, 1957).

44. John C. Shearer, *High-Level Manpower in Overseas Subsidiaries: Experience in Brazil and Mexico* (Princeton, N.J.: Industrial Relations Section, Princeton University, 1960).

45. Ibid., p. 39.

level posts are approximately four times the average costs of employing comparable nationals for the same posts.[46]

In spite of these high costs the great majority of companies in my sample depended heavily on North Americans. Although they constituted a small proportion of total employment they dominated most subsidiaries because they occupied most of the highest posts. In some large and old subsidiaries the highest national was outranked and overwhelmed by dozens of North Americans. In the subsidiaries of nineteen companies operating in both countries, Brazilians occupied only 14 percent and Mexicans only 9 percent of the five highest posts in each subsidiary. In recent years the heavy dependence on North Americans had generally been increasing, rather than decreasing, despite the claims of most home-office executives to the contrary.

The justification for the employment of more than 85 percent of the 501 North Americans in my sample was the alleged inability of the firms to recruit, develop, and retain qualified nationals. However, my investigation revealed a much more fundamental problem: the characteristic ineptness of the subsidiary in recruiting, developing, motivating, utilizing, and retaining competent nationals. This ineptness seems explainable largely in terms of the difficulty most firms have in securing high-quality North Americans for overseas service. Many home-office executives lament that they often have to send "second stringers" abroad because the best men usually have more attractive opportunities in the United States. One executive of a large firm stated that his organization had made "hundreds of mistakes" in selecting men for its Latin American operations.

Despite the difficulties of obtaining "first stringers" most firms insist on sending their executives abroad on a career basis under the assumption that they will always be more valuable than any available national. This assumption blinds firms to the likelihood that heavy dependence on North Americans may harm, rather than improve, the efficiency of their subsidiaries, especially through its strongly negative effects on the development and utilization of nationals.

46. Ibid., p. 49.

There is a strong disposition by most North Americans to protect their overseas jobs at any cost. Job protection is a natural consequence of the assignment on a career basis of second stringers to better jobs abroad than they could generally hold in the United States. It manifests itself in a stubborn refusal of most overseas North Americans to implement the standard home-office policy of "maximum use of nationals." It is not surprising that the North Americans, who dominate the subsidiaries, make little effort to recruit or develop nationals for (their) top posts. The low ceilings on opportunities for nationals, with the consequent stifling effects on their motivation, morale, and effectiveness, act as strong impediments to the efficient development and utilization of national high-level manpower by most United States companies.

A few firms, four of the twenty-three I studied abroad, do things very differently. They consider long-run dependence on Americans abroad as a costly disadvantage rather than a necessity. Their goal is completely national organizations abroad. Their very rare Americans abroad have no interest in protecting their overseas posts. They invariably serve in stop-gap and organization-building capacities only until they develop competent nationals. Their performance is judged by their effectiveness in working themselves out of their overseas posts. These few firms find it far easier than do the vast majority to recruit, motivate, develop, and retain nationals of excellent quality, for they alone offer them unlimited opportunities.

One of my major conclusions is that the great majority of firms studied would make progress toward increasing "nationalization" of their subsidiaries only when the authorities of the home office or of the host country might require them to do so. I put the following question to the chief executive of a distinguished United States firm which had operated in Mexico for more than forty years and which employed about 800 persons, including twenty-two North Americans in the twenty-two top jobs: "If your home office or the Mexican government insisted that you substantially reduce the number of North Americans, what would be the minimum number necessary to maintain efficiency?" His reply is indicative of many. He stated that the organization could manage with only two of the twenty-two: himself and the technical director. In a separate interview the technical director gave exactly the same answer.

My findings, only a few of which I have reviewed here, strongly suggest that although the inflows of high-level manpower which accompany United States investments in Latin America bring in important skills, they do so only at very high cost to the firms and to the host countries. These inflows usually seriously impede the efficient development and utilization of indigenous high-level human resources

Importation of foreigners by the public sector—I shall deal briefly with some relevant aspects of the use of foreigners contracted by the public sector for specific, usually short-term, assignments in Latin America. This is generally termed "technical assistance." Especially in recent years most Latin American countries have played host to large numbers of foreign experts, especially from the United States. These experts are often involved in major public works projects sponsored, at least in part, by United States or international agencies. In many such instances the sponsor requires that the receiving country contract with foreign firms for the engineering studies and for advisory services. In practice this often results in foreigners designing and supervising the projects.

A sound case can often be made for this mandatory importation of costly high-level human resources. They presumably bring scarce skills which they are to impart to the nationals whom they "advise." They are the "watchdogs" for the foreign sponsors. There are, however, major flaws in the system. Those of us who have undertaken technical assistance assignments abroad often find that, for a variety of reasons, we "do" rather than "advise," and that the watchdog role often creates sensitive and wasteful situations.

A recent situation in Chile suggests some problems which may often render the inflow of technical assistance experts a mixed blessing for the receiving country. The United States was a major sponsor of construction of a large international airport for Santiago, at Pudahuel.[47] The contract required the "advisory" and "instruction" services of a group of engineers from a United States firm. Late in 1963 considerable conflict developed between the Chilean and United States engineers on this major project. The Chilean College (Association) of Engineers made major and widely publicized protestations to the Chilean government concerning the role of the United States engineers. The situation became so nasty that it resulted in the cancellation of the contract, the cessation of work, and considerable resentment against the United States aid program.

The College of Engineers, citing specific circumstances and facts, raised strong objections to the importation of foreign engineers for this and other projects in an official statement of September 27, 1963 to the Minister of Public Works.[48] Their specific grievances included the poor work done by highly paid, second-rate, foreign engineers which had to be redone by Chilean engineers, the blocking of opportunities for available, qualified Chilean engineers, and the damaging impact upon the profession of unnecessary and insulting supervision by foreigners at high cost to Chile in terms of foreign exchange, professional development, and national pride.

Inflows of knowledge and skills acquired abroad—Major inflows to Latin America of high-level human knowledge and skills are represented by Latin Americans who return home after study abroad. It is generally estimated that far more Latin Americans pursue university-level studies in the United States than in any other foreign country. The 1963–1964 annual census of foreign students in the United States conducted by the Institute of International Education enumerated 12,882 Latin Americans, of whom 2,960 were identified as graduate students.[49]

47. The following information is from editions of *El Mercurio* (Santiago, Chile) of September 29 (p. 27), October 6 (p. 61), and October 10, 1963 (p. 25). Translation mine.

48. Colegio de Ingenieros de Chile, "Participación de Ingenieros Titulados en el Extranjero en Actividades Profesionales de la Ingeniería Chilena y las Int r-ferencias e Infracciones Legales que Estas Actividades Producen" (Participation of Foreign Engineers in Chilean Professional Engineering Activities and the Interferences and Legal Infractions that These Activities Produce), *El Mercurio* (Santiago, Chile), October 6, 1963, p. 61.

49. *Open Doors, 1964* (New York: Institute of International Education, 1964), p. 5.

I recently began a study of the relevance for home country needs of the United States training of Latin American graduate students. I seek a better understanding of the past and present experience with this significant movement through space of high-level human resources, especially as it relates, or fails to relate, to the development and utilization of those human resources of greatest importance to national development. Although this study is in its initial stages, tabulations based on the annual census data of the Institute of International Education provide some "first fruits" which suggest implications for development administration. These tabulations make it possible to identify certain patterns and interrelations, over time, with respect to home country, field of specialization, sponsorship, level and location of studies, etc. Although certainly not definitive, the following results of these tabulations are suggestive of further work of great potential value for development administration.

Graduate training is still rare in almost any field anywhere in Latin America. Therefore, if a Latin American is to pursue education beyond the often inadequate level of university training available in his country he usually must go abroad. It is probable that for most Latin American countries progress in most fields will depend heavily on foreign (United States) graduate training, at least until those countries develop sufficient graduate programs of their own, often through the overseas graduate training of faculty.

As a first approach to gauging, in a very approximate sense, how the patterns of training in the United States relate to development needs, I have devised two parallel indexes based on particular fields of specialization in graduate studies. The first of these I term the "technical" index and the second, the "structural" index. The construction of the "technical" index reflects the conclusions of Harbison and Myers that perhaps the highest priorities for human resource development for countries in their Levels II and III, where almost all Latin American countries are found, should be given to improving the quantity and quality of training, especially in science, engineering, agriculture, and education.[50]

On the other hand, it seems clear that the technical specialities

50. Harbison and Myers, *Education, Manpower and Economic Growth*, see esp. chap. 5, pp. 73–100 and chap. 6, pp. 101–29.

will be unable to make major contributions to the general welfare in most Latin American countries unless and until there are basic structural changes in those countries. As Raul Prebisch has stated:

> The social structure prevalent in Latin America constitutes a serious obstacle to technical progress and, consequently, to economic and social development. . . . Is it suggested that the present system, under which the energies of individual initiative are cramped by social stratification and privilege, should be kept intact? Or is the way to be cleared for this initiative by the structural reforms referred to, so that the system may acquire the full dynamic force it lacks at present? [51]

The use, therefore, of a technical index as the only yardstick for appraising the relevance of foreign training for development needs might put the cart before the horse. There is nothing inherent in the technical specialities which increase the competence of these students as potential agents for structural change. There are, however, other important fields of specialization, including the social sciences and many of the humanities, whose basic concern is precisely for man as a member of society, its various components and institutions. Inherent in these fields is a concern for the structure of society and, presumably, such specializations increase the competence of these students as potential agents for structural changes in the often moribund social, economic, political, and administrative structures which so seriously impede progress in Latin America. Accordingly, I have developed a parallel index based on "structural" specialties. These two simple indexes are presented merely as suggestive of the general relevance for development needs of each country's pattern of graduate student specialties pursued in the United States. For the technical index and for the structural index I have incorporated each of the 94 specialties identified by the Institute of International Education into

51. United Nations, Economic and Social Council, Economic Commission for Latin America, *Towards a Dynamic Development Policy for Latin America* (E/CN.12/680), 14 April 1963, pp. 4–5.

one of three levels, according to its apparent relevance for that particular index.[52]

Table 11 presents both sets of index numbers and rankings for nineteen countries for 1963–1964. This table also presents for the seven countries with the largest numbers of students (hereafter called the "large" countries) rankings of sponsors by the same yardsticks. For each country each of the five sponsor categories used by the Institute of International Education has a rank of from 1 to 5. A sponsor rank of 1 designates that its index number (based on the specialties of the students it sponsored) was higher than the corresponding number for any other sponsor.

For the technical index, Table 11 shows an all-country index number of 57.9 with the countries ranging from a high of 69.3 (Venezuela), to a low of 44.6 (Panama), with a median of 53.7 (Mexico). For the structural index the all-country number is

52. The following are examples of how some of the 94 specialties are incorporated in the indexes:

Index of Technical Specialties	*Index of Structural Specialties*
level A (best fit)	*level X* (best fit)
26 specialities, including:	28 specialties, including:
agriculture (all specialties)	economics
education (all)	education (all specialties)
engineering (almost all)	humanities (about half)
physical sciences (almost all)	law
	philosophy
	public administration
	political science
	sociology
level B (questionable)	*level Y* (questionable)
25 specialties, including:	15 specialties, including:
economics	classics
mathematics	fine arts (most)
medicine (all)	humanities (about half)
sociology	library science
level C (worse fit)	*level Z* (worse fit)
43 specialties, including:	51 specialties, including:
classics	agriculture (all)
fine arts (all)	engineering (all)
humanities (almost all)	medicine (all)
law	physical sciences (all)
philosophy	

The index numbers are determined by the formula:

$$100 \times \frac{\text{No. students in level A (or X)} + \frac{1}{2}\text{ No. students in level B (or Y)}}{\text{total No. students}}$$

Table 11. *Evaluation Indexes, Rankings, and Sponsor Rankings for "All" Graduate Students from Nineteen Latin American Countries in U.S., 1963–1964*

Country	Number students	"Technical" specialities				"Structural" specialities			
		Index [a] number	Rank	Sponsor rank [b] U.S.	Home gvt.	Index [a] number	Rank	Sponsor rank [b] U.S.	Home gvt.
Brazil	329	59.4	7	2	1	42.4	8 [c]	1	5
Mexico	326	53.7	10	5	1	29.5	16	5	2
Colombia	288	62.5	4	4	1	31.5	14	1	5
Venezuela	278	69.3	1	4	2	31.0	15	1	5
Argentina	221	50.3	14	4	1	38.9	13	2	4
Chile	190	58.6	8	5	2	62.5	2	1	5
Peru	141	67.0	2	4	5	23.7	19	1	2
Panama	84	44.6	19			39.9	11		
Costa Rica	52	45.2	18			42.4	8 [c]		
Ecuador	52	59.5	5			42.4	8 [c]		
Bolivia	39	51.5	13			39.7	12		
Haiti	38	52.6	12			52.6	3		
Guatemala	29	53.4	11			29.4	17		
Uruguay	22	47.7	15			45.5	6		
Nicaragua	21	45.4	17			52.5	4		
Paraguay	21	47.5	16			42.9	7		
Domin. Rep.	19	60.5	6			26.3	18		
El Salvador	18	55.5	9			50.0	5		
Honduras	13	65.5	3			65.5	1		
	2,181	57.9[d]				37.7 [d]			

Source: Calculated from raw data furnished by the Institute of International Education from its 1963–1964 census.
a Index # of 100.0 would indicate that *all* students were in these specialties.
b Sponsor rank of five sponsors: U.S. government, home government, U.S. college, private organization, and self-sponsored. Calculations for rankings are weighted to adjust for multiple sponsorship. After Peru, small numbers curtail useful meaning of sponsor rankings.
c Tie ranking.
d Index nos. for all countries combined.

37.7, substantially less than that for the other index. The countries range from a high of 65.5 (Honduras), to a low of 23.7 (Peru), with a median of 42.4 (Brazil, Costa Rica, and Ecuador are tied).

The considerable difference in the all-country index numbers clearly shows the much greater emphasis on technical than on structural studies, despite the possibility that this emphasis may not be the faster way to promote progress. Three of the large countries which rank very high by the technical index, rank very low by the structural index: Venezuela (1, 15), Peru (2, 19), and Colombia (4, 14), and several other countries show major inversions in rank.

Because of the composition of the indexes significant inversions in rank are not surprising; however, Argentina (14, 13) and Bolivia (13, 12) have low rankings by both indexes. Only for little Honduras, with the smallest number of students, are both rankings high (3, 1). A check of the detailed tabulations reveals that, as one might expect, a high proportion of the Honduran students (5 of the 13) are in the field of education, which counts heavily in both indexes.

Only two countries had higher index numbers for the structural than for the technical index: Chile (62.5, 58.6) and Nicaragua (52.5, 45.4). One might speculate as to whether Chile's achievements as one of the very few viable democracies in Latin America, combined with its vigorous efforts to cope with its tremendous economic and social problems, may induce its students (and their sponsors) more toward the structural specialties. To explain Nicaragua, however, some of these arguments might have to be reversed.

The sponsor rankings for the seven large countries of Table 11 show pronounced patterns. I list the rankings only for two types of sponsors—"United States government" and "home government." Of the five sponsors covered, their actions should be most responsive to public policies and national goals. On the technical side, the home government ranks first in four and second in two cases, whereas only for Peru does it rank low. The United States government, however, shows just the reverse pattern. It ranks last or next to last for all but Brazil. Clearly then, the governments of the large countries support, to a relatively much greater extent than does the United States government, the technical specialties for their graduate students in the United States.

On the structural side the patterns are almost reversed. The United States government ranks first in five of the seven cases and low only for Mexico, whereas the home government ranks last in four cases and fourth in one. Thus, the United States is giving much greater emphasis to structural specialties than are the other sponsors, and the home governments much less. Mexico, however, is an exception for both governmental sponsors. Perhaps the explanation for its significantly different situation (which appears again in other respects in Tables 12 and 13) lies in the nature of the "institutionalized" and "continuing" Mexican Revolution. Any explanation of why the Peruvian government bucks the trend of home governments by ranking high as a sponsor of structural students will have to await field investigation.

Table 12. *Percentages of Graduate Students from Seven Latin American Countries in Selected Specialties, 1963–1964*

		Specialty		
				Public admin. and
	Number			political
Country	students	Agriculture [a]	Economics	science
Brazil	329	4.3%	9.4%	6.4%
Mexico	326	13.2	3.1	0.3
Colombia	288	9.7	9.7	1.7
Venezuela	278	8.6	10.4	2.2
Argentina	221	6.3	14.5	2.3
Chile	190	7.4	5.8	3.2
Peru	141	16.3	9.2	0.0
Total, all countries	1,773	9.0%	8.6%	2.5%

Source: Tabulated from data from the 1963–1964 census of the Institute of International Education.
a Includes all six agricultural specialties: agriculture, agronomy, agricultural engineering, food technology, husbandry, and veterinary medicine.

The tabulations allow us to trace over time the emphasis by specialties of any nation's students and their sponsors. For example, Tables 12 and 13 compare the concentrations of students of the seven large countries in all six agricultural specialties combined, in economics, and in public administration and political science combined. Table 12 covers all students enumerated in the 1963–1964 Institute of International Education census. The available data for earlier years, Table 13, cover only those who began their United States studies in that year. Our time series, therefore, consists of entrants rather than of all students in the years before 1963–1964.

In some respects Tables 12 and 13 are alarming. Improvements in agriculture are generally of the highest priority for these as for most countries. Nevertheless, agriculture gets relatively little emphasis in most of the student groups. The cases of Brazil and Argentina are particularly surprising. Agriculture is probably

Table 13. *Percentages of Graduate Students from Seven Latin American Countries Who Began United States Studies in Selected Specialties, 1955–1962*

Country	Number students	Specialty		
		Agriculture [a]	Economics	Public admin. and political science
Brazil	900	3.4%	5.4%	3.4%
Mexico	718	8.5	5.4	1.0
Colombia	529	9.8	9.1	3.6
Venezuela	391	9.2	5.6	2.6
Argentina	499	8.6	6.4	0.4
Chile	466	7.9	10.3	1.9
Peru	288	10.4	3.8	0.3
Total, all countries	3,791	7.7%	6.6%	2.1%

Source: Tabulated from data from the annual censuses of the Institute of International Education.
a Includes all six agricultural specialties: agriculture, agronomy, agricultural engineering, food technology, husbandry, and veterinary medicine.

more important for these two countries, especially for their ability to earn foreign exchange, than for any of the other countries listed. Yet they had the lowest concentrations of students in agriculture in the 1963–1964 period. There had been a similar paucity of Brazilian entrants in agriculture in prior years.

For an increasing number of countries there is available reliable information on some of the critical shortages of high-level manpower. For example, after analyzing Argentina's situation, Horowitz concludes: "the most significant scarcity is that of veterinarians, agronomists, and agricultural technicians." [53] My tabulations can help evaluate the role of United States graduate training in helping satisfy such specific needs. In this instance have the large numbers of Argentine graduate students in the United States reflected the need for veterinarians and agronomists? Of the 221 Argentine students in 1963–1964 with a stated specialty, only 1 (0.5 percent) was in veterinary medicine and only 6 (2.7 percent) were in agronomy. In the previous eight years none of the 499 entrants was in veterinary medicine and only 2 (0.4 percent) were in agronomy! This dismal picture seems fairly characteristic of the frequently poor utilization of foreign (United States) training to help satisfy urgent needs for high-level human resources.

Although I regard economics as a field vital for development, I doubt that it warrants, for the seven large countries combined, almost as much emphasis as the combination of all six agricultural specialties received both in the 1963–1964 census (Table 12), and among the prior entrants (Table 13). Particularly surprising again are Brazil and Argentina, more than twice as many of whose students were studying economics than were studying agriculture—a strange and intriguing phenomenon.

Economics is a popular field for these countries. In Table 12 we note that it receives almost three and a half times the overall emphasis of the public administration-political science combination. About the same relationship exists for entrants in prior years (Table 13). Another topic for field investigation might concern the apparent Peruvian disinterest in United States graduate training in these two vital specialties.

Another important problem concerns foreign student "leakage" —that is, those students who do not return home and the costs they represent for the home country. This is widely regarded as a major problem. Although very scarce, available information tends to justify this concern. The most definitive evidence I have found for Latin America, cited earlier in another connection, concerns

53. Morris A. Horowitz, "High-level Manpower in the Economic Development of Argentina," p. 35. This is chap. 1 in Frederick Harbison and Charles A. Myers, *Manpower and Education* (New York: McGraw-Hill, 1965).

persons who received some statistical training in the United States from about 1942 through 1962.[54] My calculations reveal that of the 431 professionals who had at least six months of training in the United States, 79 (18.3 percent), were employed outside their home countries at the end of 1962. Of these 79, 48 (61 percent) were employed in the United States and an additional 10, not included in the 79, were working for United States companies or for the United States government in their home countries. Haiti lost 16 of its 32, Brazil lost only 2 of its 35, and Venezuela, the richest country, lost none of its 13.

An investigation of the "leakage" problem would probably reveal that large numbers of Latin American students remain in, or return to, the United States as immigrants. There are probably significant variations by country, specialty, and level of United States training. Impressionistic evidence suggests that Ph.D. graduates, especially in the physical sciences, have perhaps the highest leakage rates.

Some Implications for Development Administration

My major conclusions may be summarized as follows:

1. Richer areas act as magnets which attract human resources, and especially high-level human resources, from poorer areas.

2. These movements of human resources, in themselves, constitute major subsidies of the richer areas by the poorer areas.

3. The costs to many poor areas of such movements constitute significant offsets to any aid (which itself may be in the form of high-level human resources) provided to these poor areas by rich areas.

4. The movements of high-level human resources may, to a great extent, account for the persistent and often widening gaps between rich and poor areas.

54. Inter American Statistical Institute, *Latin Americans Receiving Training in the United States.*

Such movements of human resources and their consequences may be accepted, or even desired, by any given society. However, there are widespread concern and activity to reduce the great and often increasing economic and social differences within and among nations. Where this is the case, development administration must concern itself with evaluating and influencing the intra- and international movements of high-level human resources. Although these movements are rational and may tend to increase overall productivity, they can severely impede hopes and plans for achieving spatially balanced development. If the poor areas are not to resign themselves to falling further behind, one of their urgent tasks is to devise ways to reverse the heavy outflows of scarce and valuable human knowledge and skills to the rich areas.

Within a country the authorities must increase the relative attractiveness of opportunities outside the capitals. A planned decentralization of the country's pattern of capital investments can be the major means to this end. Merely to increase rural education without relating it closely to improving rural opportunities is to encourage the outflow. Chile recently established a system of regional colleges in rural areas, most of whose programs are geared specifically to regional opportunities and are generally of much shorter duration than standard university programs. A basic aim of this innovation is to reduce the regions' heavy outflows of some of their best talent for educational and career opportunities in richer areas.

With respect to international movements, efforts by Latin American countries to increase their high-level human resources will continue to be undermined by the heavy emigration to rich countries of these key people. This major subsidy by the poor countries to the rich countries contributes to the widening of the already considerable gaps between them. Short of outright prohibition of emigration of key people, governments might discourage the outflow by requiring at least partial indemnification for the public costs of the education of the émigrés. For most Latin American countries the losses of high-level manpower through emigration probably vastly exceed the gains through immigration. For example, for the period 1958 through 1962 Colombia lost 3.4

times as many professional, administrative, and technical workers as it gained.[55] Nevertheless, the countries might seek more actively, or even subsidize, immigration of persons with needed skills.

Inflows of high-level manpower to work for foreign companies or in technical assistance capacities often carry considerably less real than apparent benefit for the host country. Because these inflows may tend to impede the development and utilization of a country's own human resources, it may do well to regulate these inflows carefully. In the case of foreign companies the government might, for example, require proof of the need for foreigners to fill key posts. In the case of technical assistance experts it might insist that they act as advisers and that they be selected by, rather than be thrust upon, the host country.

The patterns of United States graduate training of Latin Americans suggest that in many instances these great expenditures have little apparent relevance for the home country's greatest needs. The evidence also suggests that high-level education, especially that obtained overseas, often constitutes an "exit visa" for pursuing better opportunities abroad. Other countries would do well to emulate Colombia's systematic efforts through the Instituto Colombiano para Especialización Técnica en el Exterior to coordinate overseas studies with national needs and opportunities and to require that students return home.

Insofar as nations are able to design the institutions and opportunities that will discourage flows of high-level human resources from poor to rich areas, their efforts to reduce the great gaps between these areas are much more likely to succeed. However, if nations are unwilling or unable to discourage them, these flows will continue to intensify the differentials.

55. From data obtained in interviews with officials of the Instituto Colombiano para Especialización Técnica en el Exterior, Bogotá, Colombia, August 23, 1965.

Chapter 6

Space-Time and Postindustrial Society

Bertram M. Gross

For our ancestors a few centuries ago earth was a vast un-explored mystery. Communication or transportation from one region or country to another was so time-consuming as to be limited to a few venturesome nomads, traders, and migrants. Even the great empire builders and "world" conquerors operated in relatively small areas. By the last third of the twentieth century, earth has shrunken to small proportions. Without significant change in its 8,000-mile diameter, there has been a revolutionary change in the spatial measure most important to men—namely, the time taken in moving information, energy, or matter over its surface. With men and equipment soon to be based on the moon, our astronauts may soon explore the solar system itself. Our scanning will probe more deeply than ever before into millions of light years of interstellar space.

In comparison with the vast space-time continuum of the universe, earth shrinks still further. Our entire solar system is little more than a tiny particle in a small cluster of a constellation within one of countless galaxies. Indeed, astronomers now suggest that in all this vast array there must certainly be innumerable other mass-energy concentrations with various forms of life and types of social systems—some similar to ours, others substantially different, many beyond our capacity to comprehend. For the time being we have a hard enough task trying to understand human life on our own planet. Along with space-time shrinkage an unprecedented increase is taking place in the number of people, the size of the social systems in which they participate (with the exception of families), and the complexity of their interactions. We thus find an overexpanding world of vast unexplored mysteries still awaiting serious probes. Within this world, many leaders, administrators, and technicians in all countries—both poor and rich—are engaged in efforts to bring about various types of significant social change. These efforts are often referred to as "development administration." [1]

In this paper, looking at technology in social system terms, I am concerned with space-time shrinkage as merely an aspect of broader processes of accelerating but uneven social change. My major purpose is to present a panoramic view of these change processes with special emphasis on certain spatial-temporal relations. This will be done by (1) briefly identifying the "mobiletic" revolution; (2) suggesting that the technology of space-time shrinkage is merely a part of *one of the great transitions in history: the transformation of industrialized societies into various forms of postindustrialism;* (3) giving special attention to two aspects of this transformation with sharp implications for space-time configurations, the organizational and urban revolutions; (4) suggesting that this entire transformation is associated with the rapid and painful birth pangs of a world society with no government and many bad neighbors; and (5) concluding with a comment on the possible loss—and discovery—of people as individuals. The entire discussion will thus deal with the changing environments of development administrators, the constraints upon them, and the goals they may hope to achieve.

To deal in an orderly fashion with the myriad types of informa-

---

1. The term "development administration" has recently been used to focus attention on administration in the sense of "getting results" or "getting things done through organizations," as distinguished from the use of "administration" to refer to specialized staff services or administrative or managerial techniques and processes. It is often used specifically to refer to the management, or administration, of major programs of social, economic, or political development. For Weidner, the term suggests the problems associated with innovational programs that upset traditional social processes (Edward W. Weidner, "Development Administration," in Ferrel Heady and S. Stokes, eds., *Papers in Comparative Public Administration* [Ann Arbor: University of Michigan, 1962], pp. 98–116). Swerdlow illustrates this usage in terms of the administration of an urban renewal program in an American city as well as economic development activities in an underdeveloped country (Irving Swerdlow, ed., *Development Administration: Concepts and Problems* [Syracuse: Syracuse University Press, 1963]).

tion relating to people, things, and their many groupings, I shall use an ambitious technique of social-system accounting. This technique—still in its early stages—is based upon a synthesis of the most important ideas developed in the past quarter-century of social science. It provides the conceptual tools with which one can —with enough skill and data—build a unique model of any concrete social system, a special model for any set of social systems or a general model applicable at a certain level of abstraction to all social systems. Rather than explain the technique fully, I shall save space by presuming that the reader interested in corroborative detail may find the time to track down the more detailed discussions of specific elements in my earlier *The Managing of Organizations,*[2] and "What Are Your Organization's Objectives? A General-Systems Approach to Planning,"[3] and in my more recent monograph *The State of the Nation: Social System Accounting.*[4]

Mobiletics

"Mobiletics" is used here as a way of referring to transportation, transmission, and communication as one process. It helps express something common to all three, movement over space. The tendency in all aspects of mobiletics has been for change to take place at exponential rates. A partial indication of what this rate of change has meant for intercontinental travel is provided by Figure 1. In the 1820's and 1830's sailing ships could rarely do better than 5 miles an hour. Sixty years later steamships could do 25 miles an hour. By the 1950's airplanes could exceed 600 miles an hour. This has meant a squaring of the maximum speed about every sixty years. This rate, it must be pointed out, can scarcely continue over the next sixty years. Like all exponential curves, this

2. Bertram M. Gross, *The Managing of Organizations,* 2 vols. (New York: Free Press, 1964); also appearing in condensed, one-volume form as *Organizations and Their Managing* (New York: Free Press, 1968).
3. Bertram M. Gross, "What Are Your Organization's Objectives? A General-Systems Approach to Planning," *Human Relations,* August 1965, pp. 195–216.
4. Bertram M. Gross, *The State of the Nation: Social System Accounting* (London: Tavistock 1966); also appearing as section in Raymond A. Bauer, ed., *Social Indicators* (Cambridge: M.I.T. Press, 1966).

Figure 1. *Maximum Speed Attainable for Travel over Intercontinental Distances, 1820–1960*

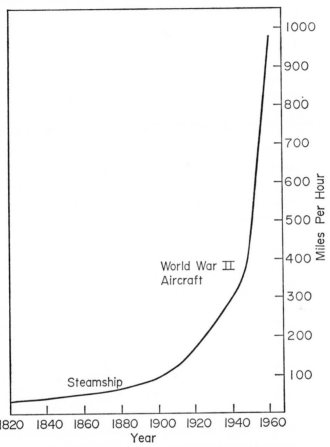

World War II
Aircraft

Steamship

1820 1840 1860 1880 1900 1920 1940 1960
Year

Miles Per Hour

1000
900
800
700
600
500
400
300
200
100

Source: Bruce M. Russett, *Trends in World Politics* (New York: Macmillan, 1965), p. 8

one also must soon level off—probably long before the speed of light is approached. Nevertheless, the change in the last fifteen years has been impressive—with supersonic jets traveling at 2,000 miles per hour and rockets reaching 20,000 miles an hour.

The transmission of energy represents a different pattern of growth. Until the development of electric power, this kind of movement was impossible. People could merely move from one place to another, the people, animals, and fuel capable of producing energy when needed. In 1900, when commercial production of electric power had just got underway, it was possible to transmit only 60 kilovolts for distances of 50 miles. By the middle of the century it was possible to transmit a few hundred kilovolts for 600 miles over one power line. But the use of single transmission lines has been largely bypassed by the development of power "grids," or networks, which may be interconnected on a vast continental (perhaps soon a multicontinental) basis. These new distribution systems make it possible to (1) bring an instantaneous supply of power to people anywhere, no matter how far they may be from the points of power generation, (2) develop a flexible combination of various sources of power (hydro, thermal, and atomic), (3) concentrate generation units at points where production is most economical, (4) economize on production by spreading peak periods over a larger number of generators, and (5) provide "back up" facilities that will provide sustained power in the case of breakdown at any few points.

In many respects the transmission of information represents the most dramatic of all mobiletic changes. The telegraph, telephone, radio, and television started out operating short distances only. Networks and interconnecting systems grew gradually. Only in the past few years have we seen direct dialing and live TV news coverage on a continental and multicontinental basis. Vast new breakthroughs are heralded by "telestar" style satellites, closed-circuit television, and household installations of teletype service and facsimile radio printing as supplemental to (or substitutes for) newspapers. The heads of giant organizations with branches all over America already conduct regular conferences with their branch heads through closed-circuit television.

While each aspect of the mobiletic revolution reinforces the others, it is also clear that there are considerable differences among them. The speed of communication and the spread of communication facilities has progressed far faster than that of transportation and transportation facilities. This is inherent in the nature of the communication process, which involves the movement of only signals, not mass. It is difficult to conceive of transportation matching this. The transmission of energy has lagged behind both. But this situation will change drastically as soon as it becomes economically feasible to transmit electrical energy by radio. The greatest unevenness, of course, is in the spread of mobiletics over the face of the earth. Most modern transportation, power transmission, and communication facilities are owned and operated by people in advanced societies. They are the "mobiletic revolutionaries." At the same time these facilities have touched the lives of people in every society in the world. Awareness of this fact will help protect us against the "scientoid" error of abstracting modern technology from the social systems in which it develops. We consider now the social system of modern mobiletics.

The Emergence of Postindustrialism

All discussions of social systems run the risk of using simplistic terms. One of the reasons is that the nature of social systems has long been—and will certainly continue to be—a major issue in international and internal political struggle. The exigencies of struggle have led to strong emphasis upon a number of dichotomies: (1) capitalist (or free enterprise) versus socialist or communist; (2) democratic versus dictatorial (or totalitarian); (3) free (or independent) versus subservient (as colony or satellite); (4) rich (or "developed" or "affluent") versus poor (the "underdeveloped" or "developing"). Scholars will use other dichotomies. An important one—hinted at in the previous section—is scientific (or technology-based) versus prescientific. Another is highly differentiated (or pluralistic) versus undifferentiated. The more sophisticated politicians and scholars recognize midpoints between the two extremes—as with mixed economy, limited autarchy, tutelary democracy, or diffracted society. With still greater sophistication, but with the sacrifice of attention-attracting labels, others may prefer to regard each of these dimensions as things to be measured on a separate continuum.

The limitation of the dimensions referred to above may be quickly suggested by thinking of the various adjectives that may be conveyed by describing the America-coming-into-being as a technological, cybernetic, service, megalopolitan, technopolitan, intellectual, leisure, educated, information-overload, long-lived, or, if we consider the potentialities of military technology, suicidal society. One could easily extend the list further.

There is value, however, in using some term which seems to provide an umbrella for all these many dimensions. One such term is "modern," which can be easily contrasted with "traditional" (or "premodern") and with an in-between stage called "transitional." For reasons that I shall soon set forth, this is highly unsatisfactory. Another all-embracing concept was provided by the term "Great Society." For Adam Smith, this meant the country as a whole, as contrasted with a single enterprise.[5] For Graham Wallas, it was a society with many large-scale institutions.[6] For Lyndon Johnson it was a certain kind of "good" society. My own choice is to differentiate between preindustrial, industrial, and postindustrial societies. In so doing, naturally, I am not using these terms as referring merely to differing modes of production, distribution, and technology. They refer to a broad set of variables that enter into every society.

The Rostow-Riggs Myths of Culmination

In the nineteenth century Hegel interpreted all of world history as culminating in the German state of his day. In the same tradition many recent writers have tended to interpret the whole course of economic and social change as culminating in their version of present-day modern society. Thus Walt W. Rostow presents a continuum of economic growth divided into five stages: traditional society, the preconditions for takeoff, the takeoff, the drive to maturity, and the age of high mass consumption. In passing, Rostow asks what will happen "when diminishing relative marginal utility sets in, on a mass basis, for real income itself?" But staying not for an answer, he contents himself with setting forth the era of mass consumption as the terminal point of his-

5. Adam Smith, *The Wealth of Nations* (New York: Modern Library, 1937), p. 651.
6. Graham Wallas, *The Great Society* (New York: Macmillan, 1920). For a more recent discussion of "great society" concepts, see the various essays in Bertram M. Gross, ed., *A Great Society?* (New York: Basic Books, 1968).

tory.[7] With considerable sophistication, Fred W. Riggs sets forth three stages of growth based on degrees of differentiation within society. According to Riggs, a society at the earliest stage of development is "fused" (that is, has very little differentiation). Later, it becomes "prismatic" (that is, somewhat more differentiated), and still later on "diffracted" (still more differentiated). Some societies may never reach the prismatic diffracted stage, according to Riggs. But once they are diffracted, that is that: they have arrived. On the question "what then?" Riggs is even more silent than Rostow.[8]

In a sense, both Rostow and Riggs present in somewhat different terms the remarkably simple flow-line from "traditional" to "transitional" to "modern." Although this set of stages has been formally set forth by Daniel Lerner in a study of social change in fifty-four societies,[9] it is inherent in a large amount of work by many others. The essence of this approach is that the present state of society in advanced industrial countries (usually the United States) is regarded as a more-or-less fixed point toward which other societies are or should be moving. This myth of culmination, in any of its innumerable varieties, provides certain conveniences for the investigator or commentator from a modern society: (1) It allows him to concentrate upon "backward" or "developing" societies without the annoyance of trying to understand his own. (2) It offers an escape from the tensions, frustrations, and social conflicts at home. (3) It promotes a satisfying sense of superiority as he contemplates people who want to, or are unable to, be like him and his peers. (4) It relieves him from the uncertainties involved in trying to find out where his own society really is at the moment or where it may be going.

On the other hand, there are some serious disadvantages to any point of view that "closes the books" on the processes of change in modern societies. Among the more obvious are the following: (1) It promotes an egocentricity that impairs relationships with elites from developing societies. (2) It prevents the mature

7. W. W. Rostow, *The Stages of Economic Growth* (Cambridge: Harvard University Press, 1960).
8. Fred W. Riggs, *Administration in Developing Countries* (Boston: Houghton Mifflin, 1964).
9. *The Passing of Traditional Society* (Glencoe: Free Press, 1958).

awareness of the cultural biases brought to the aid or study of developing societies by those from developed ones. (3) It leads to ignoring the "motes" of structural rigidity, dead-hand traditionalism, and transitional tensions in our own modern eyes. (4) It distracts attention from the processes of social change in the developed societies, including those processes that have decisive effects upon underdeveloped societies. The last point is a decisive one. If modern societies are changing rapidly, what are the characteristics of this change? What are they changing to? Does it make enough sense merely to say that they are providing more mass consumption, showing more differentiation, becoming more modern?

My own answer to this question is based upon the judgment that social change in the mass consumption, diffracted, modern societies is in many important respects much more rapid than in countries like India, Indonesia, and Ghana. This judgment seems widely spread today—particularly by those many economists who point out that economic growth is more rapid in many developed nations than in the majority of so-called developing nations. But economic measures alone are far from enough to describe the nature of social change.

One way of getting a broader picture, as already indicated, is to look at social change in terms of a continuum from preindustrial to industrial to postindustrial societies. From this point of view, we are able to see the great importance of tradition in a country like America. Our present may now be seen as a passing phase, rather than as a culmination. We are able to note what is in my judgment the central fact about American society: that America is par excellence a transitional society. Indeed, many of America's greatest difficulties—including the difficulties some Americans have created for other countries—stem from the problems Americans have in adapting to the stresses of a transitional period which is difficult to understand or accept.

The Dimensions of Postindustrialism

The Industrial Revolution which got under way in the Western world in the mid-eighteenth century brought about profound changes in social structure.

In its more obvious aspects, the "factory system," this revolution began in manufacturing. Yet it quickly spread to agriculture, transportation, finance and, despite recurring lags, to construction, distribution and the public services. It is now spreading to the "underdeveloped" countries of Asia, Africa, and South America, which by any definition still comprise from 65 to 76 percent of the world's population. . . . One may view the Industrial Revolution from many aspects. One may stress the sharp rise, although at varying rates, in living standards, literacy, and life expectancy. One may note the expansion of large urban areas and the contraction of agricultural populations. One may focus upon the abolition of chattel slavery in most parts of the world and the rise of political liberties in many parts. One may point to political and economic imperialism, new forms of organized oppression and a series of wars unprecedented in territorial coverage and destructiveness.[10]

A somewhat more orderly selection of such change facets is presented in the first two columns of Table 1. By comparing the various elements in the first column with those in the second column one may get a general impression of the kinds of structural change in the many preindustrial societies now in transition to industrialism. Neither column, however, presents a general or ideal type. A more careful detailing of the changes taking place within each structural element in—let us say—both India and Indonesia would provide "unique" models for each, models that would point up the specific nature of structural change in each.[11]

Let us now compare the second column with the third column. Here we find tremendous changes. The most dramatic ones, of course, are the "mobiletic revolution," already described, and the transformation of the old-time factory system into a system of goods production in which machinery replaces not only manual labor but even large amounts of mental labor. The combination of

---

10. Gross, *The Managing of Organizations,* pp. 37–38.
11. A detailed guide to the assembly of relevant information of each element of social structure is provided in the section on "System Structure" in Gross, *The State of the Nation.*

Table 1. Social Structure: Preindustrial, Industrial, Postindustrial

	Preindustrial		Industrial		Postindustrial
People	Low life expectancy at birth Little formal education	T R	Rising life expectancy Much more education	T R	Life expectancy above 75 "Learning force" surpasses total employment
Physical resources	Most employment in agriculture, with rudimentary specialization Hand labor, aided by tools and animals Little development of natural resources Large construction, mainly monumental	A N S	Specialization of labor force with declining agricultural component Power-driven machinery in large aggregations Natural resources more developed, depleted, and wasted Expansion of "built environment," with vast urban slums	A N S	Professionalization of labor force, with at least 70% in services Cybernation and computerization Resources more protected and conserved More rapid and concentrated growth of "built environment"
Subsystems	Extended family Large organizations, mainly intermingling of army, church, and state "Anomic" associations Villages and small towns	I T I O N A L	Nuclear family Larger and more differentiated organizations, including factory system Growth of associations and "pressure groups" Urban and metropolitan areas Clearer differentiation of government sector	I T I O N A L	Highly capitalized family Complex, mixed organizational constellations New kinds of associational networks Megalopoli and metropoli Blurred line between government and nongovernment
External relations	Colonialism and imperialism	P	From empire to bloc or commonwealth Informal penetration and infusive diplomacy	P	Polynuclear world society Extensive transnational, intersecting, and interpenetrating relations
Internal relations	Localism and sectionalism	H A S	More intergration, with growth of nationalism Vast communication and transportation networks	H A S	Decline of both sectionalism and nationalism The mobiletic revolution
Codes and values	Survival and other-worldliness Religious law and "law of jungle" Passivism	E S	Class and group conflict Cosmopolitanism and nationalism Constitutional, statutory, judicial, and administrative law Activism and secularism	E S	New forms of intense conflict Megalopolitanism and transnationalism More organizational and professional codes Decline of scarcity values Secular humanism
System guidance	Restricted elites		Multiple elites National planning systems		Dispersed elites, greater circulation Transnational planning systems

automation and computerization yields "cybernation" in all fields of activity. We must also note the growth of "complex, mixed organizational constellations" and "megalopoli and metropoli," two subjects to be discussed separately in the following sections.

In addition, the following structural changes may be briefly touched upon:

1. Increased life expectancy is creating a social structure in which there is more "generational intertwining" than ever before in history. Older people are more active. They compete with—and try to impose their values on—younger generations.

2. The learning force—composed both of those enrolled in full-time formal education and those who take part in educational refresher, extension, and development programs while working—is growing so fast that it will sooner or later become as large as the employed labor force.

3. Professionalization of the labor force, with over 70 percent in various kinds of services, brings new elites and new orientations in labor unions, trade associations and ranking systems in organizations.

4. Secular humanism in values will be based on material abundance, as contrasted with (*a*) "zero-sum" nonredistributive values in preindustrial societies (based on their limited productive potentials) and (*b*) the "scarcity economics" and "zero-sum" redistributive ideologies in industrial societies (increasingly out of keeping with growing productive potentials).

The major significance of social structure, however, is that it provides the capacity for certain kinds of performance, or activity. Let us turn to some of the changes in social performance that seem to be associated with the period of transition from industrialism to postindustrialism: [12]

Satisfying Interests: Eliminating material poverty at various absolute levels (although not of differential deprivation) and providing substantial security against pestilence, floods, earthquake, and nondegenerative diseases. Providing greater opportunities for

12. This impressionistic review is taken from Gross, *The State of the Nation,* which also provides—in the section on "System Performance"—a more specific delineation of each performance element and subelement.

leisure, creative work, and personal development, with increased blurring of the lines between work, education, and leisure. Decline in "moonlighting" and rise in "starlighting." [13] Greater opportunities for more people to satisfy the more subjective interests.

Producing Output: From vast standardization to product differentiation, with even greater attention to quality (including aesthetic aspects as well as durability and service). Vast increases in information output, information "overload," and in nonmarketed services that cannot be reflected in economic aggregates.

Investing in System: Greater utilization of machines and material inputs, with declines in work year, work week, and involuntary unemployment. Great investment in labor-saving and data-processing hard goods, but with more conscious and explicit attention in investment in people, subsystems, internal and external relations, values, and guidance systems.

Using Inputs Efficiently: Increasing attention to efficiency in terms of utilizing potentials and developing the quality of output, with declining attention to efficiency relations calculated in the more limited and old-fashioned terms of capital or labor inputs related to strictly monetary measures of output quantity.[14]

Acquiring Inputs: Greater foreign trade and international capital flows, higher domestic taxes.

Observing Codes: Substantial deviation, with changing and clashing codes. More widespread compliance with codes of honesty, truth, equity, and due process.

Behaving Rationally: Advancing and using sciences and technologies, with increasing computerization and automation. Devel-

13. "Moonlighting" occurs when people with full-time jobs take on additional after-hour jobs to augment their salary—a widespread phenomenon in industrializing societies that cannot provide enough wages or salaries to satisfy ambitious workers and professionals. "Starlighting" may be used to describe the postindustrializing phenomenon of professionals and intellectuals extending their regular "work" beyond any definable limits—to satisfy their needs for self-expression and creative activity. The probability is that anyone who has read as far as this chapter is—or will soon become—a "starlighter."

14. Galbraith has pointed out this tendency in his contention that "If the things produced are not of great urgency, it follows that the efficiency of the process by which they are produced ceases to be an overriding consideration." John K. Galbraith, *The Affluent Society* (Boston: Houghton Mifflin, 1958), p. 287. By using a narrow, single-dimensioned concept of efficiency, however, Galbraith has failed to deal with the changing nature of efficiency concepts under conditions of rising material affluence.

oping and using advanced methods of social-system guidance—with possibilities of "unitary thought" through general systems analysis. Keynesianism becomes old-fashioned "le Stop Go" (already lampooned in France and Britain) as economic planning is transformed into social-system planning.

The Uneven Transitions

All societies tend to change unevenly. Although the United States is in transition to postindustrialism, some aspects are already postindustrial while some backward sectors are still in "industrializing" transitions. Many developing societies include preindustrial village, peasant, landlord, or tribal subsystems, industries that are early or advanced industrial, and key elites who really belong to the postindustrial cultures of the advanced metropoli and megalopoli. These uneven rates of change may create serious internal conflicts. Many of them—in the United States and Europe, the non-Communist as well as the Communist countries —stem from lagging structural adaptation to new performance demands. These lags are always easier to see in other countries.

Elite leaders in many preindustrial societies, as would-be "century skippers," usually aim at improbably rapid performance levels. Their objectives on the whole are much more ambitious than was the actual historical development of today's industrialized countries. Table 2 suggests that this is the case with respect to at least one dimension of every element of system performance. Although their high objectives may often contribute to more rapid economic advance than would be the case without the pressures of attempted century-skipping, the probable outcomes by the end of the century are (1) a substantial increase in the proportion of countries and population with per capita income over $100, with great unevenness among and within countries; (2) lower living conditions relative to the postindustrializing societies; (3) large-scale conspicuous urban unemployment (15 to 20 percent of labor force) in many industrializing countries; (4) more active and organized dissatisfactions, as expectations and political organization develop faster than material consumption; and (5) greater threats to world peace stemming—in the future as in the past—

Table 2. *Western Development Performance and Poor Countries' Performance Objectives*

	Historical development in today's rich countries	Objectives of today's poor countries [a]
Satisfying interests	Unhealthy living and working conditions	"Welfare state" standards
	Growth of huge fortunes	Prevention of extreme disparities
Producing output		
Annual increases, real GNP		
Aggregate	Less than 3%, 1860–1950 [b]	At least 5%
Per capita	Less than 1.5%, 1860–1950 [c]	At least 3%
Investing in the system	Capital accumulation at expense of consumption	Capital and calories both
Using inputs efficiently	Vast social waste resulting from wild ups and downs in business cycle	Sustained use of resources
Acquiring inputs	Exploitation of colonies or dependent areas	No colonies or dependent areas
Observing codes	Conspicuous corruption in all walks of life for many decades	Modern standards of integrity in government, business, education, etc.
Behaving rationally	Slow development of science and technology	Catching up on use of rapidly accelerating science and technology of the rich countries

a The listing of these objectives, obviously, does not suggest that they have as yet been attained.
b European countries from 1860 to 1950 (e.g., U.K., 1.8; France, 1.1; Germany, 2.4; Netherlands, 2.2). R. V. Goldsmith, "Financial Structure and Economic Growth in Advanced Countries," in *Capital Formation and Economic Growth* (Princeton: Princeton University Press, 1955), p. 115. The U.S. rate for the same 90-year period, however, was 3.8.
c In most European countries the per capita rate was closer to 1% (e.g., U.K., 1.2; France, 0.9; Germany, 1.4; Netherlands, 0.7). The U.S. rate for the same 90-year period was 2.2. Ibid.

from the social changes associated with the industrializing process.

In other words, there will be many kinds of growing gaps within the industrializing nations and between them and the post-industrializing societies. To see the "widening gap" merely in terms of aggregate of GNP (or even its distribution) would be to ignore not only its sources and consequences but also the many cultural and institutional differences. It is more meaningful to focus on the major differences (some widening and some narrowing) between two sets of transitional systems: those moving from preindustrialism to various phases of industrialism and those moving from industrialism to various phases of postindustrialism.

The Organizational Revolution

Large-scale organization makes it possible for people to do many things they could not do at all, or as well, through individual action, the family, or the small organization. This increased power is provided by the capacity of large organizational systems for continuity, for the mobilization of vast, specialized resources, for the absorption, processing, and retention of great amounts of information, for cooperative or synchronized action, and, above all, for satisfying many interests. In the preindustrial societies of the West the only large organizations were armies, governments, and churches. With the Industrial Revolution came more large organizations and more administrators. This Organizational Revolution was not limited to economic production, distribution, and finance. It embraced the growth of trade associations, trade unions, voluntary organizations and federations, and large political parties. The modern society is now characterized by Big Business (whether private or public), Big Government, Big Armed Services, Big Labor, Big Agriculture, Big Science, Big Education, and Big Religion.

Economic and political development in so-called underdeveloped or developing countries centers largely on the building of such new, large-scale organizations and institutions. At the same time, the continuing Organizational Revolution in the developed countries—fed by ever-new forms of science and technology and feeding the world a volume of complex information that is increasing too fast—plays a major role in transitions to postindustrialism. This onward—but uneven—sweep of the Organizational Revolution has tremendous implications for the distribution of power in society and the rate and nature of social change. To understand these implications, we cannot rely upon old-fashioned notions of how organizations operate. We need more realistic information on their role as agents of both stability and change, and particularly on the dimensions of growth and the effects of growth on centralization and decentralization.

The Dimensions of Growth

Social demography—that is, vital statistics that go beyond the counting of people and deal with formal organizations as well—is remarkably immature. The literature on the size of business enterprises is small, sporadic, and based mainly on secondary data. Even less has been done to process the raw data available on government organizations or in the collection of basic data on associations. Nevertheless, certain impressionistic judgments—illuminated by occasional data—may be made.

The traditional measures of organizational size are output (as measured by sales revenue or added value), input (as measured by expenditures), physical assets (as measured by total value), and the number of employees or members. The first and the third of these are available in comparable terms only for organizations that sell their products. The second is available in most reliable form only for organizations whose expenditures are reflected in government budgets. Hence, the best common denominator of organizational size is the number of people. By this measure, even though labor-saving machinery provides larger ratios to output and assets to employees, there seems little doubt that there has been a major trend toward the concentration of employment and membership in large-scale organizations. One may reasonably infer, moreover, that the concentration in assets and output is still greater.[15]

Unfortunately, the traditional measures—scanty and incomplete though they may be—are increasingly inadequate. First of all, spatial dispersion is another significant measure of organizational growth, one that is particularly characteristic of the transition to postindustrialism. This may be measured by:

1. The size of organizational bases: this is a multiple of the number of people and the amount of space per person (professionalization means much more of the latter).

---

15. For a more detailed discussion of organization size, see the sections on "More Organization" and "More Large Scale Organization" in "The Rise of the Administered Society" (chap. 2) and the section on "Size" in "People-in-Organizations: Formal Aspects" (chap. 15), Gross, *The Managing of Organizations.*

2. The dispersion of bases. Modern organizations now have branches and field offices across a nation and in many other countries. The larger corporations operate in scores of nations. Any self-respecting American "multiversity" now has offices of one kind or another on a number of continents.
3. The operational range. This dimension—of increasing importance in the era of the mobiletic revolution—has rarely been considered in discussions of organizational size. With modern transportation and communication facilities an organization at one spot in the world may obtain inputs from tremendous distances and send its outputs even further. With a dispersed set of bases, operational range—in terms of both the acquisition of inputs and the distribution of outputs —is extended still further.

Second, and still more important, the formal boundaries of an organization are no longer very important in determining organizational size. Organizations tend to cluster without formal amalgamation. Thus, statistics on the size of enterprises

> underestimate the extent of horizontal and vertical integration. Many organizations consist not of single enterprises but of clusters held together by holding companies, interlocking directorates and cartels. Moreover, many thousands of smaller companies are independent in name only. They operate in fact as controlled satellites of a giant supplier (as in the case of gasoline and automobile distributors) or of a giant buyer (as in the case of factories producing products exclusively for department stores, chain stores or mail order houses).[16]

But in the universe of complex organizational forms these clusterers are pygmies. The giants are the complex systems of interrelated enterprises, government organizations, and associations. Two typical examples are the American banking system and the American air transport system. Each of these is an intricate network of relations among private organizations, government agen-

16. Ibid., p. 44.

cies at various levels, trade associations, international bodies, employee, managerial and professional groups, informal groups, and a multitude of clients. Each may be appropriately described as a giant complex constellation. Such constellations play an increasingly important role in every society moving toward postindustrialism.

"Simple-Simon" Centralization?

In a recent book, Herbert A. Simon has propounded an exceedingly simple view on the process of centralization:

> When the cable and the wireless were added to the world's techniques of communication, the organization of every nation's foreign office changed. The ambassador and minister, who had exercised broad, discretionary decision-making functions in the previous decentralized system, were now brought under much closer central control. The balance between the costs in time and money of communication with the center, and the advantages of coordination by the center had been radically altered.[17]

So much for mobiletics. He then continues by propounding the theory that the computerization of business data-processing "will radically alter the balance of advantage between centralization and decentralization." Only by greater centralization will it be possible to deal with the two main issues: (1) "how we shall take advantage of the greater analytic capacity, the larger ability to take into account the interrelations of things, that the new developments in decision-making give us"; and (2) "how we shall deal with the technological fact that the processing of information within a coordinated computing system is orders of magnitude faster than the input-output rates at which we can communicate from one system to another, particularly where human links are involved." To this, Simon adds a list of weaknesses in "most existing decentralized organizational structure." He concludes with a flat prediction that "the new developments in decision-making will

17. Herbert A. Simon, *The New Science of Management Decision* (New York: Harper and Row, 1965), p. 104.

tend to induce more centralization in decision-making activities at middle management levels." [18]

The difficulty with such a simplistic approach is that it is based in large measure upon the old-fashioned dichotomy of centralization versus decentralization.[19] It assumes that formal organizational structure can be defined in terms of hierarchical relations alone, without consideration of the polyarchic (sometimes crudely referred to as "lateral") relations without which hierarchy would collapse. It confines itself to relatively small units (such as factories) and totally ignores the larger world of complex organizational clusters and constellations.

In both industrializing and postindustrializing societies there is a major tendency toward increased differentiation of organizations into specialized subsystems. This tendency is manifest even when an organization remains the same size. It is magnified as an organization grows or becomes interrelated with a larger cluster or constellation. Computerization itself—as with all forms of technological advances—means an increasing variety of group and individual roles based upon specialized knowledge and abilities. All this provides a major stimulus to decentralization. Specialized roles provide the "authority of the position" and monopolies or quasi monopolies of the power to do certain things. To this are added the authority given by express delegation and the power acquired by the more able and upward-moving people and groups. The stimulus to decentralization is probably greatest in the case of highly differentiated expert groups located at great distances from the central base in unusual and rapidly changing environments.

Another greater stimulus to decentralization is provided by the dispersion of bases and the widening of operational range. Obstacles to communication and face-to-face contact make it more difficult for top executives to exercise power, authority, and responsibility over dispersed subsystems or to acquire enough of the internal and environmental information needed for such exercise. These difficulties tend to vary with distance in space-time and the

18. Ibid., pp. 104–107.
19. The dangers of this dichotomous approach to government organization are well set forth in James W. Fesler, "Understanding of Decentralization," *The Journal of Politics* 27 (1965): 536–66.

special characteristics of a subsystem environment. When central office executives try to maintain tight control under such circumstances, the effects are usually impaired effectiveness in the subsystem's operations and de facto breakdowns of tight central control through informal—and even illegal—assumptions of power, authority, or responsibility by field subsystems.

As Simon correctly points out, mobiletics make it possible to overcome distance. But mobiletics by itself cancel out two important kinds of role differentiation which Simon entirely ignores:

1. Overlapping regional boundaries (or multiple grids), which are created when different field units operate in overlapping territories. This makes it impossible for regional offices to coordinate all activities in their region.

2. The multiplicity of subsystems at the center. In part, this decentralization at the center is promoted by natural tendencies toward differentiation and the necessity for specialized units to mirror (or at least handle) the multiple regional breakdowns. In part, it is directly promoted by the new requirements of computerization for new groups involved in the production, interpretation, and use of larger amounts of information. The threat of serious information overload cannot be handled without increased specialization. Many of the specialized units, in turn, particularly with the new communication and transportation facilities, will join hands with regional and local subdivisions, thereby adding to the decentralization of power.

An indispensable centralizing factor, of course, is provided by hierarchic (superior-subordinate) relations. These facilitate the inclusion of smaller within larger subsystems by providing legitimation for central power, formal channels for communication, conflict resolution and personal advancement, and symbols of system unity. On the other hand, even simple hierarchy provides an instrument of decentralization through delegation. The complexities of central planning and control require multiple hierarchy—particularly conspicuous in the multiple lines of subordination on the part of field office subsystems but no less crucial in the operations of central bases themselves. Any realistic description of large-scale organizations shows a very considerable dispersion of power—usually shifting from issue to issue—among and within the highest level governing directorates, the top executives, the bureaucrats, and (particularly where formally recognized) workers' representatives.[20] This dispersion probably increases within complex clusters and constellations.

But no differentiated formal organization can be held together by hierarchy alone. Polyarchic relations, both formal and informal, are also needed to provide a multiplicity of "lateral" interactions. These may be provided through the "joint responsibility" polyarchy of committees and councils and the "dispersed responsibility" polyarchy of budgetary and clearance procedures and other work flow arrangements. These relations are powerful centralizing factors in that they tend to knit subsystems together by recognizing and building upon their decentralized power.[21]

The response to these difficulties and tendencies is often characterized by pendulum swings of decentralization and recentralization. One major swing is provided by the modern doctrine of decentralization in giant organizations—as developed under the pressures of necessity by General Motors, Du Pont, Standard Oil (N.J.), and Sears, Roebuck,[22] now being extended by many government agencies. Centralized, functionally departmentalized organizations (themselves representing a pendulum swing from loose combinations) are converted into decentralized multidivisional structures. Field offices are given a larger role in government agencies. But in both cases this requires sophisticated central planning, indoctrination, training, and control. With the expansion and growing complexity of the organization, the central organs build up their power, authority, and responsibility—at first informally, later more openly. This centralizing swing is facilitated by computerized information processing and the shrinkage of space-time distance.

Under these circumstances, the only decision that can be lo-

20. Gross, *The Managing of Organizations,* chap. 3, "The Dispersion of Power in Organizations."
21. Ibid., sections on "Polyarchy: Coordinates" and "Hierarchy: Superiors and Subordinates" in chap. 15, "People-in-Organizations: Formal Aspects."
22. Alfred D. Chandler, Jr., *Strategy and Structure* (Cambridge: M.I.T. Press, 1962).

cated at any given spot is a tiny point in one small stream of many simultaneous sequential processes. Central power to make major decisions with significant consequences depends upon the development of subsystems with significant power. These subsystems are both the product of centralized power and the major internal restraint upon its continued exercise. Herein lies the double paradox of organizational centralization and decentralization: Namely, that (1) every act of centralization (or decentralization) is usually associated with some act of decentralization (or centralization), and (2) long-range trends within an organization usually indicate major pendulum swings between various forms of de- and re-centralization.

The Urban Revolution

The growth of organizational clusters and constellations has been roughly paralleled by the growth of urban areas with high population concentrations and spreading land areas. In the earlier stages of industrialization urbanism was characterized by overcrowded, festering slums. In the latter stages we see transportation congestion, air pollution, and lags in providing adequate housing and other basic facilities and services needed by an expanding population with ever higher demands. These difficulties customarily give rise to nostalgic visions of preserving the village (as with "garden cities"), or maintaining low population densities (as in the "class" ideology of city planning and public housing). Such visions represent an unwillingness to adjust to the inevitability of the advancing urban revolution and an underestimate of the urban advantages that can counterbalance the difficulties.

Yet, with time, the internal difficulties in urban areas are gradually—although unevenly—worked through. Although new difficulties are thereby created, the very improvements in urban living conditions and the new greater advantages afforded to large-scale organizations (even with a certain amount of dispersion to once rural areas) result in accelerated urban growth. Thus, the large city becomes Metropolis—or Technopolis. And many metropolitan areas spread far enough to merge into polynuclear urban regions that may be called "megalopoloi." Urbanists with a "city planning" focus may help handle the internal problems of Metropolis and Megalopolis—particularly as they learn to accept the inevitability of increased urban concentrations and to analyze urban entities in terms of intersecting social systems. But the larger problems of Metropolis and Megalopolis may well turn out to be not those of internal rationality but rather the urban revolution's implications for the secularization of society and the great leap of man from small spaces to space-time. To help understand some of these implications let us reflect a moment on the decline of the hinterlands, the rise of the Megalopolitans, and the spread of geographic entities without governments.

The Decline of the Hinterlands

The migration from the nonurban hinterlands results from two complementary forces. On the one hand, increasing numbers of people are "pushed" out of agriculture. As the technology of agricultural production improves, fewer people are needed on the farms. Full-scale industrialism, indeed, with the production of chemical fertilizers, mechanized farm equipment, and the ethos of the factory farm, often leads to greater long-range increments in agricultural efficiency than in any other sector. During the transition from preindustrialism farm population sooner or later declines from over 70 percent to less than 20 percent. In the United States the farm population fell from 35 percent in 1910 to less than 7 percent in 1965. Some time before 1980 it will fall below 5 percent. This will be one of the many signals that the United States has at last left the transitional and entered the postindustrial period.

On the other hand, people are pulled to the great urban areas because they provide: (1) a large, skilled, and varied labor force; (2) an infrastructure of basic public services; (3) suppliers of needed inputs; (4) ready access to communication and transportation media; and (5) opportunities for face-to-face communication with associates, competitors, and government controllers. In addition, they offer individuals and families greater opportunities for education, occupational choice, privacy and mobility,[23] culture, and recreation. These opportunities become increasingly important as modernizing agriculture needs fewer and fewer people.

One of the paradoxes that plague both industrialism and post-industrialism is that people desire simultaneously physical separation and physical proximity. The desire for physical separation within the home, the office, and the factory is associated with personal and group needs for differentiation. The desire for physical proximity is associated with psychological needs for togetherness and social needs for cooperation and interdependent action. The large urban area goes far toward meeting these apparently conflicting interests. This is done by a combination of: (1) high-rise construction (will there be much more low depth construction?), which increases the ratio of people to area; (2) horizontal spread (or sprawl), which at first glance may seem to decrease people-land ratios but, in effect, expands the overall area of high population concentration; and (3) intra-urban transportation and communication, which facilitate both population concentration and spread. Indeed, the urban area provides opportunities for men, women, and children—in the privacy of the individual family—to be in touch with the entire world. "Technopolitan man," writes Harvey Cox, "sits at a vast and immensely complicated switchboard. He is *homo symbolicus,* man the communicator, and the metropolis is a massive network of communications. A whole world of possibilities for communication lies within his reach. The contemporary urban region represents an ingenious device for vastly enlarging the scope of human communication and widening the scope of individual choice. . . ."[24]

In a mature postindustrial society, a more advanced mobiletic revolution will someday render obsolete many of the advantages of the spatial proximity provided by urban concentration. Low-cost, universally available, closed-circuit television will someday make it possible to have face-to-face communication with any-

23. In his profound *The Secular City* (New York: Macmillan, 1965), Harvey Cox regards anonymity (privacy) and mobility as the main elements in the "shape" of the new "secular city" or "technopolis," chap. 2. Pragmatism and this-worldliness (profanity) are regarded as the secular city's "style."
24. Ibid., p. 40.

one, or any willing group, in a matter of seconds. Low-cost rocket transport and vertical takeoff and landing aircraft (both large-scale and individual) will make it possible to get anywhere in the world, or move things anywhere, in remarkably short periods of time. Together, these developments will drastically counteract present tendencies toward the concentration of population.

In the meantime, however (and the "meantime" will probably last through the end of this century), we are sure of seeing increasing dominance of urban areas—in politics, economics, arts, and sciences. Villages, towns, and small cities, in fact, will be increasingly drawn into the web of urbanization [25] and become psychologically suburbanized. Under these conditions decentralization programs become little more than minor political payoffs to nonurban areas to alleviate the adjustment of growing urbanism. Or else the banner of "decentralization" is sagaciously waved in efforts to promote and control the growth of a very small number of new urban concentrations—as in the "new look" in French national planning.[26] This might be called "dispersed centralization" or "concentrated dispersion."

The Rise of the Megalopolitans

A megalopolis may be roughly defined as a geographical area with a highly concentrated population of at least 30 million people and a high concentration of governmental, financial, scientific, and cultural activity. In this sense the term was first used by Gottmann with reference to the urban sprawl on the Northeast coast of the United States from Boston to Richmond.[27] Wattenberg and Scammon point out that the "statistics formed by the northeast megalopolis are staggering." Their analysis of the latest census data leads to a still more staggering conclusion: "what is already apparent is that the eastern megalopolis will not stand alone for too much longer." [28] Most city metropolitan planners are still

25. Arthur J. Vidich and Joseph Bensman, *Small Town in Mass Society* (Garden City, Doubleday, 1958).
26. Commissariat du Plan, *Reflexions sur 1985* (Paris, la Documentation Française, 1965).
27. Jean Gottmann, *Megalopolis* (New York Twentieth Century Fund, 1961).
28. Ben J. Wattenberg and Richard M. Scammon, *This U.S.A.* (Garden City, Doubleday, 1965), p. 86.

afraid to think in the terms they use to detail the growth of America's future megalopoli:

> We can see the beginnings of other megalopoli in different areas. One is clearly forming along the southwestern end of Lake Michigan, comprised of Gary-Hammond–East Chicago, Chicago, Kenosha, Racine and Milwaukee; another smaller megalopolis is growing from Miami north to Fort Lauderdale and beyond; still another megalopolis may one day connect Los Angeles and San Francisco–Oakland (with Fresno in the middle) but this will take a long time in the coming; and a fifth urban belt may eventually link Detroit and Cleveland with Toledo in the middle, or Cleveland and Pittsburgh with Youngstown in between.[29]

One may dispute the exact location and composition of these future megalopoli. One may even disagree with Wattenberg and Scammon on the exact number. Yet the framework of the debate will certainly be within the 3-to-5 range. In other words, it seems certain that the United States will soon become a "multi-megalopolitan" nation. When one considers that a megalopolis is a huge concentration not merely of people but of wealth, science, influence, and prestige, this may be seen as one of the most significant facts in the distribution of power throughout the world. After all, there are very few other countries—probably only the Soviet Union, China, and India—that can be expected to attain "multi-megalopolitan" rank. Most of the nations with large, growing, and prestigious capitals can never expect to include more than one megalopolis. These will consist of the vast urban regions growing up around such capitals as Paris, London, Tokyo, and Rome. As suggested in Table 3, the number of "uni-megalopolitan" nations by 2000 A.D. will probably be no more than nine. To provide leeway for error in the prediction, one may add the qualifying phrase "plus or minus three." Yet it is highly improbable that twelve nations will ever reach uni-megalopolitan rank. It is much more likely that some of the major megalopoli will merge one into the other—as with the possible linkage of London and Paris in a vast

29. Ibid., p. 87.

Table 3. *Estimated World Distribution of Megalopoli, 2000* A.D.

Nation types	Total	North America	South America	Europe	Asia and Middle East	Africa
Multi-Megalopolitan	4	1: U.S.		1: U.S.S.R.	2: China Japan	
Uni-Megalopolitan	9		2: Brazil Argentina	5: France Britain Germany Poland Italy	1: Japan	1: Egypt
Demi-Megalopolitan	2			2: Belgium Netherlands		
Non-Megalopolitan	All the rest (about 100 of present-day countries)					

urban region within which the English Channel (soon to be bridged by a tunnel as well as by plane and boat) would be a pleasant waterway instead of a divider. Such developments would increase somewhat the number of "demi-megalopolitan" countries, those which share a single megalopolis with other nations. In any case, it is highly unlikely that many more than fifteen of the present nations of the world will be megalopolitan, multi-, uni-, or demi-. The great bulk of the world's nations will unquestionably be non-megalopolitan.

The megalopoli of the future will transcend national boundaries. They will provide the home bases and regional offices of organizations engaging in operations that encircle the world. They will become the major "reference points" in the minds of elites from non-megalopolitan areas throughout the world. Around the megalopoli will develop a megalopolitan culture much broader and more diverse than the cosmopolitan culture which developed in the large cities of the past. The elites based in one megalopolis will develop intimate associations with people and organizations in many other megalopoli. Indeed, they will get to know other megalopoli much better than the hinterlands of their own country. The term "Acumenopolis" has been used to describe the interconnections between the world's megalopoli by the time that supersonic air transport makes certain that no megalopolis is more than an hour or two away from any other.[30] A far cry from the "City of God," by 2000 A.D. the mobiletic community of "Acumenopolis" will probably be the "City of the Elite Man."

Territorial Entities Without Governments

As the metropolitan areas grow, there is a sharp decline in the number of "over-bounded" and "true-bounded" cities: that is, cities whose legally fixed geographical areas are larger than or equal to the urban aggregate. The typical city in a metropolitan area is "underbounded."[31] For decades urban reformers have sought to solve this problem by extending the boundaries of core cities—through consolidation or annexation—so that city government may become the governments of metropolitan areas. As Roscoe Martin and others have repeatedly pointed out, such efforts have not been successful. Thus, in the United States "212 metropolitan areas have not 212 governments but 87 times that number."[32] The conversion of large metropoli into megalopoli administers the coup de grace to the vision of the true-bounded urban region with a local government capable of unified action throughout the area.

Even where old city boundaries are extended—as in the recent case of London—the new boundaries will not contain (in the sense of stop) urban spread. In a short time, in fact, the territorial boundaries of the new metropolitan government may include a smaller proportion than before of the expanding metropolis. For boundary expansion to keep up with urban spread, metropolitan government would probably then require decentralization among —or devolution to—a number of smaller territorial unts. A multiplicity of localized government would thus be recreated.

30. This term was first used by C. A. Doxiadis of the Athens Institute of Ekistics.
31. These concepts are set forth in greater detail in Kingsley Davis et al., *The World's Metropolitan Areas* (Berkeley and Los Angeles: University of California Press, 1959).
32. Roscoe Martin, *The Cities and the Federal System* (New York: Atherton, 1965), p. 182.

The political boundaries of the urban governments within metropoli and megalopoli are rendered still less significant by another fact that has received little attention: the boundary-transcending nature of the major subsystems within the urban region. Any territorial entity is an aggregation of the other social systems —individuals, groups, and formal organizations. The variety of possible territorial entities, together with the other social systems included within them, is set forth in Table 4. From the village, local community, and neighborhood, we move on to the larger entities such as towns, urban regions, larger subnational regions, regions, nations, international regions, and the world itself. In the present-day world even the peasant village in Asia or Africa is an extremely open system—with many inhabitants moving back and forth between village and town, and with many local offices and representatives of nationwide government agencies or enterprises. As already suggested, the megalopolis is an open system par excellence. Many of its most important people have only one foot (or one finger) in this megalopolis. They spend much of their active time in other megalopoli. They may live in the remote hinterlands. Their loyalties are not geographically determined. This boundary transcendence is even stronger with respect to large organizations, with bases in many other urban regions and with operational ranges embracing much larger areas. The megalopolis is thus a very segmented community, a convenient intersection of overlapping social systems with interests far beyond its boundaries. Accordingly, the problems involved in planning, financing, and providing basic services and facilities in metropoli and megalopoli become nationwide problems.

Accordingly, there can be no simple, ready-made pattern for the government of huge urban regions. Governmental activity in these areas will inevitably be characterized by polyarchic relations among (1) many local (or intermediate-level) governments, the national government, and the many agencies of each (with all sorts of representative bodies for mutual consultation), and (2) an increasing number of functional authorities and planning groups (public or mixed) cutting across many local boundaries. Within any such area major power and the major sources of initiative and

Table 4. Varieties of Social Systems

Levels	Groups[1]			Formal Organizations[1]				Territorial[2] Entities
	People[1]	Informal groups	Families	Associations	Enterprises	Govt. agencies	Govts.	
1. Micro-systems	Individuals	Small groups	Nuclear families	Single associations	Single enterprise units	Single agencies	Local govts.	Villages Local communities Neighborhoods
2. System clusters		Mobs Crowds	Extended families	Local, state, & regional federations	Multi-unit enterprises or groups	Agency groups	Inter-govt. bodies, state & regional	Towns & cities Metropoli Megalopoli Intranational
3. System constellations			Tribes	National federations	National multi-unit enterprises or groups	Nationwide agencies	National states (unitary) or fed.	States and regions Nations
4. Macro-systems				International federations	International multi-unit enterprises or groups	International agencies	Internat'l regional systems "World-wide" govt. federations	International regions World

1. These columns include only simple systems. Complex systems are networks composed of formal organizations (usually different types), groups, and individuals.
2. As here defined, "territorial entity" includes a variety of other social systems within its spatial boundaries. Almost every territorial entity is a complex system.

growth will tend to be distributed among a number of overlapping complex clusters.

The Birthpangs of a World Society

For centuries idealists have dreamed of some future world society. With or without a "parliament of man," this dream has usually been seen as some blissful state of utopian rationality. For "anti-utopians" it has been seen as a new form of regimentation. Today, unheralded and uncelebrated, a world society is slowly and painfully coming into being. It is characterized by the growth of increasingly interdependent nations, both industrializing and postindustrializing, of world-spanning organizations, of urban world centers, and of world-oriented elites. This growing interdependence is facilitated by communication-transportation systems that, for some activities, are continuously decreasing the space-time distance between Washington and Moscow more rapidly than that between Washington and Wichita or Moscow and Minsk.

The emerging "one world" hardly conforms to the visions of the utopians—any more than does the giant organization to "classical" ideas of administration, the megalopolis to the models of city planners, or the "great societies" to Keynesian theory. The world society includes a bewildering variety of subsystems increasingly locked together in conflict-cooperation relationships. The world polity is characterized by polycentric conflict, intersecting coalitions, continuing outbreaks of localized violence, many possibilities of "escalation," and spreading capacities for nuclear destruction. The political instrumentalities of conflict resolution and regional and world integration operate—as in nations, states, and cities—in an atmosphere of pressure and power politics, behind-the-scene lobbying, rotten borough representation, moralistic double-talk, deception, and self-deception. The world economy tends to be disorderly—neither free nor planned. The world culture, on the one hand, tends to submerge national characteristics and values in a homogenizing flood of material goods and international styles. On the other hand, it includes vast value differences and sharp value conflicts. Like Megalopolis, the world society is a territorial entity without a government. It is an all-inclusive complex macrosystem with remarkably complicated and unpredictable— although increasingly structured—mechanisms of mutual adjustment.

Let us explore this strange new world by taking a brief look at some transnational (albeit latent) functions of nationalism, some aspects of national boundary transcendence, and the emerging structure of world power.

Nationalism As "Ego Maturation"

How can a world society be emerging at a time when nationalism is rampant? Is it not likely that the nationalistic forces at work in the preindustrial nations driving toward industrialism will prevent a world society?

One answer to these questions is that rampant nationalism, at worst, will make the world society a dangerous place in which to live. In less somber terms it will give our "one world" a more heterogenous set of subsocieties. Another answer is to suggest that even the most utopian form of internationalism would be meaningless without territorial subdivisions. If we had a world government, the first thing it would have to do would be to create territorial subdivisions. But these would be meaningless without the breath of life within them—and that breath would mean substantive equivalents of nationalism or regionalism, probably both.

In a more fundamental sense, we may view nation-building in Africa and Asia as an important step in the building of more intimate transnational relations. At the level of the individual (who may also be regarded as a social system) we see a parallel phenomenon, albeit with smaller compass. With individuals, according to modern psychology, a sense of personal identity is a prerequisite for cooperative relations with others. Yet the emergence of the ego usually leads to considerable difficulties in the period of adolescence. The stormy period of nation-building might thus be regarded as "national" adolescence."

The Sturm und Drang of national adolescence may take much

longer, and lead to far greater difficulties, than personal adolescence. In Western Europe the nation-building process covered centuries of recurring bloodshed. Today the experience of Africa, Asia, and the Middle East suggests that this process, though less prolonged and less bloody, will precipitate one world crisis after another. It will also hold back the process of building supranational regional groups. A clear example of this is East Africa, where each nation is interested both in nation-building and in the development of their resources through an East African federation. The conflict between these two goals has been described as follows:

> The two efforts compete for the time and energy of a small minority of leaders and for the meager resources at their disposal. If state planning to construct a nation may be likened to the conduct of a war, an effort to build a transnational system at the same time would be like conducting a war on two fronts. It could mean defeat on both. Indeed, one might even offer the hypothesis that peaceful transnational federation is possible only if the units that federate are really nations. . . . nation-building and nationalism may be seen as a prerequisite of international cooperation. Although it may lead in some cases to totalistic or aggressive nationalism, it also provides the building blocks for subsequent transnational groupings and produces more mature actors in an emerging world society.[33]

The Transcendence of National Boundaries

Despite the vigor of nationalism, the last half of the twentieth century is witnessing an unparalleled amount of transnational activity. On the basis of the mobiletic revolution itself, we can readily agree with Bruce Russett in his perceptive comment that today " 'one world' has a meaning beyond the understanding even of those who lived just a generation ago." [34] Beyond mobiletics, how-

33. Bertram M. Gross, "The Gamesmanship of National Planning," prefatory comment to Fred G. Burke, *Tanganyika: Preplanning* (Syracuse: Syracuse University Press, 1965), p. xxii.
34. Bruce M. Russett, *Trends in World Politics* (New York: Macmillan, 1965), pp. 17–18.

number of multinational organizations. Among the latter are inter-organizations that operate in many countries and by the growing boundary-transcendence provided by wide-ranging nation-based formance facilitated by mobiletics. One of these is found in the national organizations, functional regional agencies, international cartels and commodity agreements, professional associations, labor federations, and international churches.

A second form is provided by a variety of multinational groupings. Among these are such blocs and alliances as those represented by NATO, the Warsaw pact, the European Economic Community, and COMECOM. There are also many spatially dispersed coalitions and alliances—such as the "free world," the "Communist world," the Russian bloc, the Communist bloc, and various efforts to build a "third force."

Still another form is international conflict itself. The ultimate form of international conflict—full nuclear world war—would unquestionably integrate the planet either by leaving it a biophysical system undisturbed by much human life or providing enough crisis conditions and common interests to being the survivors together under some form of world government. Lesser forms of international conflict themselves lead to crisis that can be handled only through resort to various forms of transnational and international activity and control. Indeed, there is even a sense in which the far-reaching scale of international conflicts helps bring parties at conflict together. In analyzing social organization, Simmel long ago pointed out that conflict is the other side of the coin of cooperation. "A certain amount of discord, inner divergence and outer controversy is organically tied up with the very elements that ultimately hold the group together." [35] Similarly, in his efforts to make game theory more relevant to the real world, Schelling uses the terms "bargaining game" and "mixed motive game" to refer to the "mixture of mutual dependence and conflict, of partnership and competition" found in many international conflicts.[36]

35. George Simmel, *Conflict*, trans. Kurt H. Wolff (New York: Free Press, 1955), pp. 17–18.
36. Thomas C. Schelling, *The Strategy of Conflict* (Cambridge: Harvard University Press, 1960), pp. 83–118.

It is interesting to note that the international "gamesmanship" of nation-builders, while oriented toward welding disparate tribes into genuine nations, may nonetheless contribute to the broader conflict processes that knit the entire world more closely together.

The leaders of pre-industrial states face two inescapable facts of life. The first—well documented in innumerable reports and conferences of the United Nations—is that truly rapid development is impossible without substantial assistance from more industrialized societies. The second, although equally obvious, is one of those great secrets that everyone knows but nobody is supposed to talk about openly: the great powers seem more inclined to provide large amounts of development assistance without strings only when they believe they are offsetting the influence of a rival power. Thus, not only in Africa but throughout Asia and the Middle East, shrewd nationalist leaders have won substantial increments of assistance (and room for more autonomous maneuvering) by playing the Russians against the Americans and the Americans against the Russians.[37]

A more recent gambit in this international gamesmanship has been to play the Chinese against both the Americans and the Russians. Although this may be regarded as playing with fire, this is the kind of thing that brings different nations closer together. The proximity need not necessarily mean violence. In fact, there are conditions under which the playing of various sides against each other may lead to cooling, rather than fanning, the fires of international conflict. The donor country is inevitably interested in propaganda on its own behalf. But the most successful propaganda is the propaganda of the deed. No amount of publicity or speechmaking can cover up a downright failure. Thus, in the field of foreign aid American, Russian, and Chinese groups, with their allies from other countries, are inevitably engaged in peaceful competition. No matter how virulent the words of the Chinese may be, their actions involve them in competitive coexistence.

37. Gross, "The Gamesmanship of National Planning," p. xiv.

What is more, the logic of competition—as has so often been proved true in ordinary markets—often leads to various forms of cooperation.[38]

Let it also be added the international conflict no longer operates on the basis of interactions between nation-states as self-contained decisional units. Formal relations among states are now but a small part of statecraft. The new style of foreign policy is "infusive diplomacy" based upon informal penetration. This method of influence may be used upon allies and neutrals as well as opponents. Its purposes may range from the molding of policies and institutions and the strengthening of the nation affected to the breakdown of the nation affected. Its targets may be minority groups, political parties, key elites, trade unions, or enterprises. The techniques of informal penetration are both overt and covert. On the one hand, as Andrew Scott has pointed out in *The Revolution in Statecraft*, they include cultural exchange programs, technical assistance, economic aid, military aid, military training missions, and information and propaganda activities. On the other hand, they may include "the use of front organizations, financial subsidy of various organizations, the use of economic warfare techniques, organization of guerrilla warfare, sabotage, strikes and riots, establishment of military party formations, and the organization of *coups d'etat*." These informal access operations "are playing an increasingly larger role in the foreign policy activities of the major nations."[39] All in all, Scott concludes, they have contributed to "the progressive breakdown of the inviolable nation-state."[40]

The Triad in the Concentric Circles

Until World War I, a "multiple system" of world power existed in Europe. This system, as Hans Morgenthau has pointed out, was distinguished by "a number of units of approximately equal strength which combine and oppose each other in ever changing alignments." Its main characteristics were "flexibility, uncertainty

38. Ibid., p. xvi.
39. Andrew M. Scott, *The Revolution in Statecraft* (New York: Random House, 1965), pp. 9–12.
40. Ibid., p. 172.

as to the relative strength and future policies of its members, and the propensity for limited, inconclusive wars." [41] World War I saw the breakdown of this multiple system and its precarious balance of power.

The two world wars of the twentieth century brought more structure and less flexibility into the international dispersion of power. By 1945 there emerged a totally new international setup, a bipolar system with the United States and Russia at opposing poles. The bipolar system is characterized by "the predominance of two major powers of approximately equal strength, around which the other members are grouped in different degrees of closeness." This system is "rigid and stable as long as the approximately equal distribution of power between its two predominant members persist. Any marked shift in that distribution threatens the system with destruction." [42] By 1966 the bipolar system had been destroyed. In part, this has been brought about by polycentrism on both sides. Within the Russian orbit, there has been a major split between the Chinese and the Russians. Considerable independence is being exercised by most of the Communist countries in Eastern Europe. In the American orbit the Atlantic alliance has weakened considerably. Britain has been split off from Europe. NATO, considerably weakened, faces a major reorganization, perhaps replacement.

But the central fact in the destruction of the bipolar system is something far more significant than polycentrism within the two blocs. It is the slow but steady emergence of China, the largest nation in the world, as a third center of world power. This emergence has been marked by active Chinese diplomacy and foreign assistance in Africa and Asia, by the seizure of Tibet and the border conflicts with India. It has been characterized by direct conflicts with the Russians within the international Communist movement and direct confrontations with the United States through its support for North Vietnam and the Viet Cong.

By 1975, it has been estimated, the population of the mainland

41. Hans J. Morgenthau, *The Restoration of American Politics* (Chicago: University of Chicago Press, 1962), p. 168.
42. Ibid., p. 198.

China will exceed 915 million. This means that of every 100 people in the world at least 23 will be mainland Chinese.[43] By the same date, it is likely that China's GNP will rise to 7 percent of world GNP—as contrasted with about 2.1 for India.[44] The only countries with a larger GNP will probably be the United States, Russia, and West Germany. Unlike West Germany, however, there is no doubt that by that time China will be a major nuclear power. More specifically, by 1975 China will probably be able to hit any country in the world with nuclear bombs carried by intercontinental ballistic missiles. As distinguished from such "second class" members in the Nuclear Club as Britain, France, and other countries that may "get in," by 1975 China will be a "first class" member alongside the United States and Russia.

In my view, the emerging world society cannot be understood without recognizing the new triadic relationship that is developing among the big three: the United States, Russia, and China. Yet I am not suggesting that an understanding of the world ever develops automatically among world leaders. In the case of both the United States and Russia, there is reason to suspect that many top leaders are so uneasy about China's rise to power that they are unwilling to accept the facts of life. Many American leaders are still unwilling to give de jure diplomatic recognition to China or to withdraw objections to China's entry into the United Nations. Some are reputed to favor the bombing of China's nuclear installations before the Chinese develop their delivery capacity. Many Russian leaders cannot adjust at all to the fact that in the world Communist movement Russia can no longer be the "socialist fatherland." They feel they must "contain" China's drive for leadership among the more militant Communist parties. Accordingly, it may take some time before either Americans or Russians face up to facts and begin to adapt their policies to the realities of world power.

On the other hand, the world power structure cannot be understood only by focusing upon the new triad. As suggested in Figure 2, the Big Three are surrounded by an intermediate circle com-

Figure 2. *The Triad in the Concentric Circles*

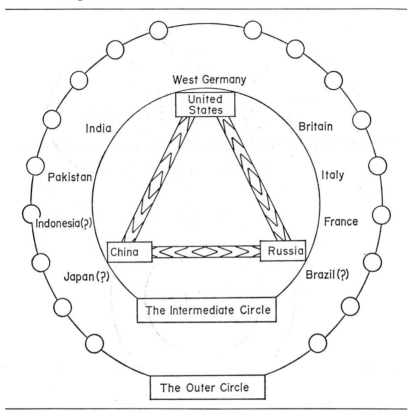

posed of six to nine great powers. These, in turn, are surrounded by an outer circle composed of all the other nations. The place of any nation in these concentric circles, naturally, may change sharply from time to time. Indonesia, Japan, and Brazil may never enter the intermediate circle. Any one or two that are already there may move to the outer circle. Two or three countries from the outer circle may conceivably break into the intermediate circle. Each of the Big Three, moreover, will develop its own sphere of influence. This is illustrated in Figure 3. But spheres of influence will no longer be monopolistically controlled. The United States will develop bastions, allies, or business partners on the borders of Russia and China, Russia on the borders of China,

Figure 3. *Triadic Interpenetration*

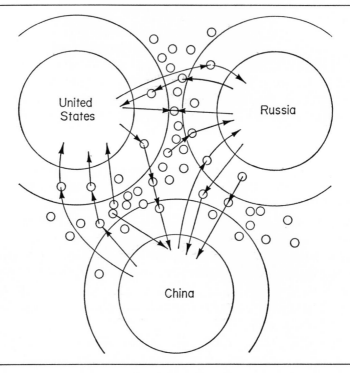

and the United States and China on the borders of the United States and Russia. What is more, each member of the triad will use the technique of penetration to influence the other two and the closest allies of the other two. Neither their own boundaries nor those of their allies will be impenetrable. This means triadic interpenetration.

Thus, in a certain sense, we are returning to a multiple system of power. Like the "balance of power" system before World War I, it too will be characterized by flexibility, uncertainty, and a propensity for limited, inconclusive wars. On the other hand, unless the Big Three can reach a working accommodation, it will be far more precarious. It will also be a truly worldwide, rather than a Europe-based system, a system whose successes and failures will determine the future of the new world society.

The Loss—and Discovery—of Man

Surrounded by giant organizations, metropoli, and megalopoli, embedded in the world society of industrializing and postindustrializing nations, stands the smallest of all social systems: man himself. With the world shrinking in space-time, will people themselves shrink—as Durkheim suggested—into anonymous specks in a cloud of dust, into tiny territorial entities with no internal self-government and boundaries shattered by the intrusion of other systems? With a totally unprecedented increase in the number of individuals, will there be a corresponding decline in the value of each one? The "literature of anti-organizational revolt"— authored by Marx, Schweitzer, Orwell, Mumford, Huxley, Kafka, William H. Shyte, Fromm, Argyris, Marcuse, and many others— accuses large-scale systems and science-based society of treating individuals like cogs in a machine, subordinating them to organizational tyranny, alienating them from truly human relations with others or promoting mental breakdown.[45] The implication is that the individuality of people will be lost.

In rebutting these attacks, Harvey Cox refers to "the peculiar psychological need our culture feels to stick pins in organization-man dolls. . . . It is a residual element of tribalism, a fetish whereby the organization people purify themselves and stay in the organization without assuming responsibility for the battle raging inside. It is a ritual by which they deny the distasteful reality, settle for a pseudo-protest, and thus abdicate the controls to others. It is a dodge."[46] In my judgment the anti-organizational revolt is something more than a dodge. The leaders of this revolt have themselves contributed to the finding of man. By giving expression and release to the dehumanizing pressures of the new world society, they have made these pressures easier to bear. Unwittingly, they have fanned the flames of individualism, which

45. This literature is rather fully summarized in "Threats to Society," chap. 3 in Gross, *The Managing of Organizations.*
46. Cox, *The Secular City,* p. 180.

can often thrive in strange and wondrous ways in the bureaucratic jungle. They have helped strengthen the case of those (Harlan Cleveland, Leonard R. Sayles, Dwight Waldo, and others) who believe—as I do—as the planet shrinks, the individual personality has greater opportunity to grow and develop.[47]

Our case, very simply, is that in the new world of giant social systems many men and women will discover themselves for the first time. We say this not merely because we know how petty and stultifying can be the tyranny of the small organization, the small town, the small village, and the extended family. We say this because, in more positive terms, we know that the "big system" world can provide: (1) opportunities for personal and family privacy in urban areas; (2) opportunities for nonconformity (sometimes masked by surface conformity), strategies of revolt, and "bureaucratic creativity" in large organizations; (3) varied opportunities for personal choice in complex systems, including opportunities to escape domination by one system through membership in many; (4) valuable prerequisites for widespread self-development and self-fulfillment: material security, commergence (belonging), and differentiation (status, respect, power); and (5) the expansion of individual "life space" (or "life space-time") in terms not only of home base territoriality but of operational range through increased physical mobility and communication inputs from the past and all over the world.

All this adds up to the possibility of a rebirth of individualism—but organizational individualism rather than the isolated individualism of withdrawal or irresponsibility.

Moreover, in postindustrial societies the potentialities of this new form of individualism will probably become more widespread with (1) advancing education, specialization, and professionalization; (2) the more humanized relations that may result when

47. This point of view has been set forth in the series of essays and studies in Leonard R. Sayles, ed., *Individualism and Big Business* (New York: McGraw-Hill, 1963). "Dinosaurs and Personal Freedom" (chap. 2 in his book) by Harlan Cleveland deals with big organizations generally, not merely Big Business. In this classic piece Cleveland contends: "The result of bigness is actually a diffusion of the decision-making and decision-influencing process far beyond the wildest dreams of those worshippers at the shrine of Louis Brandeis, who wanted to keep power diffused by keeping the units of society small" (p. 11).

machines take over routinized work and leave nonroutinized work to people; (3) the increased blending of work, education, and leisure; (4) the decline of authoritarian management and control; (5) the greater tolerance for diversity that seems to accompany urbanization and secularization; and (6) the improved understanding of the needs of men, which are the only sound basis for the "rights of man."

On the other hand, some people will be crushed spiritually because of the discrepancies created by uneven rates of change and their inability to cope with the conflicts, complexities, and uncertainties always associated with new freedoms.

This is not a case of either-or. Bodily destruction through nuclear or postnuclear warfare is probably the only circumstance under which supersystems and superscience can destroy the human spirit. If human life on the planet survives, the circumstances will surely be mixed. Many people will be crushed or torn apart by new agonies of internal conflict, new forms of dictatorship and imperialism. More people than ever before will be liberated from the tyranny of hunger, disease, and ignorance. Most people will probably—at one and the same time—be subjected to new constraints and enjoy the possibility, if not the actual fruit, of new freedoms. The old Four Horsemen of Poverty, Ignorance, Pestilence, and Squalor will in part be replaced by the new Four Horsemen of Pride, Self-Satisfaction, Satiety, and Aggression. At the same time, many people will find new horizons of self-fulfillment, self-actualization, and self-development on behalf of interests broader than themselves. Although on our shrunken planet everyone will be closer together than ever before, this will still be a world in which the human condition (despite apparent uniformities) will be tremendously varied. The new world society will still be a place in which the true condition of man will not be known by man.

Chapter 7

Conclusions

James J. Heaphey

The preceding chapters indicate the significance of the spatial dimension in development administration. In this concluding chapter we will attempt to interrelate concepts put forward in the introductory chapter with materials from the chapters following it. We do so with no expectation that we will be definitive. All that this volume can do is to take a step, hopefully a large one, into the spatial dimension. Surely there is more about that dimension not covered in this volume than is covered. But we believe that the aspects with which we have dealt are crucial to development administration.

In all the preceding chapters malleability of spatial realities and development is stressed. From the microcosm of Henry Hart's village to the macrocosm of Bertram Gross's universe it is apparent that man can, does, and must change his spatial world as he participates in the process of development. Hart writes about small, incremental changes, whereas Gross points to tremendous, rapid, and wholesale changes. Where one conceives himself on the scale may itself be a primary indicator of developmental stage. It was the Americans' ability to manage spatial change that accounts for American development, at least in part, documents Emmette Redford in his chapter. If the early Americans had been willing to settle for northeastern United States, if they had not experimentally yet systematically taken advantage of the "rest of the country," then, of course, the story of American development would have been quite different. It is illuminating also to note the obverse, that what are generally regarded as America's most serious internal development problems are associated with America's failure to be spatially flexible. Despite all the efforts given to the conceptualization of spatial readjustments for our major cities (concepts involving metropolitan government, different relationships between suburbs and inner city, and so forth) America has simply failed to make any significant spatial readjustments, and we need not dwell on the misery of the cities to make the point. Similarly, there are many who feel that our international political theory suffers from a lack of precision in America's relationship to other areas of the world, such as, of course, Southeast Asia.

Increased productivity, in both the American and Russian cases, appears to have been a value that enabled the Americans and Russians to deal with space as a resource and strategy rather than as a traditionally fixed entity. As Redford points out, the spatial strategies for economic development that occurred in the United States were not inherent in the spatial dimension itself. A variety of other strategies might have been developed. What is important is that a strategy was developed. From the first inefficient years of experience with the Articles of Confederation, Americans knew that they lacked ways to articulate rationally land, water, routes, and individual state boundaries. They knew that a national strategy, imposed upon the individual states, was required. Yet flexibility—what we termed "nontransitivity"—was maintained, essentially because there was never the opportunity to have it otherwise. There was no possibility of imposing a completely national approach on the country at that stage of its growth. And even if there had been the opportunity, it is probable that the pragmatic orientation of the Americans would have militated against a passion for transitivity and fixation on certain spatial approaches.

Jerry Hough's analysis of the Soviet experience will probably come as a surprise to some. The Soviet spatial strategy appears to be less rigid, transitive, and unyielding to common sense than some might have supposed. The similarity between the Russian pragmatic production orientation and that of the Americans, and the effect of that orientation on spatial problems, is striking. One might essay a pseudo-geopolitical hypothesis suggesting that the vast sizes of the United States and Russia forced the people of those countries to adopt spatial strategies around the concept of production. But such a hypothesis could not survive for long. More plausible is the hypothesis that because in both countries there were ample resources to encourage a productively oriented development vision, and because it was in the nature of the ideology of the peoples of both countries to adopt such a vision as an action imperative, the United States and Russia pursued the spatial strategies that Hough and Redford have analyzed. This hypothesis might explain those two cases, it surely cannot predict other cases with certainty. Although, for example, Indonesia cannot rival the United States or the USSR in natural resources, it does enjoy considerable resource wealth and it does need a spatial strategy for rational articulation of its parts. As yet, that strategy has not emerged, though recent developments suggest it may do so.

Perhaps there is something in space-time vision which helps account for the orientation of the United States and USSR as we have been discussing it. In both cases a sense of mission, history, and change was predominant. Americans, at least American leadership, saw themselves as acting out the steps of a historical mission. When the Communists took over in Russia, they did so with their own vision of a historical mission. An interesting manifestation of this is the way in which both Americans and Russians are able to think in terms of two different temporal dimensions simultaneously. Hough points out that violation of rules leads to criticism, yet not necessarily punishment; indeed, the criticism might be followed by reward. In one temporal framework a man can be wrong (the present), whereas he could be right in another (the future). He is wrong in the present because he violates a current ruling, and what would life be like if all people did as they pleased rather than followed rules? He is right in the future, because if his action is successful, it is a step toward development. Is not American life very much this way? Was it not particularly this way during this country's history of intensive industrialization? Were not the robber barons both criticized and praised simultaneously? Criticized for what they were doing in the present, praised for what they were doing for the country (i.e., the future).

Another thing which is strikingly similar between the United States and USSR is the insistence upon a vast system of overlapping controls. This system has led more than one observer to criticize both countries as having unnecessarily confused, inarticulate, authority structures. The first Hoover Commission referred to the American administrative scene as an old farm where various bits and pieces had been added with no concern for overall plan and neatness of authority. Hough says that for purposes of deconcentration the USSR is not Weberian. And we certainly know that the United States system is not (through all governmental forms) one hierarchy of clearly stated authority.

In any case, it is wise to heed Hough's admonition that we not forget what Weber said about rationality. We should not expect it to emerge, coupled to a production-process orientation, in every culture. Hart's analysis of caste-culture in India and Pakistan reinforces this. Perhaps the major error of some community-development efforts was the presumption that every cultivator in every village desires to increase his agricultural production. There appears to be sufficient evidence to establish the proposition that at least some villagers in some cultures do not want to increase their production beyond the subsistence level. And, when it is suggested to them that they really do want to do so, it is possible that they seriously mistrust the person making the suggestion.

Hart indicates that "demonstration effects" with new technologies manifesting productivity is a way to escape the connotation of limited good. When, for example, diesel pumps and tractors are introduced into a static economy, there is the possibility of avoiding the perception that one man's gain must be another man's loss. This is quite compatible with the analyses of Hough and Redford, both of whom stress the massive introduction of new technology with the capacity for dramatic increases in production. In addition, Hough stresses the concentration upon technological rather than legal training in Soviet administration, and the emphasis on technological rather than legal goals and processes in the administrative process.

Hart's paper reveals problems of spatial inflexibility at the most basic and fundamental level of operations, just as it demonstrates possibilities for flexibility at that level. The idea of playing upon the villager's appetite for more goods and services and using that to foster new and productive spatial dimensions through which production, marketing, and distribution can take place is wrought with difficulties. Culture and space are interwoven in village culture in such a way that changes in the physical space in which human interaction takes place can be major threats to the integrity of the culture. Professor Hart's observations take us a long way toward understanding why, as we noted in a statement by Albert Waterston in the introductory chapter, planning for economic regions is frequently unsuccessful.

In the case of India, Hart points out, the new regions had to be bridged by an old prestigious civil service system which was not very anxious to be reformed from the bottom up. And there is suggested here something more fundamental than the question of whether or not established administrative systems can implement development programs involving new spatial dimensions, namely, the question of whether or not the spatial dimension should even be decided by the national government. The success of Comilla appears to rest partly on the fact that villages became involved in development and new spatial arrangements in terms of their own action based upon a desire that was supported by the social fabric of the village. Similarly, in the United States, the spatial dimension, in part, developed out of a process rather than being declared by fiat. Furthermore, the process identified with Comilla appears to be considerably more intransitive than the Indian experience, which was so dependent upon a highly transitive bureaucracy.

The experiences related by Hart also suggest some interesting things about exchange theory. There is considerable agreement in social change theory that patterns of social behavior are most effectively changed when persons whose behavior undergoes change regard themselves as involved in a meaningful exchange relationship. Social behavior pattern changes, it is fairly commonly held, are more likely to persist under conditions of satisfactory exchange relationships. Thus, a man who has quit smoking and who conceives himself as being in a satisfactory exchange system—he feels he is getting more out of it than he is giving up— is more likely to continue not smoking than is a man who has quit smoking because of fright or admonishment. Of course, if the man in the latter case begins to think of his not smoking in terms of an exchange system and feels he is benefiting more than he is losing, then his change in behavior is more likely to persist. The Indian approach appears to have failed in establishing the exchange concept, whereas the Comilla approach appears to have succeeded in doing so. As Hart tells us, the village as a social system became involved in the Comilla approach. The village reached out to the development program, not vice versa, because it saw something in doing so for itself as a village. The expertise of Comilla was like a store that had something to sell to someone who had decided he needed it, rather than like a missionary who goes to the village to educate it. What is suggested by this is that village space should be entered only after the village decision-making structure has asked for such entrance. And perhaps it is better that the space never be entered, but that persons leave it and go to places of training, such as Comilla. The very presence of any nonvillager in village space may disrupt the exchange system that must develop if social change is to occur and persist. Perhaps it is like the situation where a marriage counselor tries to work with the unhappy marriage by living with the troubled couple.

There are two major difficulties in the idea of flexibility. First, development elites are prone to think they know what must be done throughout the country, and not prone to think about discovering the developmental potential of the country. Second, development cannot take place in the absence of order. Development requires mobilization of available energies. John Shearer has recorded some problematical dimensions of mobilizing human energies at the right place. Internationally, a flexible approach would suggest free movement of people throughout the world, as the people desire. But the needs of developing countries suggest a need for restrictions on such movement. Intranationally, flexibility is also problematical. Flexibility suggests the capacity to react undogmatically to needs, promises, and problems as they appear on the scene. But problems of spatial movements may not present themselves temporally suitable to this strategy. If the brain drain from village to city is a serious problem, this problem may only emerge when it is too late to be stopped. The American experience with large cities is an immediate and sorry example. New York City's mayor in 1969 is a very flexible individual, and in many ways the administrative structures of that city are unusually flexible; but the problem is beyond the flexible approach.

Looking at the spatial dimension of development administration forces one to realize the horrendous complications of development. Development is a strategy to change spatial arrangements and to utilize as resources current spatial arrangements, simultaneously. Put this way, the contradiction is obvious. But if we do not put it this way, we do not see the contradiction because we fail to see that space is a vital dimension in culture and society. People relate to one another in spatial terms, and those terms become givens, even sacred symbols in some cases, of existence. Development ideas are challenging in that they threaten such current modes of existence. A further challenge to the information-gathering capacity of a developing country is found in the suggested need for "flexible statistics," that is for keeping unaggregated data of local economic activity ready and available for aggregation at whatever spatial dimension might be in demand. Thus, statistics on crime might be kept unaggregated at the level of a small town because if they are not kept distinct but aggregated at a higher level of government, call it x, they would not be available for aggregation at another level which does not entirely use the x data. For example, suppose statistics on agricultural yield in Albany village are not kept separate but are aggregated in the report on yields of twenty villages in Imaginary province. The chapters of this book indicate that development requires aggregation of Albany village agricultural yield statistics in other ways for specific purposes. Thus, in a country of twenty villages, one may need for one purpose to aggregate statistics from villages, 1, 8, 10, and 14. For another purpose it may be necessary to aggregate statistics from villages 1, 8, 11, and 19. For another purpose, statistics from villages 8, 19, and 20 may be aggregated. No one of these aggregations is sufficient for the other, so the individuality of the statistics for each village must be maintained. And this requires considerable resources, which may simply not be available in some countries. Even in the United States there is a necessity to derive regional income estimates from national income figures, for reasons of available research resources.[1] The reason for this, as John R. Meyer has noted, is "regional economies are almost invariably more open, in the sense of being more reliant on external trade and institutions, than national economies."[2]

The chapter by Gross raises an interesting question. Will human space be determined by technological ("mobiletics") revolutions? Hart stresses cultural obstacles to spatial changes; Gross writes as though culture will make no difference. Gross is talking about national elites as they will probably relate to national elites of other countries. Hart is talking about how national elites deal with internal community development programs. Both visions are relevant. Culture must, and will, bend to technology under certain conditions. Technology will be changed through cultural interpretations. In the United States we find two different and contradictory answers to the Gross question. One answer is that the society has been determined by technologies, alas. The other answer is that the society has, in rude persistence, resisted the improvements promised in technology, alas.

Shearer's chapter suggests that large leaps in mobiletics may lead to greater shortages of important human resources in underdeveloped places. Increases in mobility of important human resources across nation-state boundaries is a potential impediment to development in some countries. What Gross refers to as the "coming world" may be an antidevelopment model for some countries. For if what Shearer describes is accurate regarding trends, then facilitation of mobility will bring about even greater disparities between the developed and underdeveloped parts of the world and parts of a country. Perhaps nations will throw up

1. For a proposal to keep unaggregated records of regional accounts, see E. M. Hoover, *The Location of Economic Activity* (New York: McGraw-Hill, 1948).
2. "Regional Economics: Survey," *The American Economic Review* 53, no. 1 (March 1963): 24.

restrictions against mobility. Increases in the ease of mobility may lead to severe restrictions against it, which will create an inflexible spatial condition. Our suggestion throughout this volume has been that maintenance of flexibility in the spatial dimension is vitally important to development. Something like severe restriction of human movement might be a disaster. While it is obvious that mobility creates problems such as one finds in large urban areas, it is equally true that the ability of people to move from place to place has been a basic factor in the development of every country regarded today as developed. This is not to say, of course, that the allowance of easy movement by people guarantees development.

The irony is that mobiletics represents, simultaneously, the problem of "too much" and "too little." Hough talks about how leadership in Russia dealt with the problem of getting good men into the field, and out of the large cities, not that good men are not also needed in large cities. When we are talking about the flow from the countryside to the city, mobiletics seems to be at work in every country; as it is when we talk about international brain drain of human resources from less developed cities to more developed cities in other countries. When we are talking about the mobiletics from city to countryside, or from developed city to less developed city, then we talk about a problem, a blockage, a nonmovement. Hough suggests consideration of the Russian techniques for handling this, which were, and are, based upon incentive systems. Specialists, Hough says, must share the prestige and responsibilities formerly reserved exclusively for the elite administrative services. This has certainly been the case in the United States. Indeed, one of the most ubiquitous complaints in American administrative circles is that we have failed to develop a respectable profession of general administration, that we have failed to establish an administrative elite in the country. There are a myriad of studies made by institutions such as Brookings, and by high-level commissions, such as the second Hoover, calling for, and proposing ways to achieve "an American administrative elite." Students from developing countries with such elites, visiting the United States to study administration are often taken aback by the low esteem of the administrative generalist in American administrative circles.

Areal coordination is still another phenomenon providing an interesting subject for comparison of the Soviet Union with the United States. As Hough says, the Russians use the most powerful and dramatic institution in the country, the party organization, for areal coordination. The coordination of American economic development, which was originally much more a private than a public affair, took place at the individual state level. Thus there was areal coordination and it took place at the level which, at the time, had the most power to do so. It is interesting that despite the great trend toward centralization in Washington, D.C., there still is a very strong feeling in the United States that the individual states should be primary areal coordinators. India appears to have a problem experienced in the United States regarding unevenness of the areal coordination provided by individual states. Hart points out that each state followed its own approach in establishing *panchayats*. Some constituted a *panchayat* for almost every census village; some averaged six or seven, or even twenty villages in a *panchayat*.

If such differences in approach were results of consciously conceived strategies of development, we would note them as examples of fruitful outcomes of a flexible condition. But flexibility is a condition that enables rational spatial strategies to emerge, in that it does not prevent them. It does not guarantee fruitful outcomes. As Hart tells us, these differences were not based upon careful thinking about development goals in the light of meticulously gathered statistics. This is very similar to what happened in the United States. However, American development, Redford makes quite clear, was essentially a result of private enterprise, which did follow spatial strategies of placement and coordination ruled by a logic of increasing production and efficiency. In a sense, the Russian approach to areal coordination was a functional substitute for American private enterprise with regard to development of rational spatial strategies guided by the value of economic growth.

The question of decentralization is answerable in terms of

professionalization and value-integration, as suggested in the first chapter. (We might note that we are using the word "decentralization" to include "deconcentration," the term discussed by Hough, and "devolution," which Hart treats, inter alia. Deconcentration, here, means delegating authority to staff situated outside of headquarters so that they can adequately discharge specified functions. Devolution, here, means legally conferring powers to discharge specified functions to a noncentral authority. Decentralization is either or both.) As we have already mentioned, American and Russian decentralization were furthered by increasing the prestige and responsibility of specialists. Our point in the first chapter was that decentralization sometimes comes about because certain professions will not live with centralization if it hampers them in carrying out their function. As the prestige and responsibility of specialists rises, so, apparently, does their concern for doing the job correctly, by the standards of their specialty. This concern can override the imbecility of a rule in a particular context. The specialist knows that he is first and foremost to perform as a specialist—building the bridge correctly, applying the vaccine in the best way possible, spraying the crops in the most effective way. He is oriented to the task, not to the rules.

Value-integration also appears important for decentralization. Hough emphasizes psychological preconditions in his analysis of development in the Soviet Union, one vital dimension of which is the common viewpoint shared by members of the party organization. What is most impressive about a great deal of what has been written above is that the goal of productivity, developmental productivity, is the key to everything else in development. Development is the dependent variable of the goal of development. Value-integration for a decentralization that is conducive to development appears to revolve around development as a goal. This suggests that the proposition "Development requires decentralization" is inaccurate until we add "which is based on a value-integration toward development."

Thus, what we now have is a hypothetical view of development and decentralization which interrelates the two in terms of professionalization (increasing the prestige and responsibility of specialists) and value-integration on the goal of productivity. We can see how both professionalization and this specific form of value-integration leads to decentralized behavior conducive to development.

We hope we have presented an agenda for future research as well as having generalized in a relevant way regarding interrelationships of "space" and "development." There are, of course, many important interrelationships not dealt with in this volume. The more one works on an enterprise such as this, the more he finds lying outside his net. But there is no way to include these things without making a net that is already perhaps too large, larger still; at least no way conceivable to this writer. The most realistic claim that can be made at this terminal point is that though the catch has not been hauled on board, it is in the net on the water's surface, and what we can see of that catch is reasonably interesting.

Index